Wage-Earning Women

INDUSTRIAL WORK AND FAMILY LIFE
IN THE UNITED STATES, 1900–1930

LESLIE WOODCOCK TENTLER

OXFORD UNIVERSITY PRESS
Oxford   New York   Toronto   Melbourne

Oxford University Press

OXFORD   LONDON   GLASGOW
NEW YORK   TORONTO   MELBOURNE   AUCKLAND
DELHI   BOMBAY   CALCUTTA   MADRAS   KARACHI
KUALA LUMPUR   SINGAPORE   HONG KONG   TOKYO
NAIROBI   DAR ES SALAAM   CAPE TOWN

and associate companies in
BEIRUT   BERLIN   IBADAN   MEXICO CITY   NICOSIA

Copyright © 1979 by Oxford University Press, Inc.
First published by Oxford University Press, New York, 1979
First issued as an Oxford University Press paperback, 1982

Library of Congress Cataloging in Publication Data
Tentler, Leslie Woodcock.
Wage-earning women.
Bibliography: p. 241
1. Women—Employment—United States—History.
2. Women—United States—History.   3. Sex role.   I. Title.
HD6095.T44   331.4′0973   79-12802
ISBN 0-19-502627-6
ISBN 0-19-503211-X (pbk.)

Printing (last digit): 9 8 7 6 5 4

Printed in the United States of America

For Tom, Sarah, Daniel and Gregory

Acknowledgments

It is a genuine pleasure to acknowledge the debts I have acquired in the course of writing this book; it is easy to forget, in the isolation of the note-card strewn study, just how much one's colleagues contribute to even a modest scholarly undertaking. My oldest debt is to Sam Bass Warner; his imaginative teaching of American social history was important to me as a graduate student. I thank Robert Sklar, Gerald Linderman, Louise Tilly, and Elizabeth Pleck for their criticism of the original dissertation in its various drafts, and thank especially Louise Tilly for her encouragement to revise the thesis for publication. She made helpful suggestions for revisions, as did my colleague Peter Amann. Sidney Fine and Jonathan Marwil read the revised manuscript at a later stage, and offered important suggestions for its improvement. And throughout the writing, Thomas Tentler gave editorial advice, sensitive criticism, and moral support. My debt to him is very great.

People who write books with infants and small children underfoot accumulate special debts. Tom Tentler has been patient, energetic, and nearly always cheerful during the hectic past few years. Kate Tentler gave her services as a childminder lovingly and responsibly. Sarah Tentler grew up astonishingly, her self-reliance a source of comfort and aid to her mother. And Luberta Collins cared for my children so effectively that I was able to work with real peace of mind, and so affectionately that she often reminded us too-harried parents that twins are indeed "life more abundantly." My colleagues at the University of Michigan-Dearborn have been understanding and generous in protecting me from excessive demands on my time.

Cause and effect in their case work in a circle. Expectation of marriage, as a customary means of support, stunts professional ambition among women. This lack of ambition can have no other effect than to limit efficiency, and restricts them to subsidiary, uninteresting, and monotonous occupations. The very character of their work in turn lessens their interest in it. Without interest, they least of all feel themselves integral parts of the industry and in consequence assume no responsibility, affect no loyalty. They do not care to learn; opportunity to learn is not given them; both are causes and both are effects. Women see only a fight for place, and a very uncertain advantage if they gain it; wages are low, again both cause and effect of their dependence on others for their support. They shift around on lower levels of industry from packing room to metal work, from metal work to laundry work; a very few, through unwonted good fortune, unwonted determination, break through the circle and rise.

Elizabeth Beardsley Butler,
from *Women and the Trades*

Contents

Introduction

American women began to work outside the home in significant and increasing numbers after 1875. Until well into the twentieth century, most of these pioneering workers were the daughters of the working class. This study attempts to explore their experience, to reconstruct the day-to-day realities of life on the job, in the working-class home, and in the industrial neighborhoods of major cities. It attempts as well to analyze the impact of paid employment on the lives of working-class women. Did the employment interval—generally the six or eight years between school-leaving and marriage—alter in fundamental ways the values, behavior, and expectations of young women? Did the work experience, for example, deter early marriage among working-class girls and cause them to center their adult lives less exclusively around the family than their mothers had done? Is it correct to say, with William Leuchtenburg, that "By 1930 more than ten million women held jobs. Nothing did more to emancipate them."[1]

To understand fully the meaning of employment in the life of the working-class woman, we must understand her periods of paid work as integral to a series of life experiences. Employment followed schooling, generally terminated with marriage, and continued—if at all—intermittently and casually during the long years as wife and mother. Paid work was not the primary focus of most women's lives. But employment was a particularly important aspect of socialization for a majority of urban working-class youth, because paid work normally began in and continued throughout the significant decision-making years of adolescence. Employment experiences could either ratify or undermine the values and expectations undereducated boys and girls brought to workshop, store, or factory.

Employment, however, was nearly always a sex-segregated experience, and, as such, tended to reinforce in powerful ways separate roles for male and female in adulthood. Indeed, I will argue that paid work often afforded working-class women more persuasive lessons about the inevitability of a circumscribed female role than did the typical experiences of home, school, or neighborhood social life. It is as an ultimately conservative aspect of socialization that we best understand the meaning of employment for working-class women. The connections between work and female emancipation are inevitably subtle and elusive, for the work experience normally served to direct the restive young toward conventional maturity.

I have limited this study to the three decades between 1900 and the outset of the Great Depression for several reasons. These were decades of significant female participation in the labor force, but, more important, these were the opening decades of a truly mature industrial economy. Young urban women went out to work in stores and factories and offices that were discernibly modern, though vestiges of older modes of production survived throughout the 1920s. These were also decades of important investigations into the nature and conditions of women's work—investigations, both publicly and privately sponsored, that are invaluable for reconstructing the working-class experience. And these were decades of enormous assimilative pressure on a largely immigrant working class. Daughters of immigrant families learned at work a thoroughly "American" version of feminine adolescence, apparently freer in manners and morals than many immigrant parents found acceptable. The work experience of young people in these decades helped to alter working-class culture in important ways. But assimilation largely failed to achieve for working-class women an adult role significantly less limited by familial priorities than was the norm in tradition-rooted European cultures.

Additionally, an important transition to present-day patterns of women's work was beginning to occur by 1930. Female labor force participation increased more rapidly after 1930 than before, and the female labor force after 1930 began to age significantly.[2] The decades between 1900 and 1930, then, can be seen as a first and critical chapter in the history of modern female industrial employment. In this period, important precedents regarding women's work were established or confirmed: enduring patterns of occupational segregation by sex, a consistently inferior female wage, a broadly popular interpretation of the reasons for female employment. An understanding of these decades, in short, is essential to an understanding of women's place in the labor force today.

I have limited this study to the experiences of women in the major industrial cities of the East and the Midwest, principally but not exclusively Boston, New York, Philadelphia, and Chicago. These were industrially mature cities with diversified economies. The employment opportunities they afforded their residents, both male and female, were thus representatively modern. The study is limited, moreover, to manufacturing, sales, and nondomestic service occupations, employments for which, throughout the period, a minimum education was sufficient. I have not discussed private domestic employment, though it was the single largest female occupational category in 1900, because it declined rapidly thereafter as young women's work and was increasingly the province of women who, because of age or race or marital status, could not easily secure higher-paying jobs in the factory or office. Nor have I discussed clerical employment, which assuredly increased in importance as women's work and especially as a favored work choice of the young. Particularly during the 1920s, as educational levels rose among working-class youth, many working-class daughters took clerical jobs. Indeed, by 1930 manufacturing was rapidly becoming the work choice of relatively low-status women—most notably the foreign-born—and an occupational category of declining importance for all women.

Nevertheless, I have chosen to focus principally on factory employment because it seems paradigmatic of the work experience of the majority of working-class women in the decades under study. Factory work, like clerical work, was generally sex-segregated and relatively low-paying; unlike clerical work, factory work was also physically taxing and governed by a harsh, even abusive, style of work authority. For a great many women at work in these decades, employment— whether as factory operatives, service workers, or even domestic servants—was both physically and psychologically onerous. This important fact shaped women's attitudes toward paid work and affected the ways in which the better-educated working-class woman calculated the satisfactions of routine white-collar employment. This is not to say that clerical work need not be studied—it is the principal means by which working-class women in the twentieth century have achieved occupational mobility—but that clerical work is beyond the scope of this study, for carefully considered reasons. Finally, I have ignored the work history of black women, for theirs is a unique history that merits separate investigation.

Notwithstanding, the subject of this study is still a large and heterogeneous population. And because this is true, at least three important questions about the validity of my conclusions will quite reasonably occur to many readers. First, can an historian describe with sufficient precision the experiences and attitudes of a population as geographically and ethnically diverse as the population that is the focus of this study? Might the investigation not profitably have been limited to the experiences of a single ethnic group in one industrial city? Second, does not the nature of the evidence—fragmentary, impressionistic, overwhelmingly middle class in authorship—cast serious doubts on conclusions about the nature of working-class life experience? And, third, is there not a danger that in dealing with so general a category as working women, one neglects the exceptional individual? If the study concentrates on the vast majority of working women who were indifferent to organized labor, does this not do disservice to those women who were conscious agents of social change? Let me deal briefly with each of these questions.

I chose not to limit my study to a local ethnic group because I am convinced that sex and class shape most Americans' lives more decisively than does their residence or nationality. For women, especially, the normal life cycle and the social expectations that define it transcend ethnic divisions. To a more limited extent, the common experiences of femininity span barriers of class. The Italian daughter in New York and her Polish counterpart in Chicago had much in common despite differences in home language, customs, and affective styles. Americans, moreover, are and were a geographically mobile population. Our identities have often of necessity been drawn from sources other than the current place of residence. And by the early twentieth century, the children of immigrant parents were being assimilated to a larger working-class culture. They did not lose all distinctive ethnic traits, but they came to share with one another attitudes toward personal conduct, family life, and political behavior that were broadly characteristic of a class rather than of a particular ethnic group.[3] Indeed, this important process of assimilation to a class culture occurred in part at work, especially in the conviviality of the small work group.

A local focus also obscures the reality of a national industrial system. Urban working-class women, save perhaps in the South, entered essentially the same world of low-skill work whether they were garment makers in New York or packinghouse workers in Chicago. Wages and working conditions could vary considerably, but they varied within cities as well as between cities. Essentially the same labor market existed for women in nearly all major industrial centers in the East and the Midwest. Only single-industry mill towns or towns dominated exclusively by heavy industry created unique employment situations for working-class women.

The nature of the evidence employed in this study is potentially more troublesome than the issue of the study's focus. Evidence is neither as complete and systematic nor as representative of working-class opinion as I would like. I have drawn heavily from the work of contemporary social investigators, middle-class women and men who recorded the work and sometimes the home experience of employed women. At times, their observations are unashamedly subjective, particularly with reference to the attitudes and behavior of the young.

Wherever possible I have used the written legacy of working-class women themselves. But this precious testimony is scant indeed compared to the wealth of available investigatory material.

Essentially, my dilemma is a perennial dilemma of the social historian. Few working-class women have testimony deposited in archives; those who do are immediately suspect in their "typicality." Much information about working-class life must come from middle-class pens. This will be nearly as true fifty years hence when the working-class history of our own decade is compiled. Moreover, suspect as "middle-class" evidence may be, it can be subjected to empirical criticism. Middle-class authorship does not automatically discredit testimony, nor are working-class sources unimpeachable.

In this study, I have rejected as obviously class-biased information that is openly contemptuous of working-class culture, and have rejected as well material that assumes the inferiority of women. Very few sources, in fact, fall into these categories. In many cases, observers are at once sensitive to certain aspects of working-class experience but remarkably obtuse in other judgments. I have made assessments of the worth of their statements based on my own sensibilities, sharpened, I hope, by reading in the sociology of class. And I have reasons to be confident about my sources. They yield a good deal of agreement among diverse observers about broad areas of women's work and home experience. Either class bias is sufficiently powerful to homogenize the perceptions of very different individuals, or elements of working-class life were striking and evident to the engaged observer. As recorders of work environments and wage data, moreover, middle-class investigators were painstaking and skilled. And often, precisely because they were less consciously "objective" than today's sociologists, early twentieth-century observers were unusually sensitive to the detail and variety of individual life histories. Used with caution, middle-class investigatory material can prove enormously valuable.

The final objection has, for me, no truly satisfying solution. In dealing with so broad a population as employed working-class women, one produces a group portrait that inevitably slights the exceptional individual, particularly the active member of the labor movement. In pursuit of representative working-class experience, I have, of necessity, ignored the complexities of exceptional lives. But the group portrait is not thereby seriously distorted. The vast majority of working-class women were not overtly political in their concerns, and they were not activists. This does not, of course, diminish the courage and the achievements of women who were active trade unionists. Indeed their task as organizers was far more formidable than that confronting their male counterparts.

Finally, by describing the typical working-class woman as a nonactivist, even a passive worker, I am probably vulnerable to charges of sexism. But I write from a generally feminist perspective. Where I have characterized working women in stereotypically feminine terms, I do so only because the overwhelming weight of evidence warrants this judgment. Ultimately, I feel a deep respect for the women I have studied. They made fundamentally humane choices and created in the midst of poverty lives that are often moving and courageous. These women were not, however, the same social creatures that men were, either as workers or as family members. It is hardly sexist to affirm what was admirable in women's lives while analyzing the cultural and institutional forces that supported a distinctive femininity.

I have indicated already that I believe employment to have been an important and conservative aspect of working-class female socialization. Women's work experience was different from that of men, and their particular experience of work helped to validate for most women conventional life choices. Women's wages were very low, often deliberately calculated to be less than living wages, as we shall see in chapter one. Working women were thus condemned to financial dependence on men—fathers, brothers, husbands. Life outside the family for most women was economically precarious, as we shall see in chapter four; and it was also socially isolating. Moreover, women's low wages often reinforced a self-image of dependence and passivity in the world outside the home. The social message of the woman's wage reaffirmed her domestic destiny even as she tended complex modern machinery. The same message was reflected in the very limited nature of the female job market and the sexual division of labor in predominantly female trades. The realities of the work experience, in short, did not for most women challenge the lessons about femininity learned at home, in school, and in the community.

For most women, the work experience failed to alter significantly their role in and their dependence on the family, for nearly all women's jobs offered less security and status than did life as a working-class wife and mother. Most white women before 1930 left paid employment when they married; generally only severe poverty induced a married woman to return to work. And because the working-class wife was normally full-time in the home, there was little to upset the traditional sexual division of labor in marriage, as we shall see in chapter six. Indeed, the atypical employed wife had little social support for a lightening of her considerable work and family burden.

The employment interval for most working-class women, then, had relatively little impact on the essentials of the female life cycle. Women moved from school through employment and into marriage, much as their mothers and grandmothers had passed through a domestic apprenticeship on their way to husbands and child-bearing. During the brief years of adolescence, however, the experience of work was important in facilitating female social freedom, as we shall see in chapters three and four. But this important change in young women's "manners and morals" had much less certain impact on the long years of domesticity that followed courtship. Indeed, if contemporary sociologists are correct, it is precisely that class of women with the longest history of employment, working-class women, that is only now beginning to respond by its attitudes and behavior to the feminist movement of the past decade. Responding to a sympathetic sociologist, a California woman, a plumber's wife and mother of three children, lamented in 1975: "When I was a kid and used to wish I was a boy, I never knew why I thought that. Now I know. It's because a man can go to work for eight hours and come home, and a woman's work is just never done. And it doesn't make any difference if she works or not."[4]

This study helps to explain why this is so.

PART ONE

The World of the Job

I

Women's Wages

When you say living wage of course I will admit that it is very hard for a woman to live on six dollars a week if she had to support herself, but I think you will find that the cases of that kind are a great exception. I know in our stores, and I think in most of the other stores, we really only like to employ people who live at home, that is of the younger people, and I do not think they are at all dependent upon the salary they make.

Benedict J. Greenhut, in testimony before the New York State Factory Investigating Commission, 1914.

Women, Mr. Greenhut tells us, are not like men: when women work, they do so not as individuals seeking a means of self-support but as dependent family members. His reasoning was shared by many Americans in the early twentieth century. And his reasoning had powerful consequences. If women were not paid enough to be independent, they would remain, of necessity, dependent for survival on membership in male-headed families. They would live in the parental home until marriage and understand marriage as essential to personal security. And women would learn from their low wages an important lesson about society's valuation of women in nondomestic roles. The world of work, they would come to understand, was a man's world, in which women were accorded a very limited place.

In their limited place, however, working women played immensely important roles in the national economy and in the economy of the working-class family. But despite their economic importance, most

13

working women in the early twentieth century failed to achieve personal economic independence. Working-class women were successfully maintained as a poverty-wage population throughout the period under study.

We need, first, to understand the economic role women played when they left the home to work at industrial jobs, and then to understand how they and their contemporaries interpreted this behavior. Women began to enter the nondomestic work force in significant numbers in the last quarter of the nineteenth century as the progressive mechanization and rationalization of industry created a variety of light, unskilled jobs for low-wage labor. Sophisticated mechanization in industry required myriad assemblers, light-machine tenders, sorters, and packers. Bureaucratization of industry generated increasing—and increasingly routine—clerical employment. The immense productivity of the mature industrial economy necessitated a growing retail sales force. Increased personal wealth accelerated demand for such service industries as professional laundries, restaurants, and beauty salons. Women entered the nondomestic work force to meet these needs, and they were employed at work not ordinarily performed by men. Men and women were rarely in direct competition for jobs, and despite changes in the kinds of jobs open to women and men, a high degree of labor market segregation by sex has persisted, if not actually increased, from 1900 to the present.[1]

From the first, then, women inhabited a distinct and separate labor market, one characterized by low pay, low skill, low security, and low mobility. In their characteristic work role, women were inestimably valuable to their employers and to the larger society. Employers of women benefited from low labor costs and from the flexibility gained by employing workers reportedly more tractable than men and who rarely organized into unions.* The vast majority of working women

---

* Even in 1920, the high point for membership in American unions until the late 1930s, only 6.6% of the female nonagricultural labor force was organized. Of all non-farm workers in that year, fully 20.8% were members of trade unions. Women, it is true, were virtually never employed in construction, in the mines, or on the railroads—each a

were easily hired and dismissed from their jobs in response to the immediate needs of the employer. And society appeared to benefit from the concentration of women in low-wage jobs because most women, as supplementary rather than primary family breadwinners, could earn small and uncertain wages without causing massive economic suffering or political unrest. No other group could be segregated into low-wage employment with so few adverse social consequences.

Indeed, the employment of women normally enhanced working-class standards of living. The supplementary wages of daughters and wives helped to cushion the working-class family against adversity and permitted a new flexibility in stringent household budgets. Only where women were economic heads-of-household or lived alone did their low wages demonstrably result in poverty. But most women worked as members of male-headed families; few working-class women and men, therefore, perceived women's low wages as a direct threat to family economic security. And women's employers, as well as many social policymakers and trade unionists, were complacent about the female poverty wage.

Employers and policymakers merely articulated what was a broad social consensus concerning women's place in the early twentieth century. Most Americans accepted as axiomatic that women's first responsibility was to bear and raise children and maintain the home.

---

stronghold of unionism—and they were heavily employed in occupations where unions were conspicuously absent even among men. The low figure for female union membership is accounted for in part by the greater concentration of women than men in clerical, trade, and domestic and personal service occupations. The major source of female trade union members in 1920 was the garment trades; fully one quarter of the total female union membership in the country in that year was in New York State, much of this a garment trade constituency. In greater New York in 1920, the importance of the garment trades in the urban economy meant that over 14% of the area's employed women were members of a union. Women, however, were consistently less well organized than men even in trades where unions were strong. In 1920, 46% of female garment workers were reported to be members of unions, although this figure would not take into account the large number of female homeworkers employed in the industry even in 1920. By comparison, 57.8% of the men who worked in the garment trades were organized. Contemporary testimony, as we shall see, argued strongly that even in the same industry, women were generally more difficult to organize than men.[2]

Few doubted that women were innately better suited to the domestic role than to paid employment, and few believed that women ought to be self-supporting, lifelong workers. If poverty forced women to work for wages outside the home before marriage, the assumption of wifely status ought to mean retirement from the work force. Women without men were by definition deviant; women who failed to marry were often ridiculed, the widowed and the deserted were pitied, and the divorced woman was stigmatized.[3] Even minimum wage legislation, first proposed in the United States exclusively for women workers, failed in its early years to set a wage standard sufficient for an individual's survival outside the family.[4] Nor did the consciously liberal employer normally consider as just or necessary a "living wage" for women. One such employer candidly reviewed his firm's wage policies before the New York State Factory Investigating Commission in 1915:

> I am the director of a small corporation employing a number of girls in Brooklyn to whom we pay less than the $9 a week which probably constitutes a living wage in that borough. On the other hand, we pay $1 to $1.50 per week more than the prevailing rate of wages in that labor market. That is to say, we can hang out a sign in front of our factory saying "Girls Wanted—$4.50 a week," and get applicants galore who are capable of doing the class of work which we require. I am convinced that they are the same girls that come to us when we hang out the sign saying "Girls Wanted, $6 per week." We pay the higher wage as a concession to our own self-respect, and because the business in recent years has become profitable enough so that we can easily afford it. If our competitors would raise their wage standards, we would be willing to go higher than they do with our wage rate, on the principle that we are strong enough to accept a certain amount of handicap in this matter.[5]

And women themselves, deeply affected by the prevailing definition of femininity, generally accepted without overt protest both their low wages and their very limited job opportunities. Wrote one investigator of the "average working woman":

> [S]he has no definite idea of the value of her services; the first place she goes to, if she is repulsed, she is willing to ask less at the

next, and when she gets a place she is so thankful that she never thinks she may be giving a quid pro quo and there is as much thankfulness due on the other side.[6]

Immigrant women were often too shy to ask about wages when they were hired, Caroline Manning noted in Pennsylvania in the mid-1920s, "and would frequently not fight when money was unfairly withheld by the employer or there were 'mistakes' in the payroll."[7] Young New Yorkers, according to the State Factory Investigating Commission in 1915, apparently found the prestige associated with saleswork satisfactory compensation for the low pay they normally received: "Applicants appear willing to start at any rate."[8] Bureau of Labor investigators detected among women workers "a lack of self-assertion which makes them willing to take low wages."[9] Such behavior was reminiscent perhaps of young immigrant men, who expected often to work in industry for a limited time and then to remigrate, but it was not characteristic of that majority of male workers who expected to achieve personal economic independence through their work and who needed eventually to earn enough to maintain a family. When a man adopted an aggressive attitude toward his employer, moreover, he risked his job but gained some psychic benefits from playing an admired masculine role. A woman risked not only her job but the core of her social identity.

The wages that most women accepted without protest were generally less than what their contemporaries defined as subsistence wages. Investigations of women's store and factory employment conducted between 1900 and the late 1920s argued that the majority of women studied earned less than was necessary for a single woman to live alone in minimally acceptable circumstances.[10] In Massachusetts, for example, the State Minimum Wage Commission in 1912 set "the lowest total for human living conditions for an individual in Boston" at $8.28 per week, though this estimate made no allowance for savings or medical care. Women employees in the industry under study, the brush industry, most often mentioned $10.60 a week as a necessary minimum wage. But the industry itself paid far less than this, and the recommended though not legally binding minimum wage in the Massachusetts brush industry was finally set at 15½¢ an hour for experienced adult makers, or $7.75 for a week of fifty hours, assuming full employment.[11]

The commission's cost-of-living estimate represented less a realistic calculation than a political compromise, for the brush industry had pressed for a low minimum wage decree. Other studies of Boston women living alone produced higher subsistence budgets. A 1911 investigation set $9.00 per week as the minimum for an adequate standard of living in Boston, and a group of Boston social workers in 1912 set $10.60 as the necessary minimum wage for a woman living away from home.[12] But whether the standard employed was stringent or generous, few working-class women in Boston were earning subsistence wages. Seventy-seven percent of Boston factory women studied by the Bureau of Labor in 1908 earned less than $8.00 per week— even allowing for some inflation between 1908 and 1912, a substantial majority in this study clearly earned poverty wages—and fully 88% of saleswomen studied by the State Minimum Wage Commission in 1911 earned less than $8.00.[13]

The New York City YWCA maintained in 1915 that at least $9.00 per week was essential expenditure for room and board alone in that city, and social workers, trade union leaders, and industrialists testifying before the State Factory Investigating Commission set the minimum weekly cost of living for a New York single woman variously from $8.00 to $15.00. About $10.00 a week represented the median estimate.[14] But again, the vast majority of New York's working women earned less than adequate wages. The State Factory Investigating Commission found that New York City department store clerks, the most highly paid group studied, earned in 1914 an average of $7.77 per week, with half earning $8.25 or less.[15] Fully 71% of the department store clerks studied earned less than $10.00. Eighty-five percent of saleswomen in neighborhood stores and 97% of saleswomen in five-and-dime stores earned less than this amount. And more than 88% of women employed in the city's shirt factories earned less than $10.00 per week, as did 85.5% of the women studied in the paper box industry.[16]

Women's low wages reflected in part their segregation in low-wage sectors of the economy. But even within those industries that employed women in large numbers, women were considerably more disadvantaged than men. There clearly prevailed in these trades hiring, promotion, and pay practices that kept the female wage a consistently lower ratio of the higher male wage. In eighty-eight men's clothing factories in New York City, for example, Bureau of Labor investigators reported in 1911 that weekly earnings varied sharply by sex: men's median wages fell between $10.00 and $10.99, but women's median wages fell between $5.00 and $5.99. The same investigation found male garment workers in Philadelphia earning median wages of between $9.00 and $9.99, while females received the same low pay as their New York counterparts. Only in Chicago, a relatively high-wage city, did women in the men's clothing trade earn a median wage greater than two-thirds the standard male wage. Male workers in the bureau's study earned median wages of between $10.00 and $10.99, while the women studied earned between $7.00 and $7.99.[17]

The good fortune of women in the Chicago men's clothing trade, however, was the exception, not the rule. Women in urban manufacturing jobs normally earned from one-half to two-thirds of the standard male wage in their various industries. And although real wages rose in the period under study—particularly in the 1920s—the ratio of male to female wages was little altered. Typically, the New York State Department of Labor reported that during the year 1923–24, women employed in New York City factories earned on an average 60% of the wages of men in factory occupations.[18] In sales work the prevailing pay differentials were nearly always greater than those in factory occupations, for the relatively few men employed in retailing invariably monopolized the most lucrative jobs in supervision and prestige selling.[19]

Significantly, sharp pay differentials by sex normally existed even for unskilled labor; hence, the sex differential in industrial, sales, and service wages was explained only in part by male domination of skilled jobs. Women of course earned lower average wages than men because women were concentrated in unskilled work, but women also earned low wages simply because they were women. The male labor market encompassed not only the great majority of skilled jobs but the most remunerative unskilled jobs as well, while women were largely confined to light low-skill hand and machine work at wages unskilled men would rarely accept. A 1909 Pittsburgh study documented the consequences for women of the segregated job market and noted that neither experience nor lengthy tenure normally enabled a woman to break the sex-related wage barrier:

> Unskilled workmen who have not yet acquired a certain dexterity and familiarity with their tasks are paid $2.00 a day, or $12.00 a week. Unskilled working women, who have made themselves valuable by length of service and by familiarity with a certain operation, are paid $1.00 a day, $6.00 a week. That is, the ratio between the wages of unskilled work men and of unskilled working women is two to one.[20]

Women were, moreover, heavily employed in highly seasonal trades. "On a very conservative estimate," argued economist Charles Persons in 1915, women workers lost 10% of full-time earnings each week due to seasonal variations in actual hours worked.[21] Indeed, in many women's industries it was estimated that busy season overtime pay did not ultimately compensate for the time lost to unemployment and underemployment.[22] Women were not, of course, the only workers who suffered from excessive unemployment. Many male workers, particularly the unskilled, also knew the insecurity of seasonal work, although it is not possible to compare meaningfully male and female unemployment rates for the pre-Depression decades. But whether or not unemployment was a particularly severe affliction of one sex, it nonetheless was experienced differently by women and men. Economic insecurity had meaning and suggested compensatory strategies, often according to the sex of the worker. And unemployment clearly imposed a severe tax on the already low earnings of probably a majority of women—a tax, in short, exacted from those in the work force quite literally least able to pay.

Beyond seasonal unemployment, other factors conspired to keep women's wages low. In many shops, workers negotiated the starting wage with the employer or supervisor, although this was true as well for many unskilled men. For men and women the practice probably had similar consequences, save that women normally negotiated pay with reference to a lower wage ceiling than men did. Working women, however, because of their sex and their youth, may well have been the less effective bargainers. Certainly in many women's workrooms the individual wage gave employers great discretion in determining the pay of their inexperienced and nonassertive workers: "As one employer said, 'they generally take what we offer.' "[23] And the individual wage contract often meant that women were ignorant of the wages of their coworkers. Since many were reluctant to reveal what they earned (we shall see that wages were a forbidden topic of conversation in some shops) collective action on the issue of low wages was made very difficult, as the employer doubtless intended.[24]

The individual wage contract, furthermore, emphasized the worker's dependence on her employer or supervisor. Since he set the wage, he could as easily withdraw it. So long as the job was needed, the worker, without the protection of union membership or personal skills, normally understood herself to be at the employer's mercy. And the very act of bargaining for wages was intimidating to many women, probably even more so than to men, because women so often had to negotiate their wages with a man. The authority of the employer over the worker was enhanced by the authority of male over female, and often enhanced further by the authority of age over a youthful female work force. Indeed, in many firms a raise in pay could only be secured through personal negotiation, and many women apparently changed jobs rather than face an employer to ask for a wage increase.[25] Occasional employers, it was claimed, even fired workers who were so brash as to request a raise.[26]

Many employers of women further depressed wages by depending heavily on "learners" and apprentices in the shop and by contracting out work to women in the home. Both learners and homeworkers were tangible threats to the wages and job security of regular employees.

Ironically, since most women's jobs were low-skill ones, long training periods were rarely necessary, yet in many occupations employers regularly hired inexperienced hands at extremely low pay under the guise of teaching women a valuable trade.[27] Since the female labor force was predominantly young, the supply of willing learners eagerly seeking employment was plentiful. In New York City's garment industry, operating under a minimum wage protocol, an economist found in 1914 that from one-fourth to one-half of the workers in the different occupations investigated were earning less than minimum pay, "the employers claiming that the workers in question were learners."[28] Indeed, in high-status occupations such as millinery and custom dressmaking, apprentices often served two full seasons without pay, though many of these young women were never taught the very real skills of the custom maker: "The complaint was made frequently concerning both wholesale and retail shops that it was hard for a learner to advance, that she was not given an opportunity to learn all the processes, and that an employer would lay off apprentices after one season and take on others so as to keep the payroll smaller."[29] A young milliner concurred: "Although I went as a learner, they didn't teach me anything. So I guess you oughtn't call it learner but errand girl."[30]

Homeworkers, who were usually the wives of poorly paid blue-collar workers, commanded even lower wages than learners.[31] Well into the 1920s, many businesses depended heavily on the labor of women in the home to perform simple tasks of finishing and assembling. Homeworkers finished garments, strung tags, carded pins, crocheted dolls' and babies' clothing, made artificial flowers, and much more.[32] Despite the extremely low pay, the supply of homeworkers in industrial cities was virtually inexhaustible. Women confined to the home by children and housework yet in need of extra cash were grateful for paid employment that accommodated the domestic schedule, and no workers were less capable of organizing among themselves than isolated homeworkers.[33] Competition for homework in hard times and eventual permanent decline in the availability of homework after the mid-1920s further undermined wages. In 1930, in Greenwich Village, women who coveted the by then scarce homework available locally "kept the place where they secured work secret from their neighbors—sometimes even trying to conceal the fact that they were doing homework at all—lest their neighbors should get the work away from them. Yet piece rates were so low as to net only a few dollars a week, perhaps three or possibly five dollars, from constant labor."[34]

The vast majority of homeworkers were women, and they performed tasks that would otherwise have fallen to women workers in the factory. Their extremely low rates of pay inevitably depressed the wages of unskilled women in those industries that used homeworkers extensively. No comparable group of men served to depress male wages, just as none but the very youngest male workers served probationary periods on the job at scandalously substandard pay. The narrow range of jobs open to women, the relative youth and inexperience of most women workers, and the needs of older women for work that proceeded on family rather than factory time created a work force uniquely divided against itself.

Finally, women's wages, particularly in the garment trades, were sometimes diminished by payments to the employer for work materials. Women, heavily employed in light manufacturing and service industries, were probably more vulnerable than men to this kind of wage loss. Garment workers, for example, frequently had to supply their own needles and thread. These were often purchased from the employer at prices higher, not uncommonly, than those in neighborhood stores. Some garment employers charged operators for the electricity that powered their machines. Some even required workers to purchase their own sewing machines.[35] Handworkers in other industries sometimes had to supply their own tools. Box makers, for example, were often required to own the necessary knives and awls.[36] Women who worked in the various food processing and food service industries usually bought their own uniforms. These were only sometimes sold at cost by the employer, and the expense of laundering the uniform was generally borne by the employee.[37] Striking waitresses in Chicago in

1914, Agnes Nestor recalled, complained bitterly of the one dollar per
week deducted from their pay to cover laundry costs. They also had to
pay the busboys a weekly fee, and were charged for food that dis-
satisfied customers returned to the kitchen.[38]

For the marginal entrepreneur, especially, these petty economies
represented valuable savings. The survival of many a business was
probably insured by what was in effect a subsidy paid regularly to the
employer by already underpaid workers. To those workers, however,
the voluntary subsidizing represented a discouraging drain on
their slender wages. "By working hard we could make an average
of about $5 a week," Rose Schneiderman remembered of her work
in a New York cap factory early in the century. "We would have
made more but had to provide our own machines, which cost us
$45, we paying for them on the installment plan." When her factory
burned, the machines were destroyed. "This was very hard on the
girls who had paid for their machines." They were never compen-
sated.[39]

It is significant that women's wages do not, on admittedly limited
evidence, appear generally to have increased with firm profitability.
Women's wages varied considerably within cities and industries, reflecting highly individual labor policies, and the larger and presumably more profitable firms were not invariably the more generous
employers.[40] The Women's Bureau in 1921 found that among large
Chicago candy factories median rates of pay varied by nearly 50%.
In Massachusetts a major state investigation of women's employment
concluded that neither firm size nor profitability guaranteed maximum wages:

> No generalization about the wage level in different localities holds
> good any more than it does for factories making the same grade of
> goods or different grades of goods or for large or small factories.
> The only conclusion is that a firm's policy in hiring labor, and no
> other factor, determines its wage scale.[41]

Many employers thus chose to pay prevailing "women's wages" for
reasons other than strict necessity, and they chose as well to assign

women only to the unskilled jobs that shop tradition and sometimes union pressure defined as exclusively female.

But whether they chose to do so for the sake of sheer economic survival or to secure greatly enhanced profits, most employers made decisions about women that helped to perpetuate existing status and power relationships between the sexes. Women's work rarely provided the means to true economic independence; this meant that fundamental change in women's status in the family could not occur. The women's wage confined the vast majority of women workers to the family; and life within the family shaped most women's values and behavior in essentially conservative ways. The woman's wage communicated to women their inevitable inferiority in nondomestic spheres. The woman's wage confirmed "female" as an immutable social category, and taught women that mobility and independence were cultural goals not appropriate to their sex. And the woman's wage underscored the individual woman's need for male economic protection, thus directing women, quite literally on each payday, to devote their best energies to social life and eventual marriage. The ultimate effect of the woman's wage was to reinforce the docility, the pervasive sense of marginality, that kept most women immobile, poverty-wage workers.

Women's low wages were the most critical factor rendering women's employment a unique experience. But the experience of work entailed more than pay. Also defining a singular female work world were the nature of the jobs open to women, the physical environments of those jobs, the social environments women themselves created at work, and the cultural messages about work and femininity women brought to the job from home, school, and community. Subsequent chapters explore these various dimensions of female experience. We will turn first to the physical and social environments of the "woman's job."

II

"Women's Work" and Work Environments

Spacy, erect, stands a building in which daily workers float in and out.

Without, the wall is decorated in countless signs of different firms in industries, signs in large staring letters "Operators Wanted."

Within, the halls are narrow, dark, the walls filthy, pencil marked, against which lean daughters of the poor, "News Ads" under their arms, waiting for the shops to open.

Their worried wistful faces tell of weary job huntings.

In the gloom of this building people work.

In the factory, at a long row of machines sit girls toiling at dresses, so many dresses hanging, lying about or at work.

How swiftly they work!

Pressers, stamping, pressing, swiftly passing the irons over the iron-boards.

Perspired, sickening faces, eyes dulled with pain of work's long strain.

Worker, how great is the power that binds you to work!

A faint sunbeam uninvited, sets a button glimmering.

And a piece of cloth is flung over the window,—to shut it out.

Thru a crack of the window-pane a vague breeze sends in the fragrance of summer.

Oh, worker does not your heart ache with longing for the sweetness of summer, for the happy out-door sounds, for the light that you have shut out?

Rose Hecht, student, Bryn Mawr School for Women Workers
(Hilda Smith papers)

We have just seen that working-class women were confined to a segregated world of work, one characterized by low wages and limited employment opportunities. But we have yet to see how unusually restrictive that world was even for working-class women in the early twentieth century. The workroom represented a social world where one's sex mattered more than one's intelligence, personal resourcefulness, or physical attractiveness. Women were confined to a truncated job market for reasons of sex alone; talent and ambition only rarely overcame the disability of being a woman. And in those industries that employed a predominantly female work force, the jobs that conferred a measure of status and authority and relatively high wages were normally the province of men. In the world of work, sex, before all else, established the boundaries of opportunity.

But the rigidities of the work world were not necessarily characteristic of other areas of working-class female experience. Public schooling by the early twentieth century was formally uniform for boys and girls, and schools were a locus of female authority. In the home, the force of individual personality often undermined the power of formal patriarchy, and women were frequently strong and controlling figures in working-class families. Organized and informal community life often reflected—even depended on—the authority and interpersonal skills of adult women.

There might well have been ambiguities, then, in the messages about the social meaning of femininity that the young received at home and in school. The work experience was an important element in the socialization of working-class youth, not because it introduced the young to messages of male power and female dependence but because it eliminated the ambiguities encountered in earlier experiences. The sex-segregated work experience defined the limits of female power in the world outside the home; it directed young women and young men toward the distinct and formally inegalitarian sex roles of working-class adulthood. And the work experience elicited from both women and men the attitudes and the behavior that supported the continuation, generation after generation, of a labor force rigidly segregated by sex.

For integral to the world of the sex-segregated workplace were (and are) the rituals of dependence that support all segregation systems, whether based on race, ethnicity, or sex. The realities of this world of work meant for most women a singular work experience.

Certainly working women shared the disabilities of many unskilled male workers. Many men worked at industrial jobs where physical conditions were unpleasant or dangerous—often much more dangerous than the normal conditions of women's work. Men as well as women were subject as workers to the arbitrary discipline of men, machines, and markets. But the world of women's work was unique in significant ways, because for women employment was more nearly a caste than a class experience. Women at work constituted a visibly separate and unequal work community. When men were present in the woman's workroom it was often as supervisors or elite skilled workers. Men rarely if ever encountered in their work the reverse of this sexual hierarchy. Women's jobs, moreover, normally were without ladders to promotion. Even in predominantly female occupations, skilled work was usually men's work, and mobility within an occupation was often reserved for men. Finally, contemporary evidence suggests that the supervisory discipline experienced by women was frequently more pervasive, more petty, and more humiliating than that endured by men.

In sum, women rarely possessed power in the work situation, and they saw at work virtually no avenues for achieving power, individually or collectively. But women, unlike men, were permitted by the culture an acceptable personal and occupational identity entirely independent of paid employment. Most working women were encouraged to regard their paid work as temporary and to understand that the domestic role granted them the greatest possible measure of independence, personal authority, and status. In turn, women's experience of work reflected and reinforced these social judgments, and, in part because of this experience, they were different workers than their industrial brothers. It is to the particulars of the female work experience—the day-to-day encounter with monotony, fatigue, frustration, arbitrary discipline—that we now turn our attention.

"For the eyes bad, for the mind stale": The *"Woman's Job"*

Although the number of women at work in the most populous trades employing women varied from city to city, the basic work processes performed by women were remarkably similar in industrial occupations. Most women in industry operated or tended light machinery or performed such routine hand work as assembling, packing, sorting, and simple sewing. Outside the factory, in sales and service occupations, work generally proceeded under less severe time pressures, and tasks were sometimes more varied. But the work remained routine. Store clerking normally required no particular skills, and the domestic and personal service jobs open to women of limited education demanded strength, speed, and reliability rather than mastery of complex work techniques.[1]

The low skill level of women's industrial work meant monotony on the job: a single, simple task repeated again and again for the duration of a nine- or ten-hour day. A New York City button manufacturer, for example, described in testimony before the State Factory Investigating Commission the quality of the jobs assigned to women in his factory. That this was typical work at typical pay is indicated by the ease with which he secured his workers:

> When a girl has been with us six months she will have attained as much proficiency as she ever will attain. It is not the length of the years. A good deal of the work is done with automatic machines. The girl sits there, or the woman, the machines all work by power, and she puts her metals in, or materials in, and the machine goes on, and whether she is there six months or six years all she does—
>
> Q. How many buttons does she cover in the course of a day with a machine?

A. Some girls might make fifty gross, some forty, some thirty. The buttons vary in size and in the parts that compose them, and it is hard to give you an intelligent answer.

Q. How long does it take to cover a button?

A. Some buttons may be covered in three seconds, and some may take a quarter of a minute.

Q. You say they make fifty gross?

A. They might make fifty gross on these automatic machines.

Q. That would be about 5000 or 7000 a day?

A. About 7000 buttons?

Q. They do that one thing over and over again?

A. Yes, sir.

Q. About 7000 times a day?

A. Yes, sir.

Q. And how many hours are they employed?

A. Nine hours. We adhere rigorously to the restrictions.

Q. They do that every three seconds and you say they are happy?

A.   Yes, sir. I should have liked to have had you with me when I went round the plant on Christmas Eve and heard Christian and Jew alike wish me a happy season and a better season than we had last year.

   We advertised last week for a few beginners to do some work, and, gentlemen, I want to assure you enough applicants came to fill this room standing close together, looking for a $5 a week job, and our advertisement intimated what they were to do. We wanted girls to do so and so, carding buttons. . . . I suppose 500 people came to the place that morning.[2]

During busy seasons no scheduled breaks save the midday meal interrupted the rhythm of the job, while pieceworkers, to maximize earnings, sometimes worked through the brief lunch period.[3] And because most women's labor was unskilled, its profitability depended on high productivity, on speed. The most efficient power sewing machines, Josephine Goldmark noted in 1905, could set 4400 stitches a minute, necessitating constant vigilance on the part of the operative:

The operative cannot see the needle; she sees merely a beam of light striking the steel needle from the electric lamp above her head. But this she must watch, as a cat watches a mousehole; for one variation means that a broken needle is cutting the fibers of the garment, and a different variation means that the thread is broken and the seam is having stitches left unsewn. Then the operative must instantly touch a button and stop the machine. Such intent watching wears out alike nerves and eyes.[4]

Automatic knitting machines took 3500 stitches a minute; automatic presses for molding paper boxes opened and closed every two seconds; flatwork ironers in laundries usually ran at speeds of forty to fifty feet per minute.[5]

Nor did power machinery alone demand speed: workers were urged to swiftness through supervisory discipline and the powerful incentive of piecework wages. In New York City's paper box factories, for example, the State Factory Investigating Commission found eloquent testimony to the intimate link between piecework and hurrying: "If a girl is getting 10¢ a hundred for covering boxes she must turn out 6000 a week in order to make $6; that is, one about every 30 seconds for 54 hours."[6] An experienced cigarette packer, noted Department of Labor investigators, "can pack from 35,000 to 40,000 cigarettes in a day of nine or ten hours."[7] In Pittsburgh cigar factories, Elizabeth Beardsley Butler discovered, piece rates were often set to reward the production of more than 6000 stogies a week.[8] Even relatively prestigious and skilled women's work placed a high premium on production. Chocolate dippers, the "aristocrats" of the candy trade, "work at great speed, some of the fastest accomplishing on plain goods from 115 to 120 pounds a day, while the average dipper does about 75 to 80 pounds."[9]

Speed on the job was a kind of skill: it required time and effort to achieve top speeds, and experienced workers earned more, often considerably more, than learners. But speed was a skill achieved relatively quickly: after three to six months on almost any women's job, a worker attained maximum productivity. Indeed, long years on the job were widely believed to impair a woman's ability to work rapidly.[10] Achieving speed was not the sort of skill that involved increased learning about the job, nor did the ability to perform a simple task rapidly provide women with passports to more interesting, complex, and better-paid employment. Rather, the swiftest workers succeeded in securing themselves firmly to their routine and repetitive jobs. There was no economic incentive for employers to promote such efficient workers to new and different tasks. "For the eyes bad, for the mind stale; no time to think, all the time run, run," an immigrant power machine operator summarized her present job and her future job prospects.[11]

The routine nature of most women's work inhibited the development of personal interest in the job. There was often an initial sense of excitement and liberation for new, young workers. For them, the mysterious bustle of the workroom, the heady thrill of a wage packet, the camaraderie with workmates defined a world far more intriguing than home or school. But once a simple job was learned, once maximum wages were attained, there was little in the process of work itself to hold the interest of the employee or to demand her intellectual energies. Louise Odencrantz, questioning New York employers about the desirability of trade school training for women, found confirmation of the utterly simple and routine nature of work traditionally assigned to women: "When they were asked whether it would be feasible to have the work taught in a trade school, they made such replies as, 'It would be superfluous,' 'The process is too simple to make trade school training wise or useful,' or 'No training is necessary.' "[12]

Rather than discovering personal satisfaction in work itself, most women found what job satisfaction they could in relationships with coworkers and in the pride of earning a money wage—strategies characteristic of the unskilled. The wage envelope, however, usually proved for women a fragile source of self-esteem: women's wages were low, and while a woman might feel justifiable pride in helping to support her family, her brothers and her father were likely to earn considerably more than she, and they had greater discretion in disposing of their wages. Friendships at work were a more enduring source of satisfaction. But, as we will discover, the social community women created at work inhibited the development of ambition, aggressiveness, competitiveness—precisely the characteristics necessary for individual mobility or leadership of effective collective action. A male work group, on the other hand, easily sanctioned aggression as a properly masculine trait. And men, in a society that highly valued individual mobility, were less capable than women of rejecting work-related ambitions in favor of workroom camaraderie.

If the monotony of the typical woman's job discouraged work-related ambitions, so much more did the dearth of advancement possibilities in women's work. Dead-end jobs simply confirmed women in an essential indifference to their work and to social mobility through paid employment. Even those few skilled jobs reserved for women tended to be visibly less interesting and lower paid than men's skilled work in the same trade. Chocolate dipping, the most prestigious job open to women in the candy trade, was a skilled task so tedious that New York investigators reported in 1915: "Deaf mutes make good dippers, of which fact manufacturers seem aware, for one applied at asylums for workers." Indeed, the eventual mechanization of this hand-task provided a new skilled job for male confectionery workers as machine regulators, while women assumed the unskilled work of feeding the new machines.[13]

The sexual division of labor in predominantly female trades meant, moreover, that a minority of high-status men were often present in the women's workroom, effective testimony to the importance of sex in determining one's fate in the world of work. In garment shops, for example, the prestigious and well-paid cutters were always male, and men did the skilled sewing on cloaks and suits. Women were assigned simple machine operations and the various tasks of hand-finishing— adding buttons, felling, snipping basting. In garment workrooms, as in all occupations employing power machinery, the skilled machine repairmen were always male, and it was on the services of these men that the earnings of pieceworkers depended.[14] In cigar making, women workers were concentrated in the low-skill processes of simple machine operation and preparation of materials for assembly. Men dominated the ranks of the skilled handworkers; where women did the actual making of cigars, their work generally involved only the cheap stogy.[15] In the manufacture of candy, indeed, in most food processing industries, men served as the skilled preparers, the cooks, while women sorted and packed the finished product.[16] In retail stores, especially in the larger chain and department stores, the immediate supervisor was usually male.[17]

Supervisory personnel in factories employing women, especially in large numbers, were more likely to be female, although the male supervisor was a very common experience of women's factory employment. While 36.8% of all factory operatives in 1910 were women, only 8.2% of all foremen in that year were female. And though nearly half of all female supervisors were employed in garment manufacture and the textile trades, a 1915 Cleveland study found among 3308 male garment workers and 5029 female workers a total of 192 male supervisors but only 98 women in supervisory positions. The factory "forelady," however, was visibly an intermediary for male authority. Department and factory managers and factory owners were nearly always men.[18]

Sometimes, of course, men monopolized the skilled positions in women's occupations for obvious physical reasons: some skilled work was heavy, and required greater strength than most women were believed to possess. But more often, skilled workers simply invoked tradition to protect relatively lucrative and high-status jobs from female competition, sometimes with the aid of unions openly hostile to the employment of women.[19] Both organized and unorganized skilled male workers argued that women were but temporary workers outside the home. Their true vocation was marriage and motherhood, and rigorous, expensive apprenticeship training would be wasted on even ambitious females. Nearly always these arguments were persuasive to male employers. The supervisor of a magazine bindery, where women were employed exclusively on unskilled hand folding, summarized the reflexively conservative labor policy of many employers:

"I could put a girl to work operating the cutting machine," he said, "if I paid her $18 a week . . . I could have a woman tend the large folding machine if I paid her the same as the union scale for men. I don't know why I don't, except that I see no good reason why I should." [20]

The low-skill nature of women's work meant pronounced job insecurity. Unskilled women were a readily interchangeable work force, likely to be laid off arbitrarily during slack seasons in particular industries and rehired just as casually into other low-skill occupations. A majority of women's industrial jobs were characterized by extreme seasonality: garment making and such related trades as button manufacture suffered two slack seasons a year, and the majority of women employed in these industries could depend on no more than eight or nine months of work annually. [21] The millinery industry employed the bulk of its labor force only eight to ten months a year. [22] Artificial flower and feather manufacture, responding to variations in the production of women's hats, provided work for most of its employees but eight or nine months a year, while two popular women's industries, paper box manufacture and candy making, were limited by holiday-related demand cycles to two busy seasons annually, totaling perhaps nine months of full-time work. [23] Even meatpacking suffered seasonal variations, and women in this industry generally lost one to two months of work during the year. [24] Sales and service work were not normally disrupted by wide seasonal variations in employment, although retail sales forces were augmented each Christmas season with fresh recruits who were rarely kept on in the new year. And some personal service occupations, such as laundering, experienced "summer doldrums" when much of their clientele was away from the city. Clerical work, however, generally promised stable employment, barring hard times. The stability of office work doubtless enhanced its inherent appeal for the working-class young and perhaps helped to reconcile the better-educated worker to the low pay that characterized most clerical employment.

For many women, especially industrial workers, seasonal unemployment confirmed their status as marginal employees. Lacking any enduring value in the eyes of their superiors, women were customarily dismissed with scant ceremony and little advance warning, and they were often dismissed while the workroom elite of skilled male workers remained secure in their positions. At least once, frequently two or three times a year, a majority of industrial women received direct and public notice of their inferior status in the world of work, and they were forced either into a humiliating and often discouraging search for alternative employment or into a condition of semi-bondage to the employer.

Some employers of women insisted, as a condition of rehiring with the return of the busy season, that their workers report daily to the idle workroom, for even in dull months a few orders were received.[25] Particularly for a small business, this was an effective way of retaining an experienced work force, one that might resume full production immediately with the new season. Such policies reinforced the passivity and timidity of some unskilled women who, lacking experience even in the narrow world of women's industries, might come to believe that their entire working life depended on the whims of a single employer. This was a particular danger for older women, less adventurous than their young sisters by dint of poverty and the pervasive job discrimination practiced against women beyond their mid-thirties. Katherine Anthony, interviewing working mothers in Manhattan, discovered one poignant example:

> Carrying some fresh-air excursion tickets in August to a laundry worker, for herself and her children, I was told that she could not afford to use them. At that time she was working at a laundry only at odd intervals during the week, but she dared not leave home lest the foreman should happen to send for her in her absence.[26]

For a majority of working women, however, the dull season meant a lengthy search for alternative employment. Seasonal downturns in major women's industries often coincided, and during some months of the year the job market for unskilled women was hopelessly overcrowded. Looking for work was then an exhausting, disappointing and often humiliating experience. The applicant left home early in the morning, waited with a crowd of other women for an employer or foreman to make his brusque choice of a fortunate few, and then returned home defeated to a family that regarded her wages as essential to its support.[27] A young New Yorker elaborated during a 1909 study of seasonal unemployment:

> "Yes, I get the papers right away in the morning, but when you come to the place there are always so many others waiting, and then it is too late to go to any other place. Sometimes the man takes your name and says he will let you know in a couple of days. You wait, but you don't hear a word from him. Half the time he doesn't want anybody. I just hate to look for work. You always feel kind of upset like, and don't feel like doing anything at home."[28]

Unemployment was not, of course, confined to working-class women; their fathers and husbands and brothers were often regularly unemployed. But women and men experienced unemployment differently and learned from it different lessons and different responses. Both men and women learned through unemployment the insecurity integral to many working-class jobs. But men, in the labor market for a lifetime and actual or potential economic heads of household, either aspired to steadier employment, urged their sons in this direction, or developed secondary skills in response. In defeat, they might turn to drink or withdraw into a morose apathy. In any event, their families and their family role served to remind them of personal failure. Women, however, relearned at each period of unemployment the importance of home and family for women's livelihood. Even when unemployed, women did not cease to be daughters or wives; unlike unemployed men, they retained in the home useful and respected functions. The two worlds of home and work were thus dramatically contrasted: home, whatever its poverty, offered at least subsistence and certain status; the job promised neither security nor a firm and lasting sense of self-esteem.

Women's Work Environments: Working Conditions, Work Discipline, Hours of Work

THE PHYSICAL WORK ENVIRONMENT

Work environments in women's industries varied enormously. "The workrooms represented every stage in the development of the factory system," wrote Louise Odencrantz of women's employment on Manhattan's West Side in 1912:

> In one instance three women sat making candy in what had formerly been a flat in an apartment house, while a few blocks away some 500 were employed in an eight-story building where they had the latest equipment in the way of an automatic sprinkler system, fire doors, excellent light, ample space, and a ventilating system.[29]

Nor did New York boast a monopoly on dramatic industrial contrasts. In all manufacturing cities of the early twentieth century, a part of the female population was employed in barely habitable sweat shops, while other luckier women labored in the relative safety and comfort of large modern factories.[30]

Probably the most important factor in determining the quality of the work environment was the size of the firm. Large establishments—those employing more than one hundred women—often, though not always, provided noticeably superior working conditions and sometimes shorter hours.[31] Large enterprises were highly visible, and where even nominal commitment to enforcing women's labor laws existed, it was the visible firm that was obliged to cease flagrant violations of health, safety, and hours regulations. The often ephemeral small manufacturing business frequently escaped the notice of the proper legal authorities. An investigator of New York City's garment industry complained in 1915:

At present, any person who has the necessary capital or credit may build, lease, or hire any ramshackle building, engage as many workers as he can crowd into his premises, and work them under any conditions. The very existence of this establishment may not be known to the Labor Department until it is discovered by accident.

In the investigation of the Cloak and Suit Industry, made during the last year, by the Joint Board of Sanitary Control, about 30% of the shops were found unrecorded, and in our own investigation, our inspectors found the utmost difficulty in tracing many establishments which were never recorded by the Labor Department. . .[32]

The large firm, moreover, was the more likely to return a reasonably high profit; larger establishments could afford the spacious, highly mechanized plants that contributed directly to efficiency in production. But not all large firms guaranteed their employees adequate work environments. Rapidly expanding businesses, especially early in the century, often crowded growing work forces into poorly lit and hopelessly congested factories. Thus, a 1904 investigation found the vast Chicago packinghouses "for the most part old frame buildings, the result of an unconscious growth" characterized by "dark passageways, long wooden stairways, and apparently involved means of entrance and exit."[33] Women worked in these plants in dim and chilly rooms, sometimes standing in pools of water.[34] Successful New York garment shops were often located in loft buildings never intended for manufacturing purposes, as indeed were the workrooms of many New York industries.[35] Many Philadelphia textile mills, by the twentieth century vast monuments to a declining industry, were more than fifty years old, noteworthy for "their general gloom and dirt."[36]

But it was the large, successful firm that provided the most dramatic improvements in women's working conditions over time. If women's conditions of work improved in the early decades of the century—and on the whole they did—it was mainly because the firm employing women was increasingly a large, bureaucratically-managed, reasonably profitable operation. Conditions improved also because progressive economic concentration and centralization meant decline of the individual entrepreneur and the marginal sweated trades. For the mod-

ern employer, an adequate work environment was a routine business
expense, an investment in productivity. Improved conditions of work
resulted from business rationalization much more frequently than from
the organized protests of working women.

Despite progressive improvement in their conditions of work, however, a majority of women who worked in factory and service occupations before 1930 were employed in environments that were objectively
unpleasant and uncomfortable. A minority of women worked under
conditions that were positively dangerous to health. This was especially true before the First World War. Workrooms were commonly
crowded; machines and workbenches lined narrow aisles in typical
small factories, with stock and assembled products piled along the
walls.[37] "The seats on this floor [top] are so close together that look
[sic] more like sardines packed in a box," wrote a shirtwaist operator
in 1912.[38] Crowding meant intense discomfort in the summer heat and
serious, omnipresent fire danger. Factories were often very dirty. Garment workrooms were littered with the scraps and lint of several days'
work; food processing rooms were sometimes literally encrusted with
spilled ingredients; box factories were piled high with inevitable waste
paper; and even laundries—in the pursuit of cleanliness—were
frequently marked by "the unswept and rotting wooden floors, the
dirty windows, and the layer of dust and lint on everything."[39] "The
great majority of factories examined by the commission were found to
be in an uncleanly condition," announced the New York State Factory
Investigating Commission in 1915.[40] Even the workrooms of New
York's elegant Bloomingdale's were not exempt from such criticism.
"We have plenty of windows but they were never cleaned," wrote
one young employee. "The rooms is [sic] also kept very unclean
spicaly [sic] the floors are never scrubbed."[41]

Workrooms were often dimly lit and poorly ventilated. The lighting
in garment shops, binderies, artificial flower shops, millinery
workrooms, and packing houses was criticized by various investigators.[42] "Your sisters, the Employees of Cohen Brothers" wrote the
New York Women's Trade Union League in 1911: "Would like to tell

you about some of the conditions in our factory. First of all about the stairs. It is so dark in the halls that when we go home at night we fall down the stairs."[43] "One felt almost as if shut up in some dungeon of an earlier age, and breathed a sigh of relief on returning to the freer air and outlook of the street," wrote a Chicago investigator of sweatshops in that city.[44] And the New York State Factory Investigating Commission noted, with a particular eye to the health hazard:

> Of the 5,124 shops investigated, only 604 or 11.8% were provided with some system of mechanical ventilation, and this was not always in good order or properly used. . . . The industries in which the worst conditions prevail as to ventilation come under the following heads: chemical, textile, printing, tobacco, artificial flowers and feathers, and human hair.[45]

Poor ventilation often meant discomfort at work: a study of New York laundries, for example, discovered that most were not equipped with heating systems, and in the winter they simply closed all fans and windows to retain natural steam heat. This meant, of course, that "the air of almost every steam laundry is oppressive."[46] And poor ventilation could pose a danger to health. A New York factory investigator found one feather-making workroom, inadequately ventilated, with "an atmosphere which is simply impossible to look through, so thick is the dust of the feathers floating in the air."[47] Women who worked in cotton mills and in other occupations where workroom air was constantly dust-saturated were particularly prone to serious respiratory diseases. A poorly ventilated workroom, moreover, exacerbated the physical effects of noxious fumes in some industries: " 'Four out of five girls can't stand the smell of the glue,' said Mr. Finnegan of the Pioneer Box Company, 'It makes them sick as does the odor of rubber in a rubber factory.' "[48]

Some women's workrooms were excessively hot or cold; laundries, for example, were often uncomfortably warm. A study of the work environments of flatwork ironers revealed that some of these operators worked in 95° heat, though temperature measurements were taken in the early spring.[49] During the summer months, many crowded and poorly ventilated workrooms were stifling. Other women worked for most of the year in abnormally cold surroundings. Candymakers, for example, often worked at temperatures of 65° or even less, for chocolate would not harden properly at higher temperatures, and some packinghouse occupations were carried out in rooms so cold that women wore coats and gloves at work. These workers frequently complained that they contracted continual colds on the job.[50]

Women's workrooms were often noisy. Even light machinery produced a deafening roar in a small shop filled to capacity with machines. This was a particular problem in the garment trades.[51] "More than half of the shops visited were noisy," noted Louise Odencrantz of Manhattan's West Side, "and a large part of these were in the sewing trades, where the power machines pound away at great speed." A "practically noiseless" sewing machine was available, she argued in 1912, but was rarely used because of the expense of conversion to the employer.[52] Noise in the workroom was often a source of acute physical discomfort to the employee, and the constant din of machinery made tedious and tiring work even more exhausting. A young Russian immigrant left her garment factory after six months because "the machines were so close, so noisy, there was no breath."[53] "The whole scene is dominated by the clamor of the machines making a noise like rolling thunder," wrote a garment worker in 1927:

> The machine for hemstitching when in operation sounds like a heavy truck going up hill on a paved road with a screeching, rasping, rattling noise. The rest of the sewing machines buzz and drone continuously.[54]

And noisy workrooms made difficult the conversation and singing among employees that normally sped the long day. Machine operators were rarely silent—one garment worker remembered "quarreling, singing, and the hum of voices above the drone of machinery"—but the power machine disturbed easy and intimate sociability.[55] "I turn my head away and begin to sing," ran a poem by a young operator, "And it seems to me that the machinery/Gets noisier still."[56]

The women's workroom was, however, much safer than the work environments of many male trades. Women worked at hazardous occupations much less frequently than men, relatively few women came into contact with industrial poisons, and virtually no women worked in the industries with the nation's highest industrial accident rates—railroads, mining, and steel. The industrial accident rate for women was much lower than that for men, and most injuries sustained by women were not seriously incapacitating. Notwithstanding, the misfortunes incident to "women's work" sometimes left lasting scars. "Her left hand had been pierced through when as a girl she had worked in the infamous Triangle Shirtwaist Factory on the East Side," Alfred Kazin wrote of his mother. "A needle had gone straight through the palm, severing a large vein. They had sewn it up for her so clumsily that a tuft of flesh always lay folded over the palm."[57]

Working women were a population particularly threatened by fire, as the 1911 Triangle Shirtwaist Factory disaster so tragically illustrated. Light industry, the employer of the majority of factory women, could often be conducted in quarters not originally built for manufacturing. These premises as industrial sites were generally overcrowded, often of highly flammable construction, with insufficient provision for fire prevention or efficient building evacuation. In the winter of 1909–10, an investigation of the premises of the strike-bound Triangle Shirtwaist Company by *The Survey* magazine uncovered personal testimony that was "like a forecast" of the subsequent disaster:

> "Once on Sunday—we had to work on Sunday from eight to four—there was a fire on the eighth floor. I was on the ninth. They locked the door on the ninth floor and kept us there till the fire was out. It was awful. Some of the girls got their fingers stuck in the needles, they were so frightened."[58]

Women also comprised the great majority of the labor force in large retail stores, many of which were virtual firetraps. In the aftermath of the Triangle fire, investigations of fire safety on commercial and industrial premises were carried out in a number of cities, and in New York, Chicago, and Boston investigators confirmed that a majority of women at work in these cities were employed in stores and factories inadequately protected against fire.[59]

Fire was a hazard normally removed from workers' immediate concerns and discontents in the workroom. In the aftermath of the Triangle fire, and especially in New York, however, many working women became aware of potential fire danger in their own workrooms, and what little we know of their response to this issue is revealing. The New York Women's Trade Union League published in several New York newspapers an employee questionnaire concerning conditions of work, especially fire hazards, in stores and factories employing women. A variety of responses were received by the league, many describing serious fire danger in individual workplaces and many expressing genuine fear that the respondents might suffer the fate of the Triangle victims. But nearly all the extant letters expressed as well a profound sense of helplessness. Despite the individual or collective act of writing in protest to the league, the respondents plead for help from the outside. No mention was made of workroom protest; many respondents were anonymous for fear of employer reprisal. "Please see to this as we can't stand it any longer. *Please,*" wrote "your sisters, the Employees of Cohen Brothers" of conditions in their Brooklyn paper box factory.

"Be a friend to us if you can," wrote "an employee" of a New York steam laundry, "and see that we get more than the window and one exit—Elevator is broken all the time and for days has not been able to be used in case of fire poor girls and old woman would all be burned to death." "I would cheerfully sign my name, but I do not want to lose my job, as I support my mother," wrote a bindery worker. She believed that her employer was bribing the local fire inspector. "I would be afraid to sign my name and address it might cost me my life otherwise I should be glad to comply with your request," wrote an employee in a paper box factory. Her loft building housed a steam laundry in the basement:

> Our boss should allow the basement to be free from fire traps.
> Laundries are very dangerous to be at the bottom of a great big fac-

tory as we work in every day. We could never escape to the street or Elevator as ropes and elevators are both rotten and would break and we would all be killed instantly and the boss keeps the roof locked all the time and basement, also boiler room in the basement. The engineer says [it] is in a very bad condition, likely to burst at any time and heat of the Mangles is bound to set fire to this factory before long.

And Hattie Rosofsky wrote of the Weisen and Goldstein shirtwaist factory: "Am well acquainted with several girls of the place and also with the conditions. I'm compelled to do so [to write], because the girls are all cowards. They are perhaps . . . afraid of losing their job." [60]

Doubtless these women understood correctly their precarious job security; doubtless economic need prevented many from considering collective action an appropriate response to dangerous conditions. And certainly there were many men who resigned themselves, sometimes without protest, to hazardous conditions on the job. For women, however, a sense of powerlessness at work reinforced dramatically the sexual stereotypes they brought to the job; they learned through their own painful experience that women were ineffectual and vulnerable once they ventured beyond the home and neighborhood. Men did not have recourse to a simple sexual explanation of their own fate. And dangerous or unpleasant work environments probably enhanced for women the prospect of eventual domesticity. As mistress of a home, a young woman might hope to control her own work environment, to create a refuge from dirt and noise and crowding, though poverty might ultimately frustrate her aspirations.

WORK DISCIPLINE

Supervisory discipline in the woman's workroom reinforced the lessons of the physical work environment. Pervasive and arbitrary discipline was an important aspect of the work experience of most unskilled women. If they shared this disability with many unskilled men, women were both less capable than men of individual or collective resistance to supervisory prerogatives and more sensitive to the personal affront conveyed by a supervisor's over-zealous exercise of disciplinary authority. Women were less well unionized than even unskilled men. Perhaps more important—given the rarity of industrial unions in this period—the woman's work group often undermined sustained aggressive challenges to supervisory authority. But women did resent, often bitterly, the disciplinary practices they encountered on the job; these constituted major grievances against the employer in those rare moments of women's collective protest. The endurance of a hated discipline, then, was for many women an important affirmation of their impotence and low status as workers. And because authority relationships on women's jobs were so often determined by sex, the experience of work discipline was for many women a constant ritual acquiescence to male dominance with the possibility, at least in some situations, of threatened or actual sexual exploitation. For unskilled men, authority relations at work were class relations or ethnic relations, but these never, save for black workers, bore the aspect of a caste relationship.

Most women's employers assumed the necessity of rigid work discipline because they employed a largely young and unskilled population. The unskilled, and particularly the young unskilled, were widely believed, not without reason, to be transient, indifferent, even deliberately careless workers.[61] Women, furthermore, were heavily employed in labor-intensive industries, where, in the absence of machinery, work discipline was imposed principally by stringent supervision. Women were also believed to be more easily disciplined than men, and male supervisors were readily persuaded that their authority over a female work force was natural and appropriate. The temptation to supervisory excess was therefore considerable. "Every time a new foreman came in he demonstrated his authority by inaugurating a new set of petty rules which seemed designed merely to irritate us," Agnes Nestor remembered of her work experience in Chicago glove factories.[62]

The supervisor was a potent disciplinary agent because he normally possessed the power to hire and fire. And he established the emotional atmosphere in which his authority was maintained. Many supervisors, according to contemporary reports, asserted their authority over women as aggressively as possible. They shouted and swore, and very probably indulged liberally in sexual innuendo: "Abusive and insulting language is frequently used by those in authority in the shops," complained striking Chicago garment workers in 1910.[63] Given the conventions governing normal male-female interaction, a foreman's verbal abuse represented a potent assault on a woman's self-respect, and verbal violence could scarcely help but threaten those who sensed themselves to be physically inferior to the aggressor.

In unorganized shops, moreover, supervisors possessed great freedom to invoke discipline in arbitrary and capricious ways. Complaints of supervisory favoritism were very common among workers. "When there is not much work the girls do not get the same amount, some only get five pair and others get ten pairs," ran the grievances of striking Chicago basters. "The girls ask that they be given an equal amount."[64] Again, the possibility of sexual exploitation arises. Certainly, it was not common for a woman to buy job security in exchange for sexual availability. But very likely the attractive woman who was willing to flirt with her supervisor and laugh at his suggestive banter was often a favored worker. With some women in a shop obviously being rewarded for their femininity, abusive treatment of others might well seem to them a devastating personal affront. For all women ever confronted with this situation the job prospects for older women must have seemed bleak.

Whether or not a supervisor maintained control through sexual favoritism, however, his authority was felt throughout the long working day. Many employers, for example, forbade women the use of seats on the job, arguing that seated workers were neither alert nor attentive and that their productivity declined accordingly. Little objective data existed to confirm this prejudice, and investigators found instances of workers in the same trade seated or standing at identical occupations according to particular workroom rules. But probably the large majority

of store and factory women spent most of each working day on their
feet; for all but the physically strongest, this element of workroom discipline rendered the long day cruelly, even dangerously, exhausting.[65] "This continual standing is one of the worst features of
a large part of the work done by women in factories." noted the New
York State Factory Investigating Commission. "Much of it is quite
unnecessary and may be due to the fact that both the management and
inspection of factories are usually in the hands of men who are apt to
be ignorant or careless of the effect on women of prolonged standing."[66]

Some industrial states by the early twentieth century required seats
in stores and factories employing women. Often, the law was ignored.
But even where the more conscientious employers furnished the necessary chairs or stools, they might well forbid their employees to sit at
work, and the demands of the employer were normally more potent
than the distant protections of the law. "Most of the women say that
they are closely watched, and are reprimanded by the floor man of
their section if they sit down, even if they are not busy," wrote a federal investigator of retail clerks in Chicago in 1910*:

> In one of the leading stores a certain section was provided with
> seats in compliance with the Illinois statute. The head of the section
> is a very young man. He solved the problem by circulating among
> the women a paper upon which they were asked to sign a statement
> that they would not use the seats. The majority, fearing the loss of
> their positions, signed the circular.[67]

*Some sixty-five years later, Louise Kapp Howe interviewed the female assistant per-
sonnel manager of a large New York department store on just this issue:

> "And one final thing," I ask. "Why isn't it possible to have chairs for the
> workers? Particularly for the cashiers. But also for the sales help. Couldn't
> there be chairs so the employees would be able to rest their feet when business
> is slow?"
> "I can't answer that," Andrea says. "I don't know why. I guess it's just
> always been that way."

The New York statute requiring seats for women in retail and most factory occupations
remained nominally in force. But by 1975 neither workers nor management seemed to
know it. (Louise Kapp Howe, *Pink-Collar Workers: Inside the World of Women's Work*
[New York: G. P. Putnam's Sons, 1977], p. 91.)

Supervisory discipline enforced long working hours and constant attentiveness to speeded work. An elaborate system of fines encouraged punctuality in many stores and factories. Many firms exacted ten or fifteen cents for even a few minutes tardiness, and a group of striking Chicago garment workers complained in 1910: "If the girls forget to punch their time cards when coming in the shop they are fined twenty-five cents."[68] Other employers required more serious forfeitures: delinquent employees were barred from the shop after a certain time, thus surrendering at least half a day's pay.[69] Maud Nathan wrote to the *New York Times* in 1900:

> Some manufacturers make it a rule to refuse to admit employees if they are five minutes late in the morning, that is, if they arrive at 8:05 o'clock, but compel them to walk the streets until the noon hour. They are then allowed to enter and work a half day. Many young girls have complained to me in regard to this cruel rule.[70]

In 1915 the New York State Factory Investigating Commission reported this same practice in some New York City stores: "194 female employees out of 831 questioned in twenty New York City stores, testified to having been fined for lateness," noted the commission. "The amounts vary from 10¢ to forfeiture of half a day's pay."[71]

Fines of varying amounts punished careless work in factories and incorrect change and lost packages in stores.[72] Speeded production encouraged poor work; supervisors, accordingly, often believed that fines were necessary to preserve a semblance of quality control. But to many working women, these penalties appeared to enforce an impossible pace of work, and they believed that payment for honest errors under such conditions ought to be borne by the company.[73] In a rare and dramatic instance of sustained organized protest by women workers, striking basters in a Chicago garment factory itemized their grievances over work procedures. Prominent in this bill of particulars were various charges for mistakes and careless work:

> Ten stitches have to be taken on each side of the canvass and if the girls make less they are fined ten cents and have to rip the work.

Sometimes they are sent home for two or more days or are made [to] wait for work.

If strips fall on the floor the girls are fined five cents.

The girls have to count their own pieces of canvass, padding, and haircloth. If they make a mistake in their count they are fined for each piece they are over or short of the required number.

The fines are: for padding, fifteen cents; canvass pieces, thirty cents; and for haircloth thirty cents, for each piece.

The girls are fined five cents for any spool lost whether it is partly used or empty.[74]

In retail stores the system of fines as an incentive to honest, efficient work was sometimes supplemented by clandestine surveillance of workers by management. In New York City department stores, the State Factory Investigating Commission found detective operations designed to monitor the honesty, diligence, and loyalty of saleswomen: "Not only are 'outsiders' employed, in the guise of shoppers, etc., to test and report, but employees are encouraged to report on the delinquencies of colleagues." Some women received additional wages as a reward for reporting the transgressions of fellow workers. Many women were required, on entering employment, to sign a pledge promising to report "any act or conduct of . . . fellow-employees that you consider against the interest of our business." Such practices, suggested the commission, doubtless made attempts at collective action very difficult.[75] They were clearly intended to do so.

Supervisors often maintained a rigid discipline in the shop even when production was not directly an issue. Pieceworkers, for example, were frequently required to be present in the shop for the full scheduled day, whether or not work was ready for them to do.[76] "In slack season not infrequently a girl reported for work at the usual time and sat idle all morning, to be told at noon that she was not needed," reported *The Survey* magazine in 1909 of conditions at the Triangle Shirtwaist Company.[77] Workers thus lost their putative autonomy under the piecework system, while employers enjoyed the system's undisputed economy. The very presence of idle, resentful workers in the shop, moreover, normally bolstered supervisory authority, being eloquent testimony to the supervisor's power and to the impotence even of angry employees.

Supervisors determined under what circumstances a worker might leave the shop. In some Chicago garment firms, one investigator noted, "girls are not permitted to go home for sickness unless it is an illness sufficiently serious to frighten the superintendent."[78] The supervisor strictly regulated his workers' movements about the workroom; often, he required that they seek permission to use the toilets. Federal investigators at the Chicago packinghouses commented in 1906: "In some establishments women are even placed in charge of privies chiefly for the purpose, it was stated, to see that the girls did not absent themselves too long from their work under the excuse of visiting them."[79]

In some factories, and especially in food-processing plants, investigators found women assuming janitorial tasks in addition to their own regularly scheduled work. Some firms even required their female employees to clean the toilets. Since women were so heavily employed in light industry, where custodial work could be done reasonably efficiently by the workers themselves, they were probably much more frequently subjected to this humiliation than were men. And they regarded the work as humiliating as well as physically burdensome. For a population that considered factory work a prestigious alternative to domestic service, the weekly cleaning tasks represented temporary but very real downward mobility.[80]

Industrial cleaning chores were therefore experienced by many women as gratuitously insulting, and certainly the conditions of this work suggest that their employers were little concerned with the worker's self-image. According to a Labor Department investigator, candy workers in Chicago scrubbed the sticky floors and tables of the workroom each week and "complained of getting their dresses wet up to their knees."[81] Pieceworkers were paid nothing for cleaning chores, according to a 1919 investigation of the candy trade in Philadelphia. Even the skilled and prestigious dippers were found scrubbing in many factories—usually without compensation—for dippers were

normally pieceworkers.[82] In Pittsburgh's Heinz pickle factory, Mrs.
Van Vorst, a middle-class but perceptive participant-observer, found
in 1903 that women regularly scrubbed their workrooms on their
knees. Discontent was widespread, but no effective group protest had
succeeded in modifying the hated practice:

> When lunch is over we are set to scrubbing. Every table and
> stand, every inch of the factory floor must be scrubbed in the next
> four hours. The whistle on Saturday blows an hour earlier. Any girl
> who has not finished her work when the day is done, so that she can
> leave things in perfect order, is kept overtime, for which she is paid
> at the rate of six or seven cents an hour. . . . The grumbling is gen-
> eral. There is but one opinion among the girls: it is not right that
> they are made to do this work. They all echo the same resentment,
> but their complaints are made in whispers; no one has the courage to
> openly rebel.[83]

Mrs. Van Vorst also found that Heinz's male employees, working
in adjacent rooms, refused to scrub on their knees; men's cleaning
chores were limited each week to a more dignified hosing and swab-
bing of workroom surfaces and floors.[84] Through collective action,
then, these low-skill men had limited employer control over an important aspect of the job and had succeeded in retaining a measure of self-
respect even as they functioned each week as janitors. But despite
their example, the Heinz women remained "on their knees," reinforcing for themselves and a male audience images of male and female that
assigned to and legitimized for women absolute inferiority as workers.
That the Heinz women believed "it is not right that they are made to
do this work" is important; it is also important that they continued to
do this work, week after week. What is done at work is gradually in-
corporated into the sense of self-as-worker. Failure to rebel may then
reflect private doubt about the legitimacy of rebellion as well as the
fear of losing one's job.

Supervisory discipline in the women's workroom, in sum, kept
most women clearly at the bottom of the status and power hierarchy at
work. Often, though not always, the dispensers of that discipline were

male, and ultimate authority at work nearly always belonged to a man. The obvious contrast to this particular institutionalized relationship between the sexes was the role of adult women in the working-class family. For most women, the vocation of wife and mother provided a work environment freer from male control, freer from the humiliations of that control, than the environment of the typical woman's job.

HOURS OF WORK

Most working women exercised little control over the length of the workday. What decline occurred in women's hours during the period 1900–1930 was due primarily to legal restrictions on women's employment and to increasingly sophisticated management techniques, which recognized that excessively long hours often substantially reduced worker productivity.[85] Despite gradual reductions in women's hours in the three decades before 1930, however, the typical woman's workday was long and fatiguing, though its length could vary considerably. Overtime extended the regularly scheduled workday for perhaps four to six months of the year in many women's occupations; slack seasons often severely contracted the workday during two, three, four, or even five additional months. Many working women found the length of the busy season workday a source of physical and mental exhaustion. The variability of work hours proved additionally a source of extreme insecurity.

The scheduled workday for women varied from city to city, from trade to trade, and even between firms in the same industry. Generally, establishments in major cities had shorter hours than small-town firms; large, profitable businesses tended more toward shorter workdays than did small marginal enterprises.[86] Before 1920 a majority of women at work in the largest cities of the East and Midwest were scheduled for weeks of roughly fifty-four hours—nine- or perhaps ten-hour days, with a frequent half-holiday on Saturday; by the mid-1920s, the scheduled work week was normally about forty-eight hours. But many women, especially before World War One, were regularly employed for even longer hours, and overtime in the busy season often extended the working day beyond the legal limits.[87] "Shops that have posted fifty-eight, fifty-six, fifty-four, or fifty-one hours a week may have overtime which brings them up to and beyond the sixty-hour mark from four to six months a year," noted the New York State Factory Investigating Commission of factory women in New York City in 1915.

> Girls who have kept account of their hours in the busy season at rush time in the laundry, clothing, artificial flower and printing trades find that they have frequently worked sixty-two to eighty-one hours per week, and ten to fifteen hours a day.[88]

Frequent overtime was a serious problem because overtime work was difficult to regulate legally. Many women's shops neglected to post current statutes governing women's employment, though this was required by law, and many women, particularly immigrant women, were utterly ignorant of the laws that ostensibly protected them from excessive hours at work.[89] Where women were aware that hours laws were regularly violated, both ignorance of corrective procedures and fear of employer reprisal caused workers to accept practices they knew to be illegal. "In spite of their dislike of overtime, the employees are usually wont to protect their own interests by shielding their employer rather than by assisting inspectors in the enforcement of the law," a Department of Labor investigator wrote of Boston dressmakers.[90] Some workers who appeared before the hearings of the New York State Factory Investigating Commission claimed not to know the names of their employers; others assured commisioners that legal hours and sanitary conditions prevailed even in their sweated occupations. And some employers eluded the legal process by compelling employees to finish overtime work at home.

Overtime work was difficult for employers to schedule in advance; consequently, many women learned of the extended workday only an hour or so before normal closing time. The employer thus acquired a peculiarly intimate authority over the lives of his workers. " 'I could never make engagements,' said one much-discouraged girl: 'I never had Saturday nights.' "[91] Certainly employers did not commonly extinguish the social lives of their workers. What they could and did do during busy times at work was disrupt the normal routine of workers' lives—causing women to miss family suppers, lose needed rest, and cancel eagerly anticipated outings. In terms of the experience of everyday life, this power of the employer was enormous and important, an authority quite unparalleled in the lives of most young working-class women. The typical woman's work experience thus encompassed a unique authoritarianism in spite of the liberation of earning wages. An organizer for the International Ladies Garment Workers Union remembered in a private letter the physical and mental stress attendant on an employer's uncontrolled authority over the rhythm of life:

> Last year while working in the factory, I could appreciate the value of limiting the hours of toil. I can't bear even now to think of the ache in my shoulders and it is a satisfaction to know that the girls who are still at the job can go home at a certain hour. I want as many of the girls as possible to be spared the torture of hearing when they are tired, the forelady saying in a sweet impersonal tone, "Another hour overtime tonight girls."[92]

Overtime pay practices varied from firm to firm, but many women worked during overtime hours for less than their already low scheduled wages. Many department stores offered employees no extra compensation for overtime work, particularly during the busy pre-Christmas season. Other more generous store employers gave supper money.[93] Some industrial employers as well paid no additional wages for overtime work, though the most common method of overtime payment in industry was straight time or piecework wages.[94] But the cost of an unexpected evening meal away from home often came out of the additional overtime wages earned, and fatigue impaired the earning power of most pieceworkers during extra evening hours. Unless a shop was unionized, time-and-a-half pay for overtime work was rare.[95]

Occasionally, spontaneous protest in the workroom succeeded in eliminating at least temporarily excessive hours of overtime work. But far more often, women simply accepted the long day, their experience of time on the job testimony to their essential powerlessness at work. One Boston dressmaker confided to a Department of Labor investigator: "We were told if we did not stay, we need not come back the next day." Her story was echoed in other investigators' reports.[96]

Women could not, of course, claim a monopoly on excessive working hours; men were often subjected to involuntary overtime, and their scheduled hours were often longer than those for women. But only young women could endure the burdens of the long day through fantasies about the leisure that awaited them as wives. Though the lives of their own mothers were hardly easeful, romantic adolescents usually saw in marriage a refuge from the tensions and exhaustion of paid employment. A Yiddish folk song, sung in the sweatshops of New York early in the century, expresses protest and female hope:

> Day the same as night, night the same as day.
> And all I do is sew and sew and sew.
> May God help me and my love come soon.
> That I may leave this work and go.[97]

The hopes of overburdened men were necessarily centered on other means of deliverance.

Conclusion

The daily experience of work for women was critically shaped by the nature of the jobs permitted them, by the physical environment of the workroom, by the length and unpredictability of hours spent on the job. For most women, the excitement of the first job and the first wages rather quickly succumbed to the pressures of monotonous work in drab and uncomfortable surroundings. It is true that the physical conditions of the typical woman's job were not inferior and were often superior to those experienced by men. But in their limited access to jobs and their particular vulnerability to petty work discipline women experienced a different world of work from most men. What is important, however, is not precise comparison of the experience of males and females on the job. Rather, the object here has been to explain how the daily experience of work served to confirm for women assumptions about their inferiority and dependence in the world beyond the home and neighborhood.

As workers, however, women were not merely passive recipients of the messages of the work environment. They also helped to create that environment, for human relationships on the job affect the work experience as fundamentally as do the physical surroundings. We turn next to an examination of the women's work community.

III

The Work Community

The Song of a Factory Worker

Red brick building
With many windows,
You're like a vampire,
For wherever I go,
You know
I'm coming back to you.
You have held many under your spell,
Many who have sewed
Their life away
Within your walls.
You say to me,
"O, you may leave
But you'll come back.
You'll miss
The whir, whir of the machinery,
The click of the tacker,
The happy laughter of the girls,
Telling jokes.
You'll miss the songs

They sing,
And the tired-eyed ones,
Watching the clock.
The pieceworkers,
Sewing fast,
So fast it makes you dizzy
To watch
(They haven't time to look up.)
And under the skylight,
The red-haired girl,
When the sun sets her head aflame.
You'll miss the noise and the bustle
    and the hurry,
And you'll come back,
You'll see."
All this and more
You say to me,
Red brick building
With many windows.

Ruth Collins, in Hilda Smith, ed, *The Workers Look at the Stars* (New York: Vineyard Shore Workers' School, 1927), p. 8.

Before the Second World War, and particularly before 1930, a sizeable majority of women who worked outside the home were young and single. Fully 55% of women at work in cities of more than 100,000 in 1920 were between the ages of sixteen and twenty-four.[1] Married women in 1920 accounted for only 21.2% of the female nonagricultural labor force. And because older women and many married women tended to choose different occupations than the young and single, most young women found at work a markedly age-segregated environment. The Bureau of Labor, for example, in an investigation of factory and sales occupations in five cities in 1908, discovered that approximately 75% of female factory workers and 63% of the retail sales workers studied were under the age of twenty-five, with the largest group of workers those between sixteen and nineteen years of age.

Table 1. Ages of women employed in selected manufacturing occupations in New York, Chicago, Boston, and Philadelphia

Total female employees	Percent of total females in specified age groups			
	Under 16 years	16–20 years	21–24 years	25 years and over
4017	4.75	50.56	20.09	24.60

Table 2. Ages of women employed in selected men's ready-made clothing establishments: New York, Chicago, Baltimore, Philadelphia, Rochester

Total female employees	Percent of total females in specified age groups			
	Under 16 years	16–19 years	20–24 years	25 years and over
10,906	6.22	40.64	27.09	26.06

Excluding children under 16 years of age, 12.2% of these garment workers were 35 years of age and older.

Table 3. Ages of women employed in selected retail stores: New York, Chicago, Boston, Philadelphia

Total female employees	Percent of total females in specified age groups			
	Under 16 years	16–20 years	21–24 years	25 years and over
1584	3.16	37.56	21.97	37.31

Source: U.S. Department of Labor, Bureau of Labor Statistics, *Summary of the Report on Condition of Woman and Child Wage-Earners*, p. 16.

The youthful female work environment stood in marked contrast to the work world experienced by most men, for the male labor force was dominated numerically by men in middle life. And young, single males did not generally gravitate to different occupations and places of work than older married workers. Adolescent boys, then, entered the work world as a minority population, necessarily deferential to those to whom experience and seniority gave status. For boys, the world of work was the world of their fathers.

Young women, however, found at work a preponderantly adolescent world, and the workroom social life they enjoyed provided them with some important freedoms. It also communicated to most of them very conservative ideas about their identities and destinies as women. Young women created workroom social life in the context of a sexually hierarchical work situation, and their communal social life of necessity recognized and reflected the sexual inequities of the work world. And workroom social life was importantly influenced by the relative absence of older women workers, women whose experience might serve to counter the conservatism of adolescent fantasies about romance and marriage.

Nevertheless, the hours of work also provided many young women with unusual social freedom. The most effective industrial discipline was unable to regulate completely workroom sociability, and, particularly in the absence of large numbers of older workers, young women at work were often less supervised in certain aspects of personal behavior than they were in most nonwork situations. Since working-class girls, unlike their brothers, seemed to have no permanent street-corner groups and few single-sex social clubs, the workroom provided many young women a unique place of refuge from family and neighborhood surveillance and an opportunity for free sociability with peers.[2] It provided a chance to explore, however tentatively, new styles of speech and manners, and the chance to learn, from the more worldly-wise, about the possibilities of social and sexual experimentation open to the Americanized adolescent.

Indeed, many young women learned at work to want more freedom in social life and management of wages than the typical working-class family would willingly countenance. The romantic preoccupations of the work group, moreover, encouraged many young women to choose an early marriage as the most desirable route to freedom from parental control. But many working-class parents not only opposed early marriage for the wage-earning young, they were doubtful about the propriety of matches that had not been mediated by the older generation.

Work group associations thus facilitated conflict between parents and working daughters. Indeed, the preoccupations of the women's work group defined the central problem in young female lives as the struggle with parents for social freedom. And these preoccupations shaped decisively most young women's responses to their work. For many, the frustrations, disappointments, and physical agonies of the job were alleviated through an intense involvement w social life and workroom personal relations, although in this respect women were much the same as men. But the female work group, reflecting the special needs and narrow experiences of very young, unmarried women, endorsed an understanding of the job that placed work at far remove from the central concerns of life. The stuggles that mattered were the struggles for adolescent autonomy; the essential victories were romantic conquests. The very success of the work group in facilitating adolescent rebellion served to deflect worker dissatisfaction from overt political expression.

Much in the nature and content of work-group sociability thus reinforced a marginal work role for women and served to integrate young women into a domestic adult role. The values of the work group were not generally conducive to unionization or other forms of direct political action, nor did the group support unconventional visions of women's life possibilities. Young women brought to the job conservative values about femininity learned at home and in school. And in their very struggle for adolescent independence, they reinforced for one another an ultimately conservative orientation to their lives as women.

In their own work communities, then, young women internalized and legitimized the assumptions about male and female that undergirded the sex-segregated world of work. But this is not to argue that the creation of the work community was not an important achievement, or that this community failed to function for women in essential protective ways. The work community, particularly because of its youthful composition, failed to challenge the sexual hierarchy of the job, but it did provide women with a refuge from workroom authority, which was most often male. The work community often provided the basis for limited resistance to supervisory pressure and innovation, though the ethos of that community was generally supportive of work discipline. The work community represented a social world where women could express individuality and independence, though group values rarely sanctioned competition with men for better jobs and wages. The work community facilitated something of a social and sexual revolution for many young women, and yet it functioned too as a bridge to conventional adulthood. As we examine more closely the nature of the social environment of women's work, we must keep in mind the contradictions between the liberating and the restrictive effects of workroom social life. For the complexities of the work community teach us how subtly and deftly a culture transmits sexually stereotyped roles and values.

Most observers of women at work, and the women themselves, were impressed by the vigor of workroom social life; women formed work friendships even under difficult conditions.[3] Some women's work, mainly handwork such as millinery sewing or flower making, encouraged group association, but women also created elaborate social worlds in shops where the conveyor belt or noisy machinery erected formidable barriers to interaction: "We used to talk very loudly so as to be heard above the roar of the machines," Agnes Nestor remembered of her work in Chicago glove factories.[4] Even piecework did not generally deter sociability, despite the premium on rapid production and the competitive situation piecework fosters. Women working under pressure often sang together to ease tensions, and work groups frequently enforced informal sanctions against excessive production competition.[5] The most stringent supervision proved impotent in prohibiting all workroom social life: "You can hear talkin' all over our room when the forelady goes out."[6] Since a prohibition against laughing and talking was not necessarily conducive to maximum worker productivity, in many shops rules against on-the-job socializing were not rigorously enforced.

Indeed, a lively workroom social environment often supported effective work discipline. The small but significant freedoms of workroom social life made less onerous the petty controls of supervision. Group life endowed tedious unskilled labor with the drama of personal interaction; it created loyalties to fellow workers which often worked against the development of hostility to the employer. And where socializing on the job was officially forbidden, challenges to the rules could provide pleasurable and effective release for anger and frustration. Mrs. Van Vorst noted the disciplinary effects of work group solidarity in Pittsburgh's Heinz pickle factory:

> I am amazed at the cheerfulness of my companions. They complain of fatigue, of cold, but never at any time is there a suggestion of ill-humor. Their suppressed animal spirits reassert themselves when the forewoman's back is turned. Companionship is the great stimulus. I am confident that without the social entrain, the encouragement of example, it would be impossible to obtain as much from each individual girl as is obtained from them in groups of tens, fiftys, hundreds working together.[7]

Working-class women rarely analyzed the disciplinary functions of the work group so precisely. But their testimony makes clear that group friendships were an extremely important source of job satisfaction and that the rewards of friendship often outweighed, in the mind of the worker, the burdens attendant on most unskilled employment. The young Agnes Nestor, for example, kept a year's diary of work and home activities at the turn of the century, chronicling her experience in a non-union glove-making shop in Chicago. Her job involved a good deal of machine work, paid by the piece, but despite these barriers to sociability, workroom personal relationships were an important focus of Agnes's working life:

Nov. 7, 1900: We all felt bad about Bryan being defeated. I am awfully tired tonight. This noon all the girls at the shop went out to see Minnie Becker give Jessie Templeman a wheelbarrow ride. The result of an election bet.

Nov. 22, 1900: This has been a fine day. The power was stopped about five hours, but we had a circus around visiting.

Nov. 23, 1900: We had lots of fun today hearing the girls quarreling about having the windows open. It has been rainy.

Feb. 14, 1901: We had lots of fun today at our table. I started on welted work this afternoon.

Feb. 19, 1901: Bitter cold today. I thought I would freeze this morning. We had fun this afternoon trying to keep quiet.

Feb. 20, 1901: We had a party at our table this afternoon oranges and chocolates. Another cold day.[8]

Clearly, the comforts of companionship eased considerably the burdens of the job. Agnes was exhausted by her work, the shop was often uncomfortably hot or cold, and frequent power failures meant enforced idleness and lost wages. But the difficulties of work were experienced in the satisfying context of group friendship, and because the group was sociable and cohesive, the job was a source of pleasure as well as grievances. Sociability could make even heavy, low-status work supportable, according to a young laundry worker, probably an Eastern

European Jew. "Although the work was rather strenuous, and the hours long, the environment was pleasing. The girls were Irish, sympathetic, and independent in spirit. They welcomed me and were very friendly. That helped greatly."[9] And even where workroom authority was manifestly harsh and capricious, sociability could relieve workers' tensions and defuse resentment. An unusually vivid worker's sketch of a garment factory in the late 1920s illustrates:

> The afternoon wears on with the usual quarreling, singing and hum of voices above the drone of the machinery.
> Suddenly all is quiet. The smell of cigar smoke is strong upon the air. This smell is a warning that the owner of the shop is near. You can always smell him before you see him. Presently he enters, a tall, well-built man with slightly graying hair. He walks up and down past the girls, who are working swiftly now. No one talks except when spoken to by the boss.
> He picks up garments, inspecting each one separately and closely, looking for bad work. Everyone holds her breath for fear it is her work he is looking at. If he finds work that is poor, his temper explodes, and we have an exciting half hour. Then he stalks out swearing to shut up the place immediately. When you can no longer see or smell him, the atmosphere changes. Voices again buzz excitedly all over, and keep up until 5:30, when the bell rings and the girls slowly and wearily depart, calling good night to each other.[10]

Indeed, a truly vital social life at work might make long hours in the shop more attractive to young women than leisure in a restrictive home or neighborhood. The excessive work hours of women were a major concern of many early twentieth-century reformers, yet a disgruntled Cambridge, Massachusetts, employer believed that his youngest workers preferred socializing with their fellows to the physical benefits of shorter hours. In testimony before the Massachusetts House of Representatives in 1913, he opposed a new state law limiting to eight hours the workday for workers under sixteen:

> Our reasons for not thinking so are: children under fifteen are allowed to go out at four-fifteen. They do not go home, but usually wait outside in the street until the other girls get through at five o'clock.[11]

Like the fourteen- and fifteen-year-old workers in a later New York study, these Cambridge girls would probably have worked longer than eight hours—and done so cheerfully—were they afforded no legal protection.[12]

A supportive work group, although immensely important as a source of job satisfaction, also embodied an oblique protest. The work group normally asserted, to what extent it could, the priority of human needs over the demands of production. In a cohesive work group, for example, newcomers and slow workers were often aided in their work by more competent mates. Group loyalties were thus demonstrably more important than competitive, achievement-oriented values. Similarly restrictions on excessive production placed the interests of the group above those of the ambitious individual. But the success of the work group as a community based on values antithetical to those that governed production generally served to minimize overt conflict with work authority. "Even in the shop I was happy. My neighbors were very kind. Each one would help the other out of difficulties in the work," an immigrant garment worker in New York remembered.[13] Their kindness was at once a conscious criticism of the values symbolized by piecework production and real assistance to the employer in sustaining production and amicable labor relations.

Men's work groups, of course, generally sanctioned similar values. But for women the ethic of work-group solidarity was probably less ambiguous than it was for men, because women were not enjoined by the larger society to achieve as individuals through their work, and they saw fewer opportunities for such achievement. Working-class men were shielded by the work group from the injunction to achieve, but they were rarely deaf to it. Since women enjoyed especially strong cultural supports for work-group solidarity, there were powerful inducements for them to understand the indirect protest of the work community as satisfying and sufficient. That the protest embodied in the work community did not facilitate mobility for the individual or the group was often of little importance to women. There were men, certainly, for whom this was also true. But for many men, even some who never joined a union or went on strike, the satisfactions of such limited protest were probably less complete. That women were widely reported to be more docile workers than men may reflect, to some extent, the greater satisfactions women obtained from highly indirect forms of work protest.

The work group was additionally an important source of information about contemporary American adolescent styles of behavior for the very young worker and the recent immigrant. The work community represented an adolescent counterculture within the protective walls of the factory and the store, and it often represented a counterculture of considerable rebelliousness. Many observers found the typical young woman's workroom a boisterous place: the workers talked loudly, often of necessity, used slang and even profanity freely, and were ostentatiously boyish and careless in demeanor.[14] "In the shop, the girls were talking all at once, clothes, styles, beaux, and dances—each one trying to out-yell the other," Anzia Yezierska recalls in *Breadgivers*.[15] They behaved, in short, in at least superficial conformity to adolescent male behavior, though the group maintained careful controls on excessive aggressiveness and deviance, as we shall see. The contrast between the ordered world of school, where the model of success was a decorous female authority figure, and the explosive sociability of the factory was real and a little frightening to at least one recent school-leaver. She wrote, in 1905:

> Monday came and I went to work: I like it better than I did for the first two days. I thought I could never get use [sic] to it. Such a noise! One talks here and another talks there all a confusion! But now I'm used to it and it seems to me, when it is a little quite [sic] something must have happened. I often wonder if we were to make such a noise there in school a whole regiment of policemen would be after us.[16]

But initiation into the heady world of adolescent independence was necessary and valuable for an urban working-class girl in the early twentieth century, because it was the adolescent peer group, and not parents, that provided suitors and, ultimately, mates. And young immigrants especially needed to learn at least surface conformity to American styles of dress, speech, and behavior. The work group could provide them with an authentically contemporary model of adolescent culture, as opposed to the formal, excessively middle-class model of the schoolroom or the outdated expectations of parents. Mary Anderson, later commissioner of the Women's Bureau, in her autobiography credited the work group with important assimilative functions. She worked in a Chicago shoe factory at the turn of the century:

> I always look back on my life in that factory, where six or seven hundred people worked, as very interesting because this was my first factory experience and I learned that factory life is not just the work at a machine. You make contacts with other people. You talk to the person at the machine on each side of you, sometimes about your work, sometimes about your people and your life at home, sometimes about parties and boyfriends. If you like one another (and that is not always) you become very friendly because you spend ten or twelve hours a day together. In that factory at lunch time we used to gather together for a half-hour around one of the big stitching tables. One of the girls would make coffee or tea for which we paid ten cents a week. Then we would have our own sandwiches and plenty of conversation. Some of the girls were very amusing, especially the Irish. To me it was all great fun and was something I needed very badly, because, after all, I was a greenhorn.[17]

Mary Anderson's experience reminds us that the women's work group had to integrate into apparent intimacy women who represented a variety of ethnic and religious groups, and women who, because they were low-skill workers, changed jobs frequently. The openness and ready friendliness of many working women helped to incorporate the new employee into a social group: "On entering a new situation I found, as a rule, cordiality and friendly interest," wrote an investigator who had worked in a number of women's factories in New York.[18] But because the work group was potentially divisible by the mobility and the ethnic diversity of the female labor force, women tended to create at work a community that demanded conformity to rigid values and behaviorial norms. These values and norms were drawn from the limited life experiences of the young women who dominated the female work force. These women solved the problems of sociability in an unstable work population by organizing workroom social life around the interests and experiences shared by most young women, regardless of ethnicity—interests in boyfriends, dress, evening amusements, and work friendships. Group life tended, then, to coalesce around interests and values ultimately conservative in their meaning for women's lives, and those individual experiences, values, and aspirations that deviated from this conventionally feminine world were often rejected as dangerous to the comfortable unity of workroom social relations. When Dorothy Richardson, an impoverished but culturally middle-class worker in early twentiety-century New York challenged her workmates' exclusive interest in dances and romantic fiction, the group responded defensively. Dorothy was defined as deviant, and her restoration to the group was accomplished only through her superficial conformity to group norms.[19] Similarly, the worker who agitated for a union in an unorganized shop often aroused hostility, not only because she challenged her companions to risks they were reluctant to take, but because she threatened the supportive warmth of workroom sociability. A successful organizer learned to establish trust through participation in group life on its own terms, as the diary of an Amalgamated Clothing Workers organizer demonstrates:

> Sunday: At camp. The R. shop on vacation for a week and a bunch of girls are camping here. So am I. There are five of us in one shack. The first day was a little strained. No one knew just what to make of the situation. Of course, they know who I am. However, that night, after lights out, we lay talking in low tones—love affairs, of course—and the second day everything was O.K. We are all good friends now.[20]

And the values of the women's work community were enormously successful in integrating into group life a wide variety of women workers. It is significant that severe interethnic conflict on women's jobs was apparently rare, for in the trades where women found work, it was not usually possible to minimize ethnic contacts through job stratification based on nationality. Women of certain ethnic groups tended to gravitate to specific employment, it is true: Italians dominated flower making for a time in New York; Jews were the preeminent national group in many garment shops; boxmaking was widely known as a Polish trade.[21] The popular stereotype of certain occupations as particular ethnic strongholds limited outside recruitment into these trades, and the tendency of young women to locate jobs through friendship networks also contributed to ethnic domination of particular workrooms. But none save the tiniest shops in major cities employed women of a single national group. Employers were concerned only with maintaining a ready supply of cheap labor, and unskilled and unorganized women were unable to place restrictions on hiring practices.

There was, to be sure, tension between members of various ethnic groups in many shops. Native-born women particularly objected to working with the foreign born, according to testimony taken by the New York State Factory Investigating Commission in 1912. The investigator refers to women's industries in New York City:

> There is always a great prejudice in factories where foreign-born help is employed and they work with Americans. It is sometimes necessary to keep them in one room. We found one case in which the Italian girls were kept entirely separate from the American girls.[22]

In a few ethnically mixed shops, this investigator claimed, the dressing room was reserved for the sole use of American-born women.[23] And in other contemporary descriptions of women at work it is apparent that ethnicity sometimes determined lunchtime cliques and informed the social hierarchy of the workroom.[24] Dorothy Richardson discovered that her New York workmates defined the world in ethnic terms: all were conscious of their own nationality and that of their companions, and shop banter was liberally spiced with derogatory references to the characteristics of various national groups.[25] But in no shop did Dorothy Richardson find that ethnic consciousness led to open conflict, nor did it prevent the existence of a lively and inclusive workroom social life. Other contemporary reports suggest that open and disruptive ethnic conflict among working women was rare. The bonds of age and sex usually served to transcend the divisions of ethnicity. For as young women of various national groups pursued as fellow workers their common goals of a thoroughly American personal style and unprecedented freedom from parental control, they often had reason to feel that they had more in common with one another than with the older generation. Through their work experience, reinforcing as it did a heightened identification with mass popular culture, these young women were creating for themselves a common identity that we can call working-class.

A workroom little divided by occupational rivalries supported the evolution of a common identity. Only a few trades had skill hierarchies open to women. Garment sample-makers, chocolate dippers, and millinery trimmers, for example, were skilled workers and were accorded the envy and respect of their workmates. These aristocrats of women's labor often formed separate social groups within the factory.[26] But, normally, opportunities for genuine mobility in women's jobs were limited, and serious competition among women for achievement and promotions was not common. Instead, the values of the work community focused women's competitive energies on social relations, conventionally the one acceptable arena of female competition. Thus, while diminished competition for status on the job contributed to work-group solidarity, it discouraged women from the individualistic ambition characteristic of the economically and socially mobile male.

The basically conservative functions of the women's work group are revealed in the normal preoccupations of workroom social life. The essence of conformity in many shops was enthusiastic discussion of off-the-job social activities: "Say, you got a feller?" was a standard overture in new work situations, according to one New York investigator.[27] Many observers of women's work emphasized the universal importance of social life as a workroom topic; no other concern rivaled it—not wages, hours, or conditions of work.[28] Beaus, social events, clothing, and the romantic prospects of workmates provided more welcome diversions from the monotony of the long day, as Mrs. Van Vorst noted in a Chicago picture frame factory:

> When we have fallen into the proper swing, we finish one hundred sheets every forty-five minutes. We could work more rapidly, but the sheets are furnished to us at this rate, and it is so comfortable that conversation is not interrupted. The subjects are the same as elsewhere—dress, young men, entertainments. The girls have "beaux" and "steady beaux." The expression "Who is she going with?" means who is her steady beau. "I've got Jim Smith now, but I don't know whether I'll keep him," means that Jim Smith is on trial as a beau and may become a "steady."[29]

Young women's interest in social life is hardly surprising, and no one doubts that men at work devote a good deal of time to the discussion of sex. What is significant, however, is that the meaning of femininity—and of masculinity—is being transmitted to young working women in highly romanticized, decidedly adolescent terms. Of significance too is the illusion of intimacy and solidarity that personal gossip inevitably creates—"illusion," because hurried confidences about boyfriends and struggles with parents were rarely sufficient to create friendships capable of sacrifice, especially among a highly mobile work force. But young women cherished the illusion of intimacy; it gave meaning and dignity to their working lives. An organizational drive within a shop put work friendships to a severe test. Rather than jeopardize the comforts of easy companionship, women often declared off-limits such potentially troublesome topics as unions and politics. Indeed, it was an unwritten rule in some women's workrooms that while the most complete confidences about social life were expected, women never revealed to one another what wage they were earning.[30]

The romantic preoccupations of the work group enhanced the prospect of marriage as the logical means to material prosperity for women, as well as to freedom from parental control. Many observers, especially those who hoped to organize women, noted the exaggerated expectations of marriage that many young working women entertained.[31] Dorothy Richardson found that her coworkers in a New York box factory constantly discussed the heroes of popular novels and endowed their own prosaic boyfriends with similar characteristics. These women also adopted romantic pseudonyms from sensational fiction.[32] Frances Donovan noted that Chicago waitresses considered expensive downtown restaurants the most desirable work places because they believed that wealthy businessmen sometimes married attractive women who served them.[33] And contemporary testimony is virtually unanimous that young working women looked forward to marriage as a desired rite of passage to adult freedom.[34] Presumably, few women anticipated that marriage would mean for them the cramped and stringent home life they had experienced as children. Perhaps collective fantasies about the possibilities of matrimony helped to obscure for the young the still harsh realities of early twentieth-century working-class life, endowing domesticity with a romantic glow. "Marriage is for all these girls the final and greatest adventure of adolescence," noted Ruth True of young workers in Manhattan. "They do not look past the adventure at the responsibilities which lie beyond. The question of children is waved aside as scarcely worth a hearing.[35]

A passionate interest in social life generated conflict with parents while it minimized conflict with the employer. Many young women learned at work to want and expect the freedom of city nightlife.[36] But many parents, especially those of the immigrant generation, could not sanction the sexual autonomy implied by an unrestricted social life for women, nor could they tolerate the allegiance of daughters to the alien norms of urban mass culture. In an important way, the experience of work proved liberating to the young, for it introduced many of them to an exciting adolescent world. And it was parents, not the boss, who were perceived as frustrating the wage earner's freedom.

Work group norms also generated ambitious standards of dress and personal display.[37] Louise Odencrantz noted that immigrant women refused to wear "old country" clothing in the factory; for many, the workplace provided the first American models of fashionable female dress.[38] Mary MacDowell of the University of Chicago settlement claimed that many young women in the "Back of the Yards" district dressed for work as stylishly as possible, because going to work was for them an important social event.[39] Robert Woods of Boston's South End House reported that store clerks in the neighborhood consciously imitated the dress of their most prosperous customers.[40]

But this interest in dress, rather than creating widespread and articulated dissatisfaction with low wages, served mainly to cause conflict with parents over control of the young woman's wage. (In most working-class families it was customary for an unmarried daughter to surrender all or most of her wage to her mother, and the mother determined what limited amount of pocket money would be returned to the girl.) Again, it was the parent and not the employer who was seen as the obstacle to happiness. "The girls were not so much interested in the amount earned as in the amount given back for spending money," noted Hazel Ormsbee in 1927 of young factory workers in New York, "and an increase in weekly wage interested many of them only if it resulted in more spending money."[41]

The romantic preoccupations of the youthful work community significantly shaped women's attitudes toward work and achievement. The work community provided little support for job-related ambitions; rather, the group endorsed the tendency of most women to understand their work as temporary and extraneous to their adult lives. The work community discouraged competitiveness, directed emotional energies away from individualistic ambition toward personal relations, and emphasized the precedence of group loyalties over private achievement.

The young, for all their rebelliousness, were the principal generators of these values. Young workers were usually physically vigorous. They were cheerfully unconcerned about future security, and normally they found at work few if any older women to warn them of the economic and emotional precariousness of married life. Moreover, for the very young, the controls and frustrations of work had a peculiar novelty: particularly for children who were unhappy at school, the greater social freedom of the workroom plus the near-adult status wage earning conferred on them endowed the job with an initial glow of excitement. "I was young. I was enthusiastic," Agnes Nestor remembered of her early years at work. "I can remember operating a particular machine. The boss asked me how I liked it. I said: 'I would never get tired of sewing on this machine.' That is how I felt that day." [42] Hazel Ormsbee in New York noticed the indifference of the youngest female workers to long hours and dangerous conditions on the job:

> The girls seemed not to complain of the long workday in comparison with the shorter school-day. For most of them, especially for those who wanted to leave school, it is such a welcome change that the novelty of it obscures the effect of the longer day until the difference is forgotten, and yet the hours of work are very long for these fourteen- to sixteen-year-old girls, as long as the law permits, and longer.
>
> The fact that they were not being trained for a vocation did not concern them. Why should one be concerned about the future at the age of fourteen? The passage of time had, as yet, little interest to them. They plodded on from day to day, heedless of work, heedless of working conditions. Not one of the five hundred girls had noticed any risks or any dangers about her. [43]

Agnes Nestor, herself a successful union organizer, believed that the youth of the female labor force was one important reason that relatively few working women joined unions. [44] By and large, young working women were not directly supporting dependents; most had little control over disposition of the weekly wage. Few young women, moreover, anticipated lifelong wage earning, for most working-class wives neither expected nor were expected to work outside the home. Hence, many women failed to see in the job a source of essential income; they were cushioned from the reality of low wages by male breadwinners. And the values of the work group encouraged them to seek their identities exclusively in their personal lives.

The work behavior of most women reflected the high value they placed on personal relationships and group solidarity. Job choice, for example, was often dictated by friendship rather than private economic advantage. Young women often sought work in the company of friends, and sometimes even changed jobs together, although group

pursuit of employment lessened women's chances of securing particularly advantageous and well-paying jobs.[45] The low-wage neighborhood shop with an abundance of openings for unskilled workers
was usually most willing to accommodate a group of friends. Similarly, investigators noticed that women sometimes objected to transfers
within the factory, even where it signalled a promotion or a wage
increase, because the transfer meant separation from friends.[46] Some
women were reported reluctant to accept rare promotions to positions
of authority, possibly because supervisors were often lonely workers,
thrust outside workroom social life.[47]

The same priorities bolstered conservative attitudes among women
toward job competition with men. In many trades, real advancement for women meant challenging male domination of skilled and
high-paying jobs, yet women generally accepted without protest prevailing definitions of male and female employment.[48] Contesting
the sexual hierarchy of the work world required a higher valuation of
work achievement and its rewards than the rewards of conventional
femininity. Most young women, anticipating early marriage, were not
eager to incur male hostility through open competition for jobs. And
the rewards of a successful competition were mixed at best. In return
for higher wages and increased job status, real advancement for
women would have meant promotion into the intense loneliness of a
male occupation. Hence, most women accommodated the rigid sexual
hierarchy of the work world, and in so doing verified the conservative
view of femininity endorsed by the larger society. Spirited young
women were seemingly content to remain second-class industrial citizens, as Sophonisba Breckinridge noted of Chicago working women in
1906:

> One difficulty in securing advancement for girls is that they acqui-
> esce in the general judgement as to their own inferiority. Young
> women who are most contemptuous regarding the ability of certain
> young men will still feel themselves disqualified in some mysterious
> way from entering the profession the young men have successfully

entered. "It's good wages (75¢) for a girl" is the reply when a girl-worker is asked why she doesn't get as much as the boy across the way (85¢). Employers take girl-workers because they are more easily satisfied: "They don't ask for a raise."[49]

Preoccupation with personal relations not only inhibited an ambitious approach to the job but also shaped working women's attitudes toward authority. Women often understood work authority to mean visible, personal authority—the supervisor, against whom resentment was common.[50] Supervisors did possess considerable power at work: their behavior could make the worker's day tolerable or exceedingly unpleasant, and they sometimes exercised important discretion in establishing piece-rates and production quotas. But supervisors were not the ultimate work authority, nor could they generate fundamental change in wages and working conditions. Bitterness toward immediate, personal authority, then, was often anger deflected from the person or persons whose decisions most critically determined the realities of the job. Ruth True, investigating women's employment on Manhattan's West Side in 1914, believed that preoccupation with the personal aspects of work obscured for young women a detached, rational view of the work world and possibilities for its reform:

> The girl of this class accepts in a matter-of-fact way conditions of work that impress the outsider as very hard. Sometimes she tells of having cried with weariness when she started. But complaints of the long day, the meager reward, and the monotony are few. She has not thought out the general aspects of the factory. Comparisons between individual places are constant, as also are personal grievances, usually against a "cranky forelady." She rebels against the tediousness of her job. "You can hear talkin' all over our room when the forelady goes out. Then we'll hear her comin' and it stops short. Soon's she goes, we'll start again." As often as not she throws up her job for a personal grievance—a quarrel with another worker, a grudge against a "boss." Fanny Mullen left the Excelsior Laundry because her friend quarreled with the foreman and Fanny's loyalty would not permit her to remain. The human factor is strongest with these young girls.[51]

For many men, too, especially the young or inexperienced worker, the personality of the foreman often largely determined attitudes toward the job. But women were probably much more likely to be limited to a highly personal understanding of work authority, if only because of their youth and their relatively brief working lives. An amicable relationship with a supervisor doubtless rendered many young women content at work, despite their low wages. Less fortunate women still were less likely than men to act aggressively and effectively to check abusive work authority. Her understanding of herself and her place in the world of work encouraged a discontented woman in personal, individualistic protest, if indeed she was moved to action at all.[52] Much of what was probably protest activity simply confirmed women's industrial marginality: young women, like unskilled men and especially young unskilled men, changed jobs frequently, and women were reported even by sympathetic observers to be indifferent and sometimes careless workers.[53]

Women were certainly capable of direct collective action to improve wages and working conditions. But more often than not, these were spontaneous, disorganized actions of short duration, the highly emotional reactions of a temporarily aroused group and not the calculated action of a disciplined and self-interested collectivity. There is evidence that spontaneous work stoppages over accumulated grievances were fairly common in some shops.[54] But generally these actions were brief, lasting only until group emotion was spent. Sometimes immediate objectives were achieved, especially since work stoppages most commonly occurred over sudden violations of standard workroom practice: a reduction in the piece-rate, a sudden spate of overtime work, a change in job procedure.[55] Thus Agnes Nestor's diary records on November 12, 1900: "The power stopped twice to begin with today. This afternoon we went on a strike about being cut down on 60¢ work and we won."[56] Victories achieved through spontaneous direct action, however, were usually precarious, because women rarely followed a successful action with permanent organization. Just so, Agnes Nestor's shop failed to unionize in the year 1900, and

Agnes herself betrayed in the year's diary no interest in permanent organization or trade unions. The ephemeral nature of much of women's collective protest is suggested in this essay by a young laundry worker, herself an ardent trade unionist:

> Again I became restless. Work alone, plenty of it, could not satisfy me completely. One day, however, we had a little recreation. A new manager had taken charge of the floor, who had very little experience in the laundry business. But he soon enough began to suggest and enforce new rules. We did not object as long as our pay did not diminish; however, as soon as there was an indication of diminishing our pay we were all provoked and immediately decided to quit, and to go to the boss at once. How romantic that spontaneous outburst was! What fiery interest it aroused in all of us! Everyone was ready to sacrifice her job—of course, her job, since there was nothing more precious to any of us who were ready to sacrifice for the principles of humanity, of human rights.
>
> The starching department occupied just a corner of the entire floor; therefore, in a solid group, to the amazement of the rest of the workers, we marched down to the office at the end of the floor. As we reached the office, the boss came out, pale and trembling. I do not know whether he was angry or frightened, but we were also confused—had no spokesman. I being one of the girls in the front row, spontaneously began to tell him our demands, surprising as it may be, without losing my self-control. He listened, asked a few questions, which were promptly answered, and in about fifteen minutes, we, victorious, walked back across the floor. The girls were satisfied, but not I.[57]

Indeed, even a tradition of successful collective protest in a particular shop might not lead to permanent organization or to sympathy for trade unions. Cornela Stratton Parker, a wealthy New Yorker who worked in a number of women's factories while researching a book, found in 1922 a small candy factory where women usually refused to work lengthy overtime or on Saturday afternoons. Despite a tradition of protective action, however, there was in this shop complete indifference toward unions. The women were not prepared emotionally or intellectually to move from limited defensive action to an aggressive attempt to improve wages and working conditions:

Had I entered the factory with any idea of encouraging organization among female factory workers, I should have imagined that candy group the most hopeless soil imaginable. Those whom I came in contact with had no class feeling, no idea of grievances, no ambitions over and above the doing of an uninteresting job with as little exertion as possible.[58]

Little in the experience of these candy workers or of most working-class women prepared them to adopt assertive, class-conscious attitudes toward their employment. Their lives provided no compelling reasons for achievement at work, either in terms of wages or job mobility. And the experience of work, particularly the interpretation of that experience evolved in concert with workmates, only confirmed for most women the very limited place of work in their lives. Many working women had simply "never heard" about union activity, even in their own industries, admitted Annie MacLean in 1910, "but many more care nothing."[59]

The typical women's work community, then, was a youthful, sex-segregated social world where important conservative values about femininity were reaffirmed by women themselves. Among their peers, young working women were encouraged to seek future security and mobility through marriage rather than employment. They learned to accept a work world that defined women as dependent and marginal employees. Not all women, of course, acceded without struggle; on rare and moving occasions, workroom social ties provided the solidarity necessary for long and bitter strikes. But these moments of sustained conflict were exceptional. Most women, in their brief working lives, found in the work community the pleasures and sustenance of friendship and support as they moved from the years of work to the decades as wives and mothers.

PART TWO

Beyond the Job: Wage Earning and Family Roles

The lives of wage-earning women extended well beyond the store and factory. And what they experienced beyond the job, both before and during the years of employment, intimately affected the experience of work, just as the experience of work altered for many women relationships within the family. For it was in the home, and secondarily in the community and the school, that the young first learned the social meaning of male and female. The work experience generally ratified, but in some ways undermined, these social definitions.

Working-class girls encountered a certain paradox as they grew toward womanhood. Though working-class culture certainly assigned to women an inferior status, women were not powerless, inept, or ignorant human beings. A boy might enjoy privileges and an independence denied his adolescent sister, but both were subject, at least until marriage, to the authority of a strong and controlling mother. So too, most husbands appeared to recognize a clear sphere of female authority once they crossed the threshold separating the home from the world outside.

The actual status of women, then, depended on the context in which men and women functioned at any given moment. The domestic sphere—the home and whatever cohesive community of kin and neighbors surrounded the home—was a locus of female power. So was the school, although the female teacher was usually too remote by virtue of her middle-class values and behavior to provide a role model for any but the daughters of upwardly-mobile working-class families. ('' 'Teacher' in the vocabulary of many children is a synonym for women-folk gentry,'' noted Jane Addams, ''and the name is indiscriminately applied to women of certain dress and manner.'' [1])

But beyond the narrow world of home and neighborhood the status of women was much diminished. Men and boys knew the city streets far better and more extensively than did women and girls. Men frequented taverns and clubs that denied admission to women; the work world was the place where men spent the greater part of their lives but where women were only transient citizens. When working-class girls ventured beyond the home and the school into work, they were effectively testing the limits of female power and authority. That is why their experiences on the job were so important.

As we have already seen, the work experience rarely provided the young with means to challenge domesticity as the appropriate life goal for women. Femininity meant greater disabilities in the workroom than the schoolroom, and there were few women indeed whose power and status on the job equalled the authority of the working-class mother in the home. The employment interval proved to be, for nearly all young women, an ultimately conservative aspect of sex role socialization.

Still, the liberating element of work away from home left neither the worker nor her family relationships unchanged. A daughter's wage earning usually permitted her greater power in dealing with parents, power she most often used to gain greater personal freedom during the years preceding marriage. Modern adolescent culture thus has its roots in the workroom as well as the high school, although the sex segregation of the workplace made the working-class adolescent's experience different in important ways from that of the middle-class young. But whether increased female freedom in the years between school and marriage led to fundamental change in working-class marital relationships is problematic.

We turn, then, to an examination of women in family roles—as daughters, as wives and mothers, and as ''exceptions'': women who lived outside the protection and the restrictions of the family group. We do so to discover the experiences, values, and self-images women brought to the job, and to discover the impact a wage-earning daughter could have on existing family relationships.

IV

The Working-Class Daughter

"I never in my life had two rooms to myself."

"When you live seven people in one attic, you must do everything very carefully. If you eat an apple, you must eat it very beautifully, or it will get on someone's nerves."

From student letters, Bryn Mawr Summer School for Women Workers (Hilda Smith Papers, c. 1927)

The working-class daughter who lived in the parental home was the typical female wage earner in the years between 1900 and 1930. And the working-class daughter in this period was overwhelmingly likely to be employed at some time before she married. In Chicago in 1920, nearly 88% of unskilled workers' children at least sixteen years old and living with their parents were estimated to be working; for families of skilled workers, the estimate was close to 85%. Girls were less likely than boys to be employed, it is true, but a large majority of daughters in these families were certainly wage earners. And even in 1920, nearly one-third of the fourteen- and fifteen-year-olds in unskilled workers' families in Chicago held jobs.[1]

The adolescent girl's experience of work was inevitably influenced in important ways by her experience of family life. It was within the family that she acquired her initial understanding of the place of paid work in her life, and it was principally within the family that she formed the self-image that shaped her work behavior. If she often ventured excitedly into work as into exotic terrain, she was nonetheless an explorer heavily weighted with conservative cultural values. To understand the worker she became, we must try to understand working-class family relationships and the economic realities that supported those relationships.

The complexities of this family life can never be certainly known, but contemporary observers speak with some degree of unanimity about relationships and attitudes in working-class families. What they seem to say is this: working-class family life, while often marked by conflict, was also characterized by a high degree of cohesiveness and by strong and controlling bonds of obligation and loyalty, deriving at least in part from the marginal economic situation of many families. These ties were especially strong for daughters. For most young women, wage earning was an essentially domestic obligation; their wages belonged to the family. Neither the emotional nor the economic realities of working-class life prepared them to assume a role independent of this loyalty.

In this chapter we shall examine what contemporaries recorded about family life in urban working-class neighborhoods, both its economic and its emotional dimensions. We shall try to discover what young women experienced as they matured, attended school, and found employment. Beyond question this is a risky business; evidence is neither abundant nor free from the distortions of class prejudice. And inevitably there is distortion of reality when generalizations are made about so individual and intimate an experience as family life.

The history of domestic experience, however, will never claim precision as its forte. What a good historian can do is read the best contemporary evidence in a sensitive and imaginative way and construct a reasonable picture of what life was like—in its broad outlines—for a great many people. We cannot know the nuances of individual experience, but we can assess what observers have said about the behavior and attitudes of a group—whether that group is based on occupational, economic, or ethnic similarities—and decide whether the evidence is consistent and plausible. The exceptional individual is sometimes lost in this approach, but we approximate another truth: we learn something, however fragmentary, about the quiet routine of ordinary life and people.

It is, fortunately, not difficult to describe the economic dimension of working-class family life in the early twentieth century, even though income statistics for the period are not absolutely reliable, especially with regard to annual family income.[2] But two important facts about the economic situation of the urban working-class family are well documented, and they are facts that shaped profoundly the life options of the working-class girl. One is that the majority of working-class families throughout the period, and especially before the First World War, earned incomes that hovered near what contemporaries defined as a poverty line. The other is that even such inadequate incomes generally depended on the contributions of more than one family breadwinner.

"Poor people, not as the charity visitor knows them, but poor, as the rank and file of wage earners are poor," wrote Crystal Eastman in 1909.[3] Every major investigation of working-class family income, from 1900 to 1924, verified this poverty. Before 1915, investigators asserted, average annual incomes in families of urban wage earners ranged between $700 and $800, a sum generally described as a subsistence budget for a family of four.[4] With incomes below $800 per year, argued Robert Chapin in 1909, the families of New York City wage earners were underfed, underclothed, and inadequately housed. A yearly income of $800 permitted sufficient food and clothing, though it did not materially relieve congested housing conditions. Other investigators supported his contention.[5]

After 1915, when a dramatic decrease in European immigration and a temporary increase in industrial production due to war demand caused a general rise in wages, some investigators argued that increases in the cost of living more than offset wage earners' new prosperity.[6] Moreover, several observers claimed, the postwar decade saw a change in working-class expectations with regard to living standards. Wage earners' families, as well as families of the middle class, began to define as "necessities" a whole range of goods hitherto considered luxuries. With an expanded definition of need, a sense of economic marginality might persist despite a rise in real income.[7]

Chapin noticed in 1909 that families of New York City wage earners generally reached annual incomes above $800 only when more than one family member was at work.[8] Other investigators verified this: generally fewer than 50% of urban working-class households studied were willing or able to subsist on the income of the father alone. Many such families took lodgers; in some, the mother went to work; but the most important source of additional income in urban working-class families was the wages of adolescent children, both sons and daughters. These wages were necessary—often to insure subsistence, sometimes to provide a modest measure of comfort or security when a father's income was sufficient for food, clothing, and shelter.[9]

Many working-class families experienced the period of greatest privation when children were small and only the father was able to work. This was especially true if sickness or unemployment reduced his already inadequate wage. By the time a working-class child reached adolescence, he well understood the importance to his family of extra income, even the small contribution an unskilled young worker might make.[10] F. W. Taussig, writing in 1916, outlined the economic life cycle of the working-class family and indicated what pressures near-poverty meant for working-class adolescents:

> The young workman, just married, gets on comfortably at the wages current. During later years, when children are half-grown, there is the most trying stage. Still later, when the children begin to earn something, their earnings serve to ease the situation. A girl of sixteen who has sisters and brothers still younger, and who gets $6.00 a week, contributes to the family more than her separate "keep," and the inducement to push into employment the oldest child in such a family—girl or boy—is overpoweringly strong.
>
> Suppose that into the budget of a family whose head earns $12 or $15 a week, a girl brings an additional $6. In a working-class family the difference between $12 and $18 a week is great; it is the difference between having hardly any margin at all and something like ease. It means that the family is well above the poverty line.[11]

Hence, the apparent willingness of many working-class parents to "sacrifice" the younger generation for immediate material gain, to terminate their children's education as soon as legally possible, and to forego vocational training for sons and daughters. A majority of parents seemed prepared to condemn their children to the near-poverty of the undereducated and the unskilled.[12] But this did not happen through the parents' volition alone: many working-class children were willing, indeed eager, to assume the burden of wage earning at an early age, to dispense with formal education even where parents were anxious for a grammar school or high school diploma.[13] The reasons for this were many. They included the unhappy school experience of many working-class children, peer group pressure, and children's own sense of frustration at a cramped and penurious home environment.[14] In many working-class communities, moreover, the fact that a majority of children left school at fourteen meant that to do so seemed natural and inevitable. In these communities, the first job was widely regarded as a rite of passage to adulthood, especially for boys; even unskilled work was initially endowed with an aura of excitement. But also important was a child's strong sense of obligation to parents and family.

Many contemporary observers were particularly impressed by the intense family loyalties of working-class girls. Although they were generally more successful in school than boys, daughters left school for work or to assist at home about as frequently as their brothers. They worked at dull, ill-paying jobs more steadily than adolescent boys; they usually surrendered their entire wage to their mothers —males often returned only a portion of their pay; and they had more household responsibilities than wage-earning sons. Investigators often reported tension between parents and daughters in working-class families, especially over spending money and social freedom, but most daughters stayed essentially obedient: they remained in the parental home, they surrendered their wages, they compromised with parents on standards of behavior.[15] Interviewing working daughters of Polish families in Chicago, Louise Montgomery noted:

Girls sometimes complain that they do not have enough "returned" to them in spending money and in "the kind of clothes the other girls wear." If the mother is indulgent with her daughter's desire for evening pleasures and some of the novelties and frivolities of fashion, there is little friction; if she fails to recognize these legitimate demands of youth, the distance between mother and daughter is widened, though among the 500 girls their instinctive devotion to family claim has been strong enough to keep them obedient.

Indeed, Miss Montgomery asserted, even in those rare families where daughters earned more than sons or fathers, they generally accepted "a position in the household that forces them to coax, cry, or quarrel with the mother whenever they wish independent spending money."[16]

Jane Addams, among others, believed that the docility of the wage-earning daughter stemmed from authoritarian child-rearing patterns in working-class families. Where family income was close to the poverty line, she argued, children were inevitably regarded primarily as potential wage earners, and parental behavior was dominated by the need to produce compliant offspring. She offered an illustrative anecdote:

The head of a kindergarten training-class once addressed a club of working women, and spoke of the despotism which is often established over little children. She said that the so-called determination to break a child's will many times arose from a lust of domination, and she urged the ideal relationship founded upon love and confidence. But many of the women were puzzled. One of them remarked, "If you did not keep control over them from the time they were little, you would never get their wages when they are grown up." Another one said, "Ah, of course she (meaning the speaker) doesn't have to depend on her children's wages. She can afford to be lax with them, because even if they don't give money to her, she can get along without it."[17]

Other observers of working-class family life concurred: the absence of serious rebellion among adolescent wage earners, especially daughters, resulted from the strict discipline that characterized the treatment of children.[18] But such observations, while describing an important element in family life, neglected the bonds of affection and loyalty that also help to explain adolescent behavior. The working-class mother, usually a strong and controlling figure, was frequently the vital emotional center of the household. She created a sense of obligation in her children through her nurturant role as well as through harsh and arbitrary discipline. Certainly when working daughters themselves described the meaning and purpose of their work, the desire to "help mama" was often important.[19] "It was assumed as a matter of course that the girls' pay envelope should be turned over to the mother intact. 'It wouldn't look nice to pay board to the mother that raised you,' was the common view of the girls," wrote Louise Odencrantz of Italians in New York.[20] "The great majority of girls turn over their income without question to the family, and are proud and happy to be able to do so," echoed the compiled testimony of two thousand social workers in 1913.[21] The intimate relationship between habits of obedience and strong family affection is well illustrated in an essay written in 1926 by a Pennsylvania working woman:

> One day I ran into the house from school and found my mother looking very tired and depressed. She usually wore a look of anxiety these days, since my father had gone to the hospital, but her depression was very marked today.
>
> "What's the matter, mama," I asked. "Is papa worse?"
>
> "No, my child, he is improving, but the doctor told me this afternoon it will be at least six months before he will be able to leave the hospital."
>
> I knew at once what had made my mother so very sad now. My father's income had been cut off when he became injured, and my mother knew the little money she had would last only a short time, with four growing children to feed.
>
> Although I was but fifteen years old, I suddenly realized it was my duty as the oldest child to go to work. I tried to fight off the idea, by telling myself I probably wouldn't after all.
>
> I slept little that night and as I rolled and tossed my conscience seemed to be shouting at me, "Would you see your mother go to the factory for the sake of your school? Would this be fair?"
>
> The next morning I awoke with my mind resolved to take the step which I would do anything to avoid. Instead of telling the principal

at once when I got to school, I went to all the classes that day, and after my last class at three-ten, I told her with much reluctance.

I shall never forget how, as I walked home that hot day, my heart seemed to sink lower with each step. I walked along seeing nothing, for the thought that I had left school forever was driving me mad. Thus, the next day I entered the factory with the door to education slammed in my face.[22]

Less articulate, but no less eloquent, was the young Italian girl who confided to Louise Odencrantz, probably in 1913: "Last summer when I was laid off for nine weeks, I couldn't sleep nights. It was awful." "She tried to bridge the gap with work in other industries," added Odencrantz, "and the best that she could find was a job in a large plant preparing spices, where she worked from 7:30 in the morning until 6:30 at night for $4.00 a week." The Italian daughter "works because her family relies on her to do her part. . . . She feels her responsibility keenly and slack time is a season of horror for her."[23]

Working-class parents themselves stressed aid in family support as a natural, normal, and important element of filial loyalty. Noting that more than 84% of 347 New York City department store employees interviewed in 1910 were surrendering their entire earnings to their families, federal investigators declared:

While many of these girls were the sole or the partial support of their families, others, especially foreigners, pay the entire earnings into the family fund from a sense of filial duty. It would never occur to some of the daughters of foreign parents to withhold even a part of their wages. To a question, "How much does your daughter pay for board?" there frequently came an answer: "She gives me all of her money, of course. She is my child. When she wants to pay board she can go somewhere else to live."[24]

During the 1920s the custom of giving the entire wage to the mother was probably abandoned in many families, even for daughters. More families could afford to indulge their children, and certainly the better-educated adolescent, alert to the heightened consumption standards of the decade, was a more formidable bargainer for personal privilege than the very young wage earner of the prewar years. Even in conservative Italian and Irish families, Caroline Ware discovered in Green-

wich Village in the 1920s, some working children were permitted to
pay board and keep the rest of their pay for personal spending. But in
Greenwich Village most working-class parents expected the children
to contribute most of their pay to the family. The old norm of filial
devotion was not easily surrendered, for to do so required a radical
change in the parents' understanding of what a family was. "The older
Irish women felt that it didn't seem right 'to make a boarding-missus
out of the mother.' "[25] Indeed, throughout the 1920s, it is likely that
most working-class daughters contended with parents who were reluctant, for economic and emotional reasons, to grant them much personal economic freedom.

When a working-class girl left school, then, and ventured into
work, she did so more in the service of family and home than in
search of personal independence. Her sense of family obligation
placed severe limits on her sense of personal autonomy and her life
options. Despite the adventure of adolescent employment, it was the
working-class girl, rather than her wealthier sister, who remained
more closely tied to home, more deeply committed to a familial rather
than an individualistic ethic. Her life at school, at work, and in the
home illustrates this clearly.

Schooling in the Working Class

Poverty meant undereducation for nearly all working-class youth. It
was very common, as late as the First World War, for working-class
children to leave school before grammar school graduation. Often they
left as soon as the legal school-leaving age—usually fourteen—was attained, and sometimes before. ("I started to work when I was
twelve—six years ago," a Chicago garment worker remembered in
1910, "and I was so small that the boss could cover me with his coat
when the factory inspector came around.")[26] In New York City the
State Factory Investigating Commission found in 1914 that nearly 75%
of factory women studied had left school before the eighth grade, as
had nearly 40% of the female store employees interviewed.[27] And the
Immigration Commission in 1908 demonstrated conclusively that not

only high school but often the upper grades of the grammar school were beyond the reach of a heavily immigrant working-class. Excessive concentration of children in the early primary grades reflected not only the youthfulness of an immigrant population but also a severe degree of school retardation for many older children, especially but not exclusively those from immigrant families:

Table 4. Distribution of school population by grades for public and parochial schools in New York, Chicago, Philadelphia and Boston, December 1908

Grades	New York		Chicago		Philadelphia		Boston	
	Public	Parochial	Public	Parochial*	Public	Parochial	Public	Parochial
Kindergarten 1st through 4th	56.3%	66.9%	55.4%	—	62.2%	78.0%	45.1%	58.7%
5th through 9th	35.4	30.6	34.7	—	28.4	21.1	39.8	37.0
High schools and commercial schools	4.6	0.7	5.8	—	5.6	0.2	10.8	1.3

*no figures available

Sources: U.S., Congress, Senate, *Reports of the Immigration Commission*, Vol. 14: *Children of Immigrants in Schools*, Vol. 2, S. Doc. 749, 61st Cong., 3rd sess. (Washington, D.C.: Government Printing Office, 1911), pp. 176, 183, 544; U.S., Congress, Senate, *Reports of the Immigration Commission*, Vol. 16: *Children of Immigrants in Schools*, Vol. 4, S. Doc. 749, 61st Cong., 3rd sess. (Washington, D.C.: Government Printing Office, 1911), pp. 608, 617, 772, 779.

Table 5. Percent of public school population in high school, by race and nativity of father, New York, Chicago, Philadelphia, Boston, December 1908

Race or nativity of father	New York	Chicago	Philadelphia	Boston
Native white	7.3%	8.9%	7.3%	14.8%
Negro	3.0	4.7	2.7	6.6
Foreign-born white	3.5	4.5	4.0	8.6

Sources: U.S., Congress, Senate, *Reports of the Immigration Commission*, Vol. 14: *Children of Immigrants in Schools*, Vol. 2, pp. 179, 546; U.S., Congress, Senate, *Reports of the Immigration Commission*, Vol. 16: *Children of Immigrants in Schools*, Vol. 4, pp. 612, 775.

By 1920 rising family income, more stringent child labor laws, and heightened educational standards for even routine jobs caused many working-class children to remain in school until they were sixteen. But with the sixteenth birthday, the majority of these children left school, and most of them went to work. In New York in 1920, only 27% of the city's sixteen- and seventeen-year-olds remained in school; in Chicago all but 29% in this age group were school-leavers. And although high school attendance nationally increased sharply during the 1920s, working-class children continued to be seriously disadvantaged educationally, girls perhaps more so than boys. In three of the four cities with which this study is principally concerned, girls in 1930 failed to enjoy access to high school in as large proportions as their brothers. In Chicago and New York the discrepancies were most pronounced: 62% of Chicago's sixteen- and seventeen-year-old males were in school, as opposed to 54% of the girls in this age group. In New York 60% of the boys and only 54% of the girls of sixteen and seventeen were enrolled in school. In Philadelphia boys in this age group enjoyed a small advantage over girls, although enrollments in the upper grades in Philadelphia were unusually low for both sexes. Only in Boston were girls as likely as boys to be in school at sixteen and seventeen years of age. In 1920, however, girls had been slightly more likely than boys of this age to be in school.[28]

It is not immediately clear why working-class girls in 1930 were evidently less educationally advantaged than their brothers. When only a small number of working-class children attended high school, girls were at least as likely as boys to be enrolled. Even in 1920 rough equality prevailed between the sexes in terms of school enrollments for sixteen- and seventeen-year-olds in the four cities under study. Perhaps many working-class parents in the 1920s, with limited financial resources but an increasing respect for extended education as essential to adult security, came to regard education as necessary to sons but merely desirable for daughters. Girls, as we shall see, had few persuasive grounds on which to argue for their rights to an education.[29]

And this is significant, for girls suffered more grievously than boys from undereducation. By the 1920s, even routine retail sales jobs generally required education beyond the legal minimum, and movement into high-status, "clean" clerical work could not occur without extended education. "Girls who have not had some high-school work should not be encouraged to take business 'college' courses in stenography and typewriting," warned a 1911 Chicago study. "In general there seems to be little hope for the grammar school girl who has gone to 'college.' After a weary and most discouraging search for a position, the best that is open to her is an undesirable place at a low wage from which she cannot advance."[30] White-collar occupations rarely offered the chance to master skills through on-the-job training or formal apprenticeship; employers depended on the schools to teach the rudiments of clerical employment. But white-collar jobs represented for most working-class women the only escape from the monotony and physical exhaustion of unskilled factory work, however illusory that mobility ultimately proved to be in terms of promotion opportunities and wages. The undereducation of many working-class women was thus a greater handicap in the job market than the undereducation of working-class men, for whom apprenticeship, promotion within an industrial occupation, or union protection of seniority rights could make mobility or security possible within the blue-collar ranks.

The limited educational opportunities of working-class girls, moreover, placed them at a serious disadvantage in competition for the best paid and most interesting clerical employment. Working-class men rarely contended for skilled jobs with well-educated men from the middle class, but the rapidly expanding job market for clerical workers attracted middle-class as well as working-class women. Clerical workers with limited or inferior educations became, in effect, members of a vast white-collar proletariat. Although they escaped the factory in increasing numbers after the First World War, most working-class women found open to them only those white-collar jobs too routine and low status to be of interest to better-educated women.

Despite the economic disadvantages of early school-leaving, however, probably a large majority of working-class girls gladly left school to go to work. They, like their brothers, often found the schoolroom dull; the workroom was generally less rigorously supervised than the authoritarian, academically-oriented urban schoolroom of the early twentieth century. (Theories of child-centered education had had little impact on the public schools of Greenwich Village, Caroline Ware noted as late as 1930: "During the first six weeks of each school year, the front blackboard in the lower-grade classrooms of one school was devoted to the instructions, 'Eyes front. Hands in lap. Heads straight.' ")[31] And although there were bright and eager children whose abilities and interests made early school-leaving a personal tragedy, most working-class pupils probably experienced school in terms of humiliation and frustration. In underfunded educational systems, which were ill-prepared to teach large populations of non-native speakers of English, failure for many children was inevitable. Throughout the 1920s large numbers of urban school children were, because of academic deficiencies, in grades for which they were too old.[32]

Against the frustrations of school stood the enticements of the job. At work, the young were given easily mastered tasks, and they enjoyed, at least initially, an unprecedented sense of achievement. The first job represented a long step toward adulthood. And the prospect of spending money, no matter how little, was a powerful incentive to go to work. For those working-class girls who remained in school after most of their friends had taken jobs, a New York investigator commented in 1911, "the dresses of their employed friends are constant sources of envy." Wage earning, moreover, generally secured for the young entry into an exciting world of evening entertainments and social life with the opposite sex. The high school student, without economic leverage within the family and burdened with homework, was often isolated from his neighborhood peers. "The young high school pupil cannot help contrasting his own daily and nightly routine with that of his friend who is employed 'downtown'. In every way his own life seems hard, confined, and unnatural."[33] Indeed, for most working-class adolescents, extended schooling was probably not a happy choice until there were sufficient numbers of working-class children in high school to cause the school to become a major focus of their social lives, much as the job had once been for most youngsters in this age group. Even in 1930, however, the lure of the job generally proved greater than the lure of the high school diploma. Most working-class youth left high school before graduation.

In most working-class communities, moreover, much school policy, even in the 1920s, assumed and encouraged pupil failure. Many teachers, school administrators and politicians were actively involved in reinforcing family decisions about early termination of education. Early in the century, big city school systems were seriously over-crowded, and frequently lacked sufficient facilities for the populations they were legally obligated to serve. One solution to this problem was to discourage extended use of the schools by working-class children, and typically, in 1912, the Chicago Board of Education opposed an amendment to the compulsory education law of Illinois prohibiting the employment of children at fourteen years of age.[34] Children who decided to leave school were usually not questioned by school authorities about their decision, and they sometimes understood the ease with which they could leave as official approval of the decision to do so.[35] There was, moreover, in many classrooms a palpable cultural gulf between the teacher and her pupils. Teachers often assumed that working-class children could not master the standard curriculum, which was generally so far removed from the values and experiences of working-class children that mastery was indeed difficult for most. Even classroom discipline was made more troublesome by the failure of many teachers and educational policymakers to comprehend the cultural worlds from which their students came. Caroline Ware wrote of Italian children in Greenwich Village in the 1920s:

> The initial impact of the school upon the children often was very confusing to them. When these children first came to school, they had already learned in their homes certain habits and attitudes, and

they had been punished for failure to conform to certain standards of conduct. But the school's disregard for any home training which differed in its assumptions from that of the school frequently resulted in the children being treated as though they were personally misbehaving when actually they were conducting themselves as they had been taught. The effect of having to bear the burden of blame for cultural differences between home and school often set the children vigorously against the school.[36]

And while the tensions between Italian families and the public schools were often especially strong, these tensions were evident in virtually all working-class communities. Children were not only pulled from school by family need; many were also driven from school by inflexible and unsympathetic educational policies.

The inadequacies of the schools, however, were but partially responsible for the frequent educational failure of working-class children. The attitudes toward education that many children absorbed at home ensured that school would not often be taken seriously as a means to social mobility or self-discovery. Many working-class parents, including the foreign born, expressed to investigators the hope that their children would exceed the parents' life achievements by entering a skilled trade or obtaining clean "indoor work", generally clerical employment.[37] But fewer parents believed that education beyond the legal minimum provided a reliable means to occupational mobility, certainly not sufficiently reliable to do for years without the wages of a child of age to go to work. And the very real material needs of the family meant that respect for education was more often than not a value that, however rhetorically honored, had little to do with daily life. Louise Boland More, writing about wage earners' families in New York, commented in 1907:

> In regard to child labor, there seems to be a general feeling among parents that they would like to keep the children in school longer if they could afford it, but that they cannot, and the result to be gained did not seem worth the sacrifice. This feeling was expressed by one woman when she said: "I know Josie (13) ought not to stay out of school, but what could I do? I needed the money and she had the

chance.'' She promised to send her back to school in a few weeks, but unless the truant officer appears, these promises are soon forgotten! With an intimate knowledge of the family struggle for existence, it is easy to understand this eagerness to put a child to work as soon as possible. . . . Yet there is a universal desire that the children should become skilled workers and "learn a trade." [38]

In addition to profound mistrust of the practicality of academic education, a mistrust that had some basis in fact, the attitudes of many working-class parents toward their children's education were complicated by the immigrant's misperception of the culture. Louise Montgomery discovered in Chicago that many Polish parents believed education beyond the compulsory age was appropriate only to the "upper classes." [39] Polish, Italian, and Jewish parents alike expressed a fear that "excessive" education would render daughters unfit for marriage. [40] Many traditional Catholic parents retained an Old World ecclesiastical ideal of education, believing that formal schooling ought to terminate at the age of confirmation, generally twelve or thirteen. In a 1917 study Edith Abbott and Sophonisba Breckinridge interviewed the mother in a "very prosperous" Chicago immigrant family:

When it was suggested that they were sufficiently prosperous to keep the boy in school until he graduated from the eighth grade, she seemed greatly surprised to know that children were allowed to stay in school after they were fourteen; her other children, she said, had all left the parochial school when they were confirmed, and she had never understood that children could go to school when they were old enough to work. [41]

Finally, in many families, the desire to own property was an important motive force toward early wage earning, for even when a father's wage could adequately feed and clothe his family, the parents' fear of old-age poverty made property ownership imperative. Few working-class parents, it seems, trusted their sons, or their sons' abilities, to contribute to the parents' support once the sons themselves were married. And the self-respect attendant on an independent old age was apparently worth a considerable price to the older generation.[42]

Hence, many working-class children received little encouragement to regard education as serious, future-oriented work, or to resist peer pressure to quit school and find a job as soon as legally possible. Girls in particular suffered from lack of parental support. Especially but not exclusively in immigrant families, the education of daughters was considered of distinctly secondary importance to that of sons. Girls, ran conventional reasoning, would inevitably marry and commence an occupation for which academic training was irrelevant; since social mobility for a woman depended almost solely on her marriage prospects, extended education for daughters had no practical justification.[43] The inexperienced fourteen-year-old rarely possessed compelling counter-arguments to the seasoned logic of her elders. An articulate Brooklyn woman remembered in 1922 her own particularly female experience of school-leaving:

> I started out quite alone and unrecommended at the age of thirteen to seek my first job. Having finished grammar school at that age decided that. Coming of a family in which each member would, as a matter of course, be expected to contribute his or her share to the family exchequer just as early as possible, and who considered industry almost a religion, it was the thing to do, as inevitable as eating and breathing and finally dying. It was just part of the scheme of life.
>
> I did have other dreams, it is true. But a child of thirteen has little command over her own existence, or at least I hadn't at that time. It wasn't so much that I was ambitious as that I had a passionate love for books . . . and I begged my mother to permit me to go to high school. I went so far as to register at one of the local high schools in order to be able to attend should mother relent by the beginning of the fall term. . . . To do mother justice, she understood, a little, my longing to go and would have liked to have me continue, but it seemed neither practical nor sensible to her. She looked at the world about her (our world) and reasoned it out. I was to earn my living of course, for a time at least, and it was up to me to get as great a return as possible in the shortest time.

Had I been a boy instead of a girl, with my natural love for my studies, mother might have struggled to send me ahead, much as she needed what little I could earn. But a girl didn't need an education. In fact it might very well be a mistake to teach her too much, for several reasons. First, she would no doubt be married by the time she was twenty. That gave her family only a few years in which to expect financial return from her, and the years spent at school would be wasted. One could get the same return, in some cases a greater return, by starting out as early as one could be hired and getting practical experience that way.[44]

These assumptions about women's education were made manifest to girls throughout their brief school careers. It was common, observers claimed, for school-age girls to be kept home to do housework and care for children if the mother—or even a relative or neighbor—were ill or unusually busy.[45] Such interruptions necessarily impeded academic progress, increasing the likelihood of failure in school with its attendant humiliation for the normally compliant girl, anxious to please her middle-class teacher. And the willingness of many parents to keep a daughter from school served to reinforce the most important lesson of her socialization: that women's primary loyalty was to the family. "The claims of the school weigh against the claims of the family," wrote Josephine Roche of Italians in New York City:

While she is a little girl in the grades, having difficulty perhaps with her lessons, the disadvantages to her of being "kept out" a few days does [sic] not weigh an instant against some temporary family need in which she may be of help. Illness, financial loss, trouble of any kind, not merely in her own home but in that of an aunt or uncle, keep many a young girl out of school if only to lament the afflicted.[46]

The moment of school-leaving—an important rite of passage in working-class life—communicated very conservative messages about sexual identity. Although the age at which a majority of children left school had advanced from fourteen to at least sixteen by 1930, the reasons that young people left school were throughout the period expressed in terms of conventional sex roles. Because high school would not significantly increase their wage-earning abilities, boys left school to begin a life's work and become men. Girls left school to help the family, often as wage earners, and to wait for marriage. Girls might, it was true, argue for extended education on the ground that white-collar work increased their chances of marrying well. ("When a clerical worker at a local clinic married one of the doctors," noted Caroline Ware, "the clinic was besieged with applications for jobs, and parents who had been doubtful about permitting daughters to work there began insisting that they get clerical training on the chance of their getting in.")[47]

But when a family made sacrifices to insure the further education of a son rather than a daughter, the young girl had little choice but to accept an educational double standard: schooling beyond the legal minimum was ultimately justified by future occupational achievement, and such achievement for women was apt to be modest and temporary. High school for girls was essentially an indulgence, a luxury within the reach of many upwardly-mobile, working-class families who might choose to buy the prestige of clerical employment for their daughters, but it was rarely regarded as a young woman's right.[48] Mary Van Kleeck recalled a New York flower maker, an Italian girl whose wages helped to send a brother through a medical course. " 'When he graduated,' she said, 'I cried all day and was as happy as though I had graduated myself. I often say to my mother that we treat my brother as if he were a king. But I can't help it.' " Van Kleeck added:

> In the same spirit the oldest daughter of a Russian family left normal school after the second year in order that her older brother might attend college. Her father was a tailor. Two younger children were in school. She explained that she wanted to go back to normal college, but for her brother a college education was "a matter of life position," while for her it was not.[49]

Thus, even in families that regarded education as a serious matter and were willing to forego adolescents' wages for an extended period of schooling, daughters were often taught that their sex made personal ambition unnecessary or inappropriate. Only when the demand for women in clerical employment became sufficiently great that continued education for girls seemed to parents a sound family investment did most working-class girls attend high school as a matter of course. And even in major cities as late as 1930, their claims to a high school education, as we have seen, were less strong than the claims of their brothers.[50]

Into Work

The undereducated adolescent began his working life under a distinct handicap. Again, girls were more severely disadvantaged than boys. Investigators found that while parents might sometimes try to establish a son in a promising occupation—one where he could acquire a skill and have a chance at promotion—they rarely gave thought to their daughters' occupations. Since the girl would eventually marry and leave paid employment, it was not necessary to establish her in a job with a future. And while many parents, especially immigrants, were so ignorant of the employment possibilities of the young that effective guidance was difficult, the range of jobs available to girls remained the greater mystery, because relatively few mothers had themselves had experience of modern industrial work.[51] Robert Woods and Albert Kennedy, compiling the reports of two thousand city social workers, wrote in 1914:

> The family sense of responsibility for the girl who goes to work is universally admitted to be greatly underdeveloped, and the majority of parents are careless concerning the place and conditions under which the daughter works. Bad influences are accepted as the responsibility of the boss or of government. At best, parents are only occasionally anxious or a little puzzled. The struggle for a living is so keen that everything else is unimportant. The vital question is that of putting the girl at work; her safety is merely incidental. "I do not know where she works, but I know what she gets a week," fairly represents the attitude of the average parent.
>
> In the majority of families it is literally true that the parents have but a vague notion where the daughter works.[52]

Ernest Talbert remarked upon this ignorance among Chicago parents, and in New York, Lillian Wald wrote of her Henry Street neighbors: "The name or address of the place of employment of the various members of the family is often not known."[53]

Paradoxically, many parents were little concerned as well with the low wages of daughters. "The woman who frets over the $6 a week wage of the sixteen-year-old boy will regard with equanimity the same wage when the seventeen-year-old girl receives it," Louise Montgomery noted in Chicago.[54] The parents' attitude revealed not only the expectation of temporary employment for women; it also reflected the generally inferior status that working-class culture assigned to women in spheres outside the home. And the parents' low standards for women's wages quite naturally affected the expectations of the young.

Working-class girls, then, seldom had useful information about job possibilities when they first went to work. Their knowledge of the work world was generally limited to those stores and factories where friends and relatives worked, to other establishments in the neighborhood that employed women, and often to a sense that store employment or such "feminine" work as millinery and dressmaking was "nicer" than factory work, though not necessarily more remunerative.[55] Indeed, department stores and millinery shops were accused of exploiting their white-collar image to keep wages low.[56] Certain ethnic groups preferred or shunned various occupations, but again, they did so for reasons of status and tradition rather than economic advantage. Thus, when a school-leaver went to seek work, she was poorly equipped to choose among the limited range of jobs open to unskilled women the employment that offered the greatest possibilities of skill acquisition, advancement, and decent wages. And she rarely chose wisely, a fact of some importance if she did not marry or if financial need forced a return to work in later life.

Working-class girls often insisted on employment in a store or factory where friends worked, and they frequently sought work only in the immediate neighborhood.[57] The job was important for its social as well as its economic aspects, and work close to home meant a practical saving of carfare and time on crowded public transportation. But such arbitrary limits on employment possibilities could easily doom a girl to the lowest-paid occupations and to those jobs where working conditions were very poor—in the marginal industrial establishments that abounded in working-class districts. This narrow, highly personal view of the work world inevitably limited the control women were able to exert over their working lives.

Many young women prized neighborhood ties at work because the industrial world frightened and bewildered them. Working-class women often lacked self-confidence as workers because they lacked a sense of the world beyond the neighborhood. Like their mothers, many young women defined the knowable world in terms of kin and friendship networks. Men, however, working at jobs in heavy industry or transportation or perhaps as mobile construction workers necessarily developed a broader knowledge of urban geography. But many women, who had a variety of job possibilities close at hand, never learned to move about the industrial world with assurance, choosing the most advantageous jobs and seeking the best possible pay. This was especially true for very young workers, as Louise Montgomery discovered in Chicago:

> Girls are held to one miserable, distasteful piece of work by fear, discouragement, timidity, or the lack of knowledge of other opportunities. A few have confessed that they thought all the factories downtown made candy and there was nothing else for little girls to do except wrapping and packing confectionery. Some who had learned a single simple process in a box factory were unable to adapt themselves to other positions when laid off temporarily. One girl insisted that "pasting labels" was "her trade" and refused to consider anything else. Another said she could work only in the one department store in which she began. She had tried others but they always made her feel "strange and queer." Still another had worked a full year in fear of the forewoman who had an "evil eye."[58]

And Sophonisba Breckinridge discovered in Chicago that immobilizing ignorance and timidity characterized even the spirited young women who had organized an impromptu strike against reduction of piece-rates in the stockyards in 1900. The strike was lost, and the leaders were blacklisted:

> So limited had their industrial experience been that when they could no longer obtain employment in the yards, they seemed actually to believe that the entire world of industry was closed to them. "Going downtown to get work" was like going to a strange country, and seemed to require greater courage than they could command.[59]

Other investigators, asking young women why they had chosen a particular occupation, discovered that employment had "just happened" to many: they had accompanied a working friend to her shop and were taken on; they had applied at the small factory they passed en route to school; they had responded to the first "help wanted" sign they saw without considering alternatives. Restless or seasonally unemployed workers drifted from job to job with a similar lack of calculation.[60] Unable to choose their jobs in an informed and conscious way, many young women could not bring to these jobs critical standards of wages and working conditions that might lead to collective protest and, eventually, to improved work opportunities.[61] The very ignorance of these workers encouraged them to cling to the certainties of the personal life. Summarizing the testimony of two thousand social workers, Robert Woods wrote in 1913: "As a rule the girl does not enter on work in the same serious spirit which distinguishes the boy. . . . . Only a very small proportion of girls see in their work anything but a makeshift."[62]

The Wage-Earning Daughter at Home

In the home, the wage-earning daughter was encouraged to understand herself and her future in terms of the domestic role. We have seen that young women usually remained completely dependent economically on their families and that wage earning did not relieve them of household responsibilities. But when an adolescent boy went to work, he rapidly assumed something like adult status: often, he began to pay board, freely disposing of his additional income; he was not burdened with domestic chores; his activities were rarely restricted or questioned. A 1911 investigation of female laundry workers offers an illustrative example:

> "Eighteen years, single, Polish. Five years laundry experience. Went to work at thirteen in laundry. Lives at home with parents and gives them her wages, $5.50 a week. Father earns $55 a month, nine children in family, two besides this girl working. Brother pays $1 a week room and board. Sister earns $6 a week and gives it to parents. Rent six-room flat in brick row. Comfortably furnished and modern conveniences, but very crowded."[63]

Some observers even claimed that periodic voluntary unemployment was tolerated for sons but not for daughters.[64]

The privileges that sons enjoyed appear to derive primarily from the conviction of working-class women that men—especially young men—were unreliable, headstrong, freedom-loving creatures who had to be indulged in order to insure continued family support. Many mothers admitted that working sons were given freedom because discipline might cause them to leave home, depriving the family of needed income.[65] Relatively few working-class boys actually did so; mothers managed rebellious youths with considerable effectiveness. And husbands, secured by the bonds of matrimony and thus by the sanctions of religion, custom, and law, usually gave all or most of their pay to their wives, as we shall see. Nevertheless anxieties about the loyalties of sons were often translated into a mystique of male privilege: "Of course they don't give you all they make," an Italian mother told Louise Odencrantz, "They're men and you never know their ways."[66] Daughters, however, presented no threat. Their wages were sufficiently low that life outside the family would have been extremely difficult, and the social climate in working-class communities did not normally sanction a young woman's separate residence.

The relative freedom that many women experienced at work also helped to secure daughters to a dependent role within the family. One of the intangible benefits of employment was escape from the hot, crowded flat, from the press of domestic duties and the inevitable adolescent conflicts with parents. And this advantage was valued, for girls normally had fewer means of escape from the family than boys did. Many young women preferred work to life at home, and often failed to see in their wage earning a sacrifice justifying fundamental change in their domestic status. By the time the job became more irksome than diverting, the possibilities of escape through an early marriage were real and appealing to most young women.

That working-class daughters remained under family control in the most important matters of wages and residence does not, however, mean that their relations with parents were without conflict. Wage earning changed many adolescent girls. With employment, a young woman inevitably assumed a more powerful family role; her monetary contributions were usually accompanied by a new, if reluctant, willingness on the part of parents to bargain with her on issues of personal privilege. Most frequently, the young wage earner desired greater social freedom, increased spending money, and, sometimes, changes in the decor of the home or the parents' traditional style of life. Her parents, often deeply conservative, with close ties to an immigrant generation or immigrants themselves, generally found her demands a source of painful conflict.[67]

Contemporary observers indicate, however, that in these painful struggles over standards of female social behavior it was the young working daughter who usually emerged victorious: "Those who faithfully hold to a difficult and uncongenial occupation, bringing home the entire wage to the family and submitting to an almost patriarchal control in other matters, will demand a freedom in the use of their evening hours before which the foreign parents are helpless," noted Louise Montgomery in Chicago.[68] Indeed, with the exception of many Italian girls, young working-class women throughout the period appear to have enjoyed active social lives quite independent of direct family control. Both before and after the First World War, watchful investigators recorded—often with dismay—the gay sociability of adolescents in the industrial city. "They want something entirely different from the day's occupation," wrote Mary McDowell of Chicago working girls. "The movies and the jazz dance seem to be the only outlet offered them at a cheap rate. They turn to these and soon do not care for the quiet of home or clubs and classes offered."[69] Adolescents in the Hull House area, Jane Addams noted in a 1909 book, were utterly fascinated by the dance hall and the cheap theater. These defined an exclusively peer-oriented world that excluded adults and eluded adult control:

> This spring a group of young girls accustomed to the life of a five-cent theater, reluctantly refused an invitation to go to the country for a day's outing because the return on a late train would compel them to miss one evening's performance. They found it impossible to tear themselves away not only from the excitement of the theater itself but from the gaiety of the crowd of young men and girls invariably gathered outside discussing the sensational posters.[70]

It was probably inevitable that working daughters should defy their parents over this sort of freedom. Adolescent girls were normally interested in the opposite sex, in clothes, in good times with friends. And it was the promise of freedom in the evening, often, that helped to make bearable long hours at a dull job. "Girls are rushing all day long," explained a New York investigator in 1910. "But in spite of [their] weariness, many seek the stimulus of exciting pleasures and thus feel that they are getting something out of life."[71]

The circumstances of working-class life in the industrial city made a social life away from home especially important. Wage earners' families usually lived in severely congested housing; the privacy essential to courtship was distinctly lacking.[72] Lacking as well was a sense of spiritual space, of relief from the pressures of a near-poverty existence. "The circle of the working girl's life is cramped and limited," wrote Mary McDowell in a private paper. "A cramped home to eat and sleep in, a cramped place for work, a cramped public dance hall, where, on Saturday night, she has her only social outlet."[73]

But it was the "cramped public dance hall," the movie theater, and the amusement park that provided the space and privacy essential to many working-class adolescents. Commercial amusement places were free from parental and neighborhood surveillance. They permitted the young to explore the city and, at the same time, to observe and appropriate more daring standards of sexual conduct. Working-class adolescents in Greenwich Village in the 1920s, according to Caroline Ware, longed to escape the neighborhood in the evening. Trips "uptown" were trips to an exotic world, and the expansive youth who took his date to an expensive movie house might justifiably hope for a reward: "The distinction between taking a girl to Times Square or to the local house was pointed out by one young man, who carefully explained that if you took a girl to a Times Square movie, you could try to kiss her good night, but if you only took her to a local movie, it would be presumptuous to attempt to kiss her." [74] And once recreation had become a highly profitable business, the movie palace and the dance hall provided an element of luxury normally absent from everyday life. "These commercialized places are far lighter, airier, and more beautiful than any small home can be," noted a New York settlement worker as early as 1910. "They represent roominess, freedom, grandeur . . ." [75] Very likely the heightened consumption standards evident even among working-class families by the 1920s were to some degree shaped by adolescent exposure to this mass-produced glamour.

Certainly the adolescent girl who went freely, often from the age of fourteen, to the theater, the dance hall, or to promenade a brightly lighted shopping street was enjoying a freedom her immigrant mother had never experienced and a freedom her mother often could not reconcile with traditional requirements of feminine respectability. And there is little doubt that the increased personal power in the family that wage earning guaranteed young women helped to make this new freedom a reality. But whether the greater social freedom of adolescence represented a genuine break with the past, a radical change in the status of women in the home and the community, is a complicated question. The change is real—apparently dramatic—but it is not clear that this behavior represents something totally new.

It is well to remember that the most daring of working daughters enjoyed at best a partial freedom. She was not economically independent, and in all probability never would be. Her ultimate dependence on the protection of home and parents represented a powerful check on her behavior; so, too, did openly inegalitarian family and community standards for male and female behavior. Middle-class observers might believe that some young working girls were as free in their social lives as their brothers, but most young women were aware that improprieties could damage their ability to attract suitable male companions and, eventually, mates. Young women were not unaware that the frenetic social life—seemingly an end in itself—was also, perhaps primarily, an elaborate prelude to engagement and marriage. Noted Caroline Ware in Greenwich Village: "Various places at which dances were held were rated according to the kind of crowd—i.e., the chances that one might have of finding a good match."[76]

To some extent the new social freedom enjoyed by the working daughter simply represents an adaption of traditional courtship customs to the realities of city life. Certainly, in many instances, rebellion was necessary even to secure privacy for free association with peers, to meet available young men, to initiate properly romantic relationships with those known from school and neighborhood. The repressiveness of many immigrant parents toward adolescent daughters, argued Jane Addams, was cruel and pointless, since a changed social environment made it impossible for parents to provide appropriate husbands for their daughters. The dance hall, theater, park, and street represented the urban marriage market, definitely free enterprise in its workings but traditional in its goals.[77]

Courtship in this new setting did not necessarily generate radically altered relationships between men and women. Females remained dependent on males both in an economic sense—for the pleasures of evening entertainment—and in a more important emotional sense. In defining her life goal as the attraction of an eligible male and, eventually, marriage, the adolescent girl depended on a man to give meaning to her adult existence. As she pursued that happy goal, she was much less concerned with establishing equality between the sexes than with securing for herself the freedom to win a mate without parental sponsorship. She wished, in short, to be herself the sum of her dowry, to be desirable for reasons wholly other than those of family connection. And she largely succeeded, for personal attractiveness, stylishness, and the ability to be an easy participant in an increasingly standardized adolescent culture were, in the eyes of her contemporaries, the important criteria for choosing a bride. Her success won her greater personal freedom; it may have infused the early months or even years of marriage with a tenderness and romance her parents had not known. But this does not mean that the marriage relationship became an equitable one, or that early romance evolved into genuine companionship. Freedom from parental restraints was the single-minded goal of most young women; their vision did not normally extend beyond adolescent "good times" to include a serious reevaluation of their lives as adults.

This is not to say, however, that the experience of adolescent freedom was unimportant, or that this experience did not change young women in significant ways. The working-class daughter in the early twentieth century did not mature into the same woman that her mother had been, especially if her mother was an immigrant. But the change between generations probably appeared to be more dramatic than it actually was. Certainly, the greater freedom in dress, manners and morals that came about in the early twentieth century altered the self-image of many women, altering too their sense of what was possible in the lives they led. Young women absorbed from popular culture a highly romantic view of marriage. They hoped, according to Caroline Ware, for " 'True Story Magazine's version of 'love' and the 'Ladies' Home Journal' style of a 'lovely home.' "[78] Girls who had experienced a pleasurable adolescence and who assumed that pleasure was a veritable right doubtless anticipated a measure of leisure and self-indulgence as wives. Their heightened expectations—or the disappointment of their expectations—could not help but affect relationships with husbands and children, and very likely they affected such critical choices as the decision to limit and space the birth of children. But greater social freedom without corresponding economic freedom did not fundamentally change the life possibilities of young women. Marriage—indeed, marriage at progressively earlier ages—remained necessary to most young women in our period, necessary both economically and psychologically. Their life choices reflected directly this most basic dependence.

V

"On Their Own"

How do they manage to do it? In what mysterious ways do girls
stretch a less than living wage into a living one? is the question
which the public most often asks when it hears of girls living on
$5, $6, and $7 a week.

Miss C. W., a department store clerk, answers quickly, 'When
I have to pay for a pair of shoes or something like that, I don't
buy meat for weeks at a time.'

New York, *Fourth Report of the Factory Investigating Commission*

Not all working women lived in families; an important minority of
employed working-class women lived apart from parents or husbands,
sometimes utterly alone. Various studies between 1900 and 1930
found 10% to 25% of women interviewed living outside the immediate
nuclear family, although the lower figures are probably the more representative of most working-class communities.[1] Because they had at-
tempted self-support and had lived for a time away from the restrictions of family life, some of these women might be expected to reject
or modify the exclusively family-oriented role assigned to women in
working-class culture. But the experience of most independent women
proves to be important because it emphasizes the essential functions
that the family played for working-class women, who lacked the economic, institutional, and ideological supports for independence enjoyed by a tiny minority of their more privileged sisters.

Working-class families, as we have seen, remained intact at least in part because of economic realities. The wage-earning unit of father and adolescent children made modest prosperity and even mobility possible for many working-class families. And women, like children and the elderly, needed the economic protection of family membership. Women who lived independently often suffered severe poverty. Many women living alone, moreover, suffered as well from cruel and emotionally debilitating social isolation.

Women were generally expected—certainly in working-class neighborhoods—to live at home as the price of respectability. Working women themselves sometimes claimed that a woman who lived alone risked loss of reputation, and indeed, women's low wages often made it difficult for them to find housing in safe and respectable areas.[2] (Local boys, noted Caroline Ware in the 1920s, assumed that unmarried middle-class women who lived alone in Greenwich Village were mistresses or prostitutes: " 'How else could they live in these apartments? You know what a girl can earn.' ")[3] And few working-class women, apparently, freely chose the independent life. Many of those whom various studies found "adrift" were alone because they were orphans or because they were immigrants who had come to the United States without their parents through sheerest economic necessity.[4] The very word "adrift," widely used in period reporting, indicates middle-class attitudes about the dangerous vulnerability of women without family ties, attitudes that a heavily immigrant, family-oriented working-class surely shared. Indeed, the end of massive foreign immigration in the 1920s probably diminished significantly the incidence of non-family residence in the working-class among both women and men.

Because the great majority of working-class adolescents and young adults lived in families, there were few institutions in working-class communities to serve the needs of the minority who lived independently. Neither churches nor social settlements touched the lives of many working-class young people, including those living alone. Because women living independently were so poor, no profits could be made by offering them attractive "singles" rooms and apartments.

Even theaters, dance halls, and amusement parks—magnets for the urban young—could be impersonal and lonely for women too isolated from kin and neighborhood social networks to have friends. Women living alone found substandard housing where they could, and they found companionship, and eventually mates, through a similarly individualistic and private struggle. The most fortunate of these women were often those who became—as kin, fellow immigrants, or simply as lodgers—effective members of a surrogate family. And all but the most unfortunate eventually solved the problems of the independent life through marriage.

Low-wage women who lived outside the family survived the years alone through severe personal economy. Many subsisted on less-than-adequate diets in periods of unemployment and underemployment, bought the cheapest clothing, and spent very little on recreation and health care. Few had savings. But the most stringent economizing—from a middle-class perspective—was on housing. Independent working women shared the congested quarters of the poorest working-class families or rented rooms in the cheapest, dirtiest, and most unsafe commercial lodging houses.

Probably a majority of women living without family chose to board in private homes. Living with a family was usually the cheapest housing alternative available to the independent woman, and as a lodger she often became a member of a surrogate family, enjoying important economic and social benefits. Many women officially adrift lived with relatives or family friends; recent immigrants sometimes lived with countrymen who regarded themselves, at least temporarily, as substitute parents. And for many other women, who lived in families that took lodgers for purely economic reasons, poverty made possible a semblance of family life; economic need opened to single women—and men—families that could not afford the closed and privatized existence of the more prosperous American household.[5]

But the very poverty of most families willing to take lodgers meant for many independent women severely congested and often unpleasant living conditions. Women who lodged in private families nearly always shared a bedroom with one or more persons; sometimes they slept on cots in the kitchen or the parlor. And lodgers shared as well the inadequate sanitary facilities of the working-class poor and the monotonous diet of the low-wage family.[6]

The very worst conditions were usually found in the homes of poor immigrant families, who often kept several lodgers as a source of essential income. A 1906 New York newspaper feature sketched the living conditions of two young Galician lodgers on the lower East Side. Theirs was a life of considerable physical hardship, but the young women, in a family and successfully fulfilling their financial obligation to absent parents, seemed secure and content. Living independently in a strange, urban world, these young immigrants nevertheless remained bound to family duty as the essential focus of life and work:

> It is half-past nine when I reach Clinton street. Number thirteen is one of many tenements. It is a long way from East Broadway and the Bowery. Yetta walks it twice every day. . . . We go upstairs to Yetta's home. It is the second floor, back flat, left hand side. Like nearly all east side tenement flats, the first door leads you to the kitchen. It is a jumble of confusion, varied odors, and compressed space.

> There are seven in the Kurtz family, father, mother and five children. Yetta and her sister make nine. There are four rooms in the little back flat, and the rent is $14 a month, "very cheap," Mr. Kurtz assured me.

> The two middle rooms are bedrooms. They are dark and windowless save for inside windows opening into the kitchen and front rooms for ventilation. They contain a couple of beds, piled high with pillows and comforters, probably pulled in off the fire-escape at sundown.

> The front room is parlor, reception-room and bedroom for the boarders. There are two windows looking out on a clothesline-hung area. The mantlepiece is draped with figured lawn. On it are two tall Russian brass candlesticks and some photographs. In the corner is an iron folding-bed, the bed on which Yetta and her sister sleep.

> The eldest Miss Kurtz is entertaining her "gentleman friend" in the parlor, but they cordially retire to the doorway downstairs, and Yetta introduces her sister.

"It is a good place to board," says Saida, contentedly. "We are
the only boarders. Some places there are so many they have to sleep
on the floor. We pay only $3 a month each, and I earn five and
sometimes six. I am a corset-cover maker. It is a nice, clean trade,
much better than paper boxes. Some weeks Yetta only makes $2.
. . . We must work and get money to send home to Galicia to our
mother and father.[7]

Nor were their conditions of life unusually harsh. Summarizing an
investigation of New York women boarding in private homes, the
New York State Factory Investigating Commission declared in 1915:

Living thus usually means a tiny room with ubiquitous green or
large-flowered walls; a window opening into an air shaft or an inner
court hung thick with bedding and washing. A bed that nearly swal-
lows the room, a chair, a table, indifferent cleanliness, poor light
and ventilation. The meager wardrobe is placed in an improvised
clothes press which is simply several nails driven into the wall to
cover the suspended garments. A bewildering collection of picture
post cards or family photographs add[s] color. Most girls share a
room of this sort. Some few are fortunate enough to have a hall entrance to their rooms, so that they are shut off from the family.
Most, however, live in the very heart of the beehive. Others again
occupy the parlor—a composite of living and dining room—sharing
a lounge or folding bed with some member of the family.[8]

In other major cities as well, the housing of the working-class poor
was badly overcrowded, and so were the conditions confronting private boarders and lodgers.

The very congestion of the working-class home, however, helped
integrate the lodger into the routine and discipline and support of family life. It was physically impossible in many situations for lodger and
family to lead separate lives in the home, and the very presence of
nonfamily members in the crowded household probably diminished the
intimacy of nuclear family relationships. A family that lived constantly
with lodgers could not easily sustain an intensely private domesticity.
In many working-class families, moreover, the tiny house or flat was
effectively a woman's world: men worked long hours away from home

and enjoyed a vigorous male social life in saloons and clubs as well. Her femininity thus qualified a woman lodger for special status in the home, and many young women lodgers appear to have moved easily into quasi-daughterly roles in host families.[9]

A sympathetic host family could provide important social and economic protection to a woman living independently. Many women lodgers valued the apparent respectability of family residence; they valued as well the physical protection of life in a familiar family group. Younger members of the host family might provide entry to the neighborhood social world. Social life and courtship were easier and safer when a woman possessed a tangible family identity. And often, in times of unemployment, the landlord sustained the lodger economically, the lodger thereby incurring an emotional as well as a financial debt—a quasi-filial relationship indeed. Particularly for immigrant women, the landlord's family, who were often countrymen, provided both refuge from and introduction to a strange new world. The New York State Factory Investigating Commission in 1915 noted the importance of surrogate family membership for young women, especially immigrants:

> Many girls prefer to live with private families. "I live with a missus" is the recurring explanation of an immigrant shop girl. To her this is the nearest approach to home—for it is not unwonted that the "Missus" is a relative or friend, "landsleute"—it is more respectable, more safe than living totally apart from kith and kin. Moreover the family, which is so often driving the wolf from the door, will time and again countenance a falling behind in the board bill, when the girl is out of work. "Don't I know what it means to be out of a job" many a kindly woman will say. "She is like my own child. How could I put her out? The little we have will have to go a bit further for a while." On the other hand the girls repay in kind, giving their services in every conceivable way. To quote Jennie, who lives very closely: "When I don't work I look after the three children and the home. My Missus was deserted by her husband. She depends lots on my rent. Now I must go and live with my sister, because her husband is out of work. But first I must find someone to take this room.[10]

The landlord's generosity in times of unemployment was admired by many observers.[11] But generosity frequently gave senior family members the right to discipline the lodger and to demand from her certain behavior in the house and even away from home. Some women lodgers were burdened with domestic chores after work.[12] And sometimes too landlady and lodger were in conflict over precisely those issues of adolescent social freedom that troubled the relationships of working-class mothers and daughters. Bureau of Labor investigators, interviewing young women "adrift" in New York, Boston, Philadelphia, Chicago, and Rochester in 1909, commented on the quasi-daughterly status of many lodgers in the host family: "In these families the girl is, at least, subject to some supervision. Her landlady knows pretty well how and where she spends her time, and feels at liberty to commend or criticize."[13] The young lodger, then, ostensibly independent of the parental home, was often very much a part of conventional family life, and her freedom to experiment with values and behavior was limited.

Some women living independently, however, lived not in family groups but completely alone. These women tested, in their own lives, the possibilities of security outside the family; most discovered a world of poverty and loneliness. This was much less true for working-class men; a young man living alone might be lonely, but he could safely and respectably be the aggressor in social relationships, and he was rarely incapable of true self-support. Not until old age or ill health reduced his earning capacity was a man likely to be economically dependent on family.

Women who lived alone often paid relatively high rents for miserably substandard accommodations. The working-class rooming house was congested, dirty, poorly lit and heated, ill-provided with sanitary facilities, and was sometimes a firetrap.[14] And the cheap lodging house was always tinged with the ugliness of poverty. An immigrant garment worker who lived alone in New York in 1914 recounted in her autobiography the depressing aspects of life in a "furnished room":

I climbed up the dark, dirty stairway to the fourth floor and opened the door to a cold, unfriendly room. An old couch, two chairs, a broken white dresser furnished the small room. The only window faced a narrow court that never allowed the sunlight to break into my room.[15]

In Boston a 1903 investigation revealed that a minimum expenditure of $5.00 a week for room and board—a price too dear for the low-wage woman—meant that "the lodger will have to live in an unheated and stuffy side room, or share a poorly furnished and often untidy square room with some roommate about whom he perhaps knows very little."[16] A former laundry worker in Chicago testified, probably in 1915:

I have worked and lived in Chicago, and I know that the average rooming house where a girl can get a room, if it is respectable at all, with any kind of decently furnished rooms, kept properly warmed, and fairly clean, will not rent her a room for less than $3 a week. They ask more than $3 a week if it is a room that is at all pleasant and is in a neighborhood that is not down at the heels. In too many places girls are not welcome at any price.

Meals purchased in a restaurant, she continued, cost twenty to twenty-five cents each: "When a girl is working, she has to eat to keep well. She can't do her work and be half-starved, though some try to do that for a while."[17] And in New York the Bureau of Social Hygiene investigated the housing available to Manhattan's working women in 1922, and found that even when women paid more than 50% of their earnings for room alone, accommodations were often poor: "These rooms . . . are far from adequate for health and happiness. The light in many houses, both natural and artificial, is very poor; the gas is often so bad that the occupant of the room cannot read after dark."[18]

By 1900, and certainly by 1910, most commercial accommodations open to urban women were rooming houses, not boardinghouses. By the first decade of the century, rising food and labor costs made the big city boardinghouse an unprofitable venture for the small landlord: greater profits accrued when all common rooms were converted to bed-sitting rooms.[19] But the passing of the boardinghouse signalled the end of important non-family communal experiences for single women and men. In the rooming house no shared meals or common activities permitted lodgers to make safe social contact with one another, and the urban rooming house was a singularly lonely place. Indeed, the experience of rooming house life testifies that—denied the emotional and social supports of family membership, denied institutions that provided familial social environments—woman and many men too found few opportunities for the secure sociability that could make the independent life an exciting alternative for the young.

The rooming house population was a highly mobile one, at least partly because the variable pay of low-wage workers forced periodic changes of residence for economy's sake.[20] Certainly the shifting population of the lodging house and the lodging house district made it difficult for single people to establish enduring friendships. But the isolation of many rooming house residents was too severe to reflect only the practical problems of sociability in a mobile population. In Philadelphia, for example, an investigator of the city's rooming house districts concluded in 1912:

> There is no real social life within the rooming house. Surrounded by thousands of their own age and social position, many roomers are as much alone as a Crusoe on some desert island. There is a remarkable isolation of the individual roomer from his fellows. Lodgers of the same house usually keep to themselves.[21]

He echoed an earlier Boston study:

> Of the social conditions characterizing rooming-house life, not the least important is the remarkable isolation of the individual lodger from his fellows—the absence of all sembalance of home ties, of companionship and friendship, and, for hundreds of young men and women, even of mere acquaintances. There is no social life within the lodging house.[22]

And in Chicago, even in the 1920s, the single life was often the solitary life, according to a University of Chicago sociologist:

> The rooming-house is a place of anonymous relationships. One knows no one, and is known by no one. One comes and goes as one wishes, does very much as one pleases, and as long as one disturbs no one else, no questions are asked.[23]

Meals, at least minimally social occasions within the family, were often taken alone by rooming-house tenants. The very poorest women ate in their rooms, without companionship or amenities, as Lucille Eaves discovered in her 1917 study of Boston women living independently:

> The women paying least for food prepare all meals in their rooms and carry their noon lunches to eat in their places of employment. Preparing meals in the room did not necessitate an expensive equipment; the usual custom seemed to be to buy what was absolutely necessary at the ten-cent store, and to dispense with all superfluous utensils and furniture. A one or two burner gas plate or oil stove on an oilcloth-covered box or table, dishes kept on the closet shelf or in a bureau drawer, a dining table that was sometimes a desk, sometimes a cutting table and sometimes a lamp stand—these furnished all that was indispensable for bedroom housekeeping.[24]

Even where lodgers could afford the cheap restaurants and cafeterias that served a predominantly rooming-house clientele, meals were rarely social occasions, as a Philadelphia investigator noted: "In these dining rooms meals are eaten almost in silence. No one has a permanent seat. The mealer comes in whenever he is hungry, takes a napkin from a rack, and sits wherever he can find a vacant place."[25]

The isolation of rooming-house life was often supported by the attitudes and policies of rooming-house proprietors. Owners and caretakers frequently refused to encourage house social life or to keep a protective eye on female lodgers.[26] Indeed, some rooming-house mistresses were reputed to be singularly hostile to women tenants, whom they considered more troublesome and less reliable than men.[27] Few restrictions governed the conduct of lodgers; women as well as men were free to pattern their lives on purely individual values. Female lodgers, according to investigators who interviewed rooming-house tenants in five cities, are responsible to no one, they come and go and spend their money when and where they will. The restrictions, with the exception of a prejudice against cooking in the rooms, of the average boarding or lodging house within the reach of these women, are few. "I don't care what they do so long as they are quiet and don't make a disturbance," was the sentiment of one landlady, and "It's none of my business where they go so long as they behave themselves here."[28]

But this very freedom made social life among lodgers extremely difficult. Women without family ties were often intensely suspicious of all strangers, even refusing to have roommates.[29] Their wariness reflected the fears that women quite legitimately associated with a mobile, socially anonymous population. The inhabitants of the rooming house lacked the reassuring and visible identity that family membership bestows. It was also family membership that provided women with the best measure of protection against sexual exploitation: a woman alone was much less able than a woman with family ties to ensure that sexual involvement led to marriage. Despite the much-reduced role of parents in the mate-selection process, families continued to define for the young safe and appropriate friends and potential mates, and few working-class daughters would be courted or married by men of whom their parents knew nothing. Women without family often lacked access to reassuring social networks. And this was so because no institutions existed to duplicate the essential functions of the family in facilitating and protecting the social relations of the young. Outside the family, some women were virtually without social ties, as Lucille Eaves noted in Boston:

> The usual difficulties incident to finding women living apart from family groups were encountered. Women "adrift" have so few social affiliations that settlements, churches, and clubs could afford the investigators little help. Moreover, many of them move frequently, and tracing them was rendered difficult by the general migratory character of rooming-house neighborhoods. The isolation of a number of these women was marked. Long hours of work, coupled with the general habit of using what leisure remained for laundry, cooking, and other household tasks, left little time or strength for making friends or forming personal ties of any kind.[30]

"Those who have never had the experience of living in single rooms in boarding or lodging houses, can never really know what it means to be wholly limited to a single room," echoed the New York State Factory Investigating Commission. "And yet there are thousands of working girls whose lives are bounded by just such narrow dimensions—who go daily from the factory or department store to their little hall bedroom, and from the hall bedroom back again to the factory."[31]

A small number of women living independently found accommodations in subsidized boardinghouses, endowed by charity for the relief of women "adrift." Most subsidized houses were very inexpensive, but they were few in number and sheltered only a tiny part of the female population who lived away from home.[32] Many women living alone were probably unaware that charity homes existed. And subsidized boardinghouses were often located far from working-class neighborhoods, attracting a predominantly white-collar and student clientele. Once a house was populated primarily by white-collar workers, factory women—sensitive to their lower occupational status—generally ceded the institution entirely to the middle class.[33] Some houses, moreover, refused to accept domestic servants, often the women most likely to need protection if they could not draw on family resources.[34] Ultimately, the subsidized home functioned more effectively to relieve middle-class consciences than to relieve working-class poverty. Employers occasionally justified low wages for women on the ground that charitable institutions could support the rare employee who did not live at home.[35]

Those subsidized houses accessible to working-class women were frequently unpopular with potential tenants because they afforded little space and privacy, often imposed very strict regulations on residents, and bore the stigma of charity.[36] For economy's sake, some houses, especially before the First World War, offered only dormitory accommodations, and these houses were often dirty and overcrowded.[37] Others provided tiny individual cubicles or curtained dressing areas around dormitory beds. Single rooms, especially at genuinely low rents, were rare. Stringent economy could also mean poorly prepared and inadequate food and dismal common rooms, though this was not invariably the case.[38] Some charitable homes for working-class women were lively and sociable places.[39]

But many subsidized houses—often because of their ties to religious or philanthropic agencies—actively inhibited easy sociability among residents.[40] Religious observances were mandatory in some houses, and the social lives of residents were unstintingly regulated. Some charity houses displayed all the repressiveness of the strictest family discipline but failed to offer women the emotional supports of family life. The Bureau of Labor explained, in 1910:

> Some houses allow the girls to be out only certain evenings in the week; almost all have a definite hour for closing, generally ten o'clock, and in many cases a girl who is not in by that hour is locked out for the night. She must then spend it where she can. Instances were told to the agents of girls walking the streets all night, having no place to go.[41]

Many such agencies regarded their clients purely as a dependent population, differing little as objects of charity from the elderly or the physically afflicted. The welfare provided them was thus all too often the repressive welfare meted out by private institutions to the "deserving poor"; in return the young, employed woman was expected to surrender her ability to govern the most basic decisions of daily life. The history of one "charity home," described in 1915 by the New York State Factory Investigating Commission as the residence of a department store saleswoman earning $7.00 a week, illustrates:

> The home in which she lives is a very large one—accommodating some 100 people when filled. It used to be an asylum for deaf-mutes but some years later was turned into an old lady's home with a few working girls accepted temporarily. It has now all of the earmarks of institutionalism—a forbidding dark red brick structure on the outside, parlors, which are pointed to with pride—large, stiff, and dark. Lines of straight-backed chairs are pushed close against the wall—a table with a Bible on it standing in the middle of the room. The windows with heavy draperies excluding the light are evidently nailed or

painted down. In this parlor it is the privilege of the girls to entertain their friends on Thursday evening. The girls have two nights a week "out"—when, with special permission, they may stay out until after ten o'clock, but the rest of the week the rules of the house oblige them to be in their rooms by ten at night. Monday evening the laundry can be used by the girls—another evening is set aside when rooms are supposed to be swept and dusted. Everything down to the smallest detail is planned and scheduled.[42]

Basically, the subsidized boardinghouse was intended to provide independent women with a restrictive way-station on the hazardous journey through youth to marriage. Indeed, many houses refused to accept as tenants women over thirty, for the middle-class directors of these charities were not interested in facilitating independent lives for adult women.[43] They wished, rather, to control the sexual lives of their young clients; the stringent rules in many charity houses were rooted in class antagonism between sponsors and the clientele the homes were intended to serve. Charitable agencies did not propose to solve the fundamental economic and social problems of independent working women. And they did not.

The poverty of most women living alone was reflected not only in the housing open to them but, as we have already indicated, in diet, dress, and an inability to afford even minimal health care, recreation, and future financial security. Theirs were lives of ceaseless and damaging personal economy.[44] Women alone were sometimes hungry; many more suffered physically because of inadequate nourishment. Lucille Eaves reported that among Boston's independent working women, average expenditures for food were not sufficient until a woman reached a wage of $10 per week. Below that wage, she noted, any increase in pay was generally spent first on food, hunger taking priority over the need for improved housing.[45] Housing costs, however, could not be temporarily eliminated from one's budget, and investigators for the New York State Factory Investigating Commission and the Federal Bureau of Labor claimed that it was common for women to economize on diet when money had to be spent for clothing or medical care. This sometimes meant elimination of all meat from the diet or regular omission of a meal, usually breakfast.[46] The commission remarked that "investigators, some of them experienced social workers, frequently expressed surprise on finding how many girls were habitually going without meals because they were too poor to purchase food."[47] And in times of unemployment and severe underemployment, many independent women economized on food to the serious detriment of health. Having interviewed 212 New York City factory women living without family, one government investigator reported:

> Many girls were found whose income was more than sufficient when the work was normal, but when the season was over their savings, if there were any, went quickly for current necessities. Rebecca C., a Russian Jewess, said that during the dull season she had lived many an entire day on a penny's worth of bread, and the landlady added that she had known the girl to go without even that much sustenance for a day.[48]

Habitually or intermittently inadequate diets probably undermined the vitality of many independent women. Elizabeth Hasanovitz, writing of her life as a garment worker in New York, recalled "a weak stomach, headaches every other day, a pale face, inflamed eyes, and my nose—my nose also began to complain."[49] A conference of Boston social workers declared in 1912, "It is generally stated and believed that women wage earners living alone are undernourished."[50] Contemporary observers often described working women, even the very young, as "thin," "pinched," and "pale."[51]

The debilitating effects of poor diet were exacerbated by the inability of most independent women to afford medical care. Few had cash resources for medical emergencies. Nor could most independent women make provision for regular visits to doctors or dentists.[52] For women living at home, family financial resources usually provided medical care during emergencies; if the family was reasonably prosperous, by working-class standards, a doctor was probably called for less serious illnesses as well. But independent women often ignored symptoms of poor health and even of serious disease: "This custom of 'letting it go on' is undoubtedly one of the many explanations for the anaemic conditions of many working girls," argued the New York State Factory Investigating Commission. "They are not able to visit the doctor's whenever a new symptom of disease manifests itself, but they do let it 'run on' until the condition becomes serious."[53]

When a woman living without family suffered a serious illness or injury and was unable to work, her prospects were bleak indeed. Sometimes relatives or even friends paid medical bills; a kind landlady might defer rent until the patient was again employed. But either instance usually meant a debt that could take months or years to pay. Some women carried insurance against sickness, but benefits were small and would not usually last the duration of a major illness. Other women had no resort but to charity, and it was in instances of medical emergency that the independent woman was most likely to suffer the humiliation of public assistance.[54] Though her disability might arguably be occupational in nature, intimately related to her low wage, women's employers incurred no legal responsibility for their employees' illnesses, and few made provision for assistance during sickness.[55]

Poverty also denied independent women most of the consumer pleasures that were so important to the working-class young. The work experience generally provided incentives to fashionable dress, yet many women who lived alone made real sacrifices to afford small wardrobes of even the poorest quality. The New York State Factory Investigating Commission found them devoting long evenings to making, repairing, and laundering their clothes. "This way of economizing," noted the commission, "leaves no free time in which to enjoy oneself."[56] Some women bought most clothing on installment plans, but thereby placed themselves in near-permanent debt.[57] And many women who lived alone bought clothing with money normally budgeted for food and housing. They reduced their already meager diets and even moved to cheaper quarters when clothing needs were serious.[58]

Many spent little for recreation: "The total sacrifice of any legitimate pleasure is a common form of economy," reported the New York State Factory Investigating Commission. "In many cases among the girls interviewed, this seemed especially disastrous, because many of them were carrying a heavy burden of anxiety, in addition to their work, and particularly needed legitimate distraction."[59] Young women often depended on male friends for recreation, but an unusually shy woman or an older woman living alone might find her isolation unrelieved by any social experience beyond the job. A thirty-eight-year-old Philadelphia laceworker, American born, revealed in her own account of years of independent living that economy in the sphere of "legitimate pleasure" could mean a life of intense loneliness:

> I have never gone begging for lack of funds, but I have sometimes neglected my meals from discouragement. I have been careful to save, or would be in a fine plight now. The saving has been mostly on clothes, though I have saved on my room rent by providing the furniture and care of it, and doing my own washing as far as I could—the small pieces. Not going out much helped in this. I did not make many visiting friends, for I could not return their invitations.[60]

Ultimately, the real poverty of the independent woman is revealed in her inability to save regularly. The Boston Women's Committee on Savings Bank Insurance interviewed thirteen hundred working women in 1910 and concluded that few had adequate savings. It was only among highly skilled women earning twelve to twenty dollars a week that as many as 30% possessed "sufficient" savings. The lower-wage women—the great majority—often did not attempt to save, and those who did were able to accumulate only small sums. Other investigators also commented that women "adrift" were unable to save effectively.[61] Yet the omnipresent threat of unemployment due to seasonal work or sickness meant that women without family were in need of cash reserves, often several times a year. Without savings, periods of unemployment or underemployment meant stringent economizing on food and housing and accumulation of debt, which then reduced income during subsequent times of full employment and further exacerbated the difficulties of saving.[62] An endless cycle of poverty and deprivation was thus perpetuated. And the physical and mental strain of poverty increased as the independent working woman grew older.

For a majority of women living alone, the most obvious and possible remedy for poverty was marriage. Most independent women eventually married and, through family membership, gained financial protection, certain respectability, and a measure of emotional gratification. Particularly at the beginning of married life, the contrasts were stark between the benefits of family membership and the difficulties of feminine independence. Before children were born, the wages of most working-class men could support a couple in modest comfort, even if the wife did not work outside the home, as most did not. And the romance of early marriage doubtless contrasted sharply with the loneliness of life alone. The role of wife, moreover, provided an apparently predictable and secure future and was genuinely honored by the community and the larger society. The independent working woman, by contrast, looked ahead to an uncertain future as a low-wage worker, a future in which her already limited earning potential would decline with age or poor health. And the working-class woman who lived alone was accorded at best an ambiguous social status. If her respectability was not questioned, she clearly remained an abnormal member of the community, rewarded by society neither for motherhood nor for success in the world outside the home.

That working-class women were in real need of family protection at least through the early decades of the twentieth century is best illustrated by the experience of older working-class women who lived alone. Those relatively few independent women who never married, and those who were widowed, divorced, or deserted and forced into self-support, faced a harsh and lonely struggle for existence on diminishing wages. Evidence suggests that many women in this situation suffered physical and emotional damage.[63]

Working women in stores and factories faced a decline in wages after the age of thirty-five, and with advancing age, employment was increasingly difficult to secure.[64] Many firms did not employ older women as a matter of policy, claiming that they were less likely than their younger sisters to be efficient producers. The woman without family ties anticipated an old age where she might be unable to earn her living. This fear often prompted the older working woman to excessive, even dangerous, economy in food, clothing, and shelter; the concomitant burden of anxiety sometimes produced a pathetically timid and distorted personality.[65]

The older woman "adrift" often lived alone in the very poorest lodging houses.[66] A New York City investigator described in 1911 the home of an American-born widow of forty who was completely without family and worked as a candy packer for self-support:

> Mrs. Hallett lived in an excessively small, unheated hall bedroom, on the fourth floor of an enormous old house filled with the clatter of the elevated railroad. On the night of the inquirer's call, she was pathetically concerned lest her visitor should catch cold because "she wasn't used to it." She lighted a small candle to show her the room, furnished with one straight hard chair, a cot, and a wash-stand with a broken pitcher, but with barely space besides for Mrs. Clark and her kind, public-spirited little hostess. They sat, drowned at times in the noise of the elevated, in almost a complete darkness, as Mrs. Hallett insisted on making a vain effort to extract some heat for her guest from the single gas-jet, by attaching it to an extremely small gas-stove.[67]

Older women without family economized on food, not during occasional emergencies but regularly, year after year. An interviewer with the Manning study in the mid-1920s found two elderly sisters, once factory workers and now homeworkers, who "remarked that they bought meat once a week so that they would be seen at the butcher shop and people would not think they went hungry."[68] The health of many older women alone appeared to suffer because of poor nutrition.[69] They spent little for clothing and could rarely budget for routine medical care or for serious illness.[70] Most lived in fear of disabling sickness or injury, for disability usually meant the end of productive employment and dependence on charity.[71]

Investigators claimed that age wrought a distinct personality change in the woman living alone; the isolation of her existence and the anxiety of her fight for survival produced a woman who was timid, passive, severely limited in her interests, and beset by constant fears about security.[72] The New York State Factory Investigating Commission offered as an example a Buffalo department store employee, only thirty-one, but already aging both in terms of marriageability and employment prospects:

> The only vacation Miss T. allowed herself was the one week given by the store with pay to each employee. She could not afford to go to the country and have a real rest, so she would sit in her little attic room trying to rest there. Every day she would visit the store "just to see if any one had taken her job away."[73]

For many older women, the terror of unemployment caused uncomplaining acceptance of wage cuts and an unwillingness to seek better pay or conditions by changing jobs or bargaining with an employer; older women were rarely assertive role models for young workers.[74] For some, the loneliness of the early years adrift became a totally friendless isolation, with all energies of mind and personality devoted to the problem of survival. Lucille Eaves, investigating the living standards of independent women in Boston, wrote: "As she grows older, excessive timidity about looking for better work or asking for better pay, selfishness and indifference to anything outside the regular day's routine become characteristic of the woman worker without home ties."[75] And a 1915 Boston observer of a group of unemployed domestic servants—an occupation to which the older, unskilled woman often turned—remarked:

> Pathetically many seemed "queer," as though the isolation and drudgery of their lives had developed curious mental twists, culminating in ominous strangeness at the critical age of fifty. No doubt anxiety and low nourishment during their idle weeks had, in many instances, hastened that development. The majority of these women when not at work were lodgers, leading at best a lonely, depressing existence.[76]

For the working-class woman, then, life outside the family was apt to be economically precarious and very lonely. It was not a life of freedom and autonomy. This was so because the great majority of unskilled women earned less than subsistence wages. They needed the economic protection of family, and without it they lacked the resources to experiment with new styles of life. Yet the price of family economic protection was, as we have seen, a surrender of considerable personal autonomy. Life outside the family, moreover, was difficult for women because extrafamilial institutions did not offer them the emotional security, the social status, the easy personal identity of family membership. Ultimately, the family provided the only emotional world in which working-class women were secure and fully acceptable. The experience of most independent women taught this lesson both to women "on their own" and to a larger female audience.

VI

The Married Woman Worker

My aunt, a kind widow, about forty years old, prematurely gray and wrinkled, frail and bent almost double, with a pale frightened countenance, stammered, "Why have you been fired?" Poor woman, she herself had been working in the same factory for fourteen consecutive years, as a shirt ironer, only about sixty-two or sixty-eight hours a week. It was the only factory in the city of Philadelphia that she knew of. She had five children to bring up, after her husband's death, and naturally had no time to acquire information of any kind. Responsibility, sometimes, breeds efficient slaves. She continued to slave until some of her children were old enough to replace her in the same factory. She was a perfect physical wreck, but naturally very ambitious and energetic. She could neither rest herself, nor see anyone idle; and here I came home, fired. Oh! If only a worker fired would not have to come home without a job! She was deaf, too, and had a chronic catarrh in the head, as a result of her fourteen years of bending over a gas iron, inhaling gas and being exposed to frequent changes in temperature. So she sat, gasping for breath, unable to hear my apology, repeating in distress, "Why have you been fired?" and at the same time continuing, "Now you will not be able to get as good a job, for this is the only steady shop in the city."

Goldie Share, "My First Job"
from *The Bryn Mawr Daisy* (Hilda Smith Papers).

Before the Second World War, wage earning was rarely a major responsibility of working-class wives. A decided minority of married women worked for wages in the prewar period: 5.6% of all married women were reported at work in 1900, and 11.7% were so recorded in 1930, although the census certainly underenumerated wives employed part-time in the home. The proportions of married women reported at work in Boston, New York, Philadelphia, and Chicago between 1900 and 1930 closely paralleled national figures.[1] In most working-class neighborhoods, of course, a more sizeable minority of married women were employed, but even in working-class families the wife was not usually at work for wages. A study based on unpublished census data for Chicago in 1920, for example, found working wives in only 20% of white unskilled workers' families, and this figure included a large number of women—nearly half the sampled group—who kept lodgers and had not been counted in the census as gainfully employed.

Table 6. An analysis of Chicago census data for 1920 indicates the extent of married women's employment in working-class families after World War One, and how infrequently both wife and children were at work for wages in male-headed families. Wives generally worked only when the wages of children were not available to supplement a husband's inadequate wage.

Occupation of husband	Total families	Percent of families having specified members earning			
		Husband only	Husband and children	Husband and wife	Husband, wife, and children
Unskilled and semiskilled wage earners	5,300	54.2%	22.2%	17.2%	3.2%
Skilled wage earners	4,537	63.6	20.1	13.9	2.4

Source: Monroe, Chicago Families, p. 150.

Wives who worked normally made but a small contribution to total family income. A wife's wages, according to the Immigration Commission in 1911, typically provided about 5% of urban working-class family income, considerably less than that provided by wage-earning sons and daughters. (In New York, however, the working wife contributed on average nearly 10% of family income.)[2] To be sure, as the numbers of married women at work increased, their importance as contributors to the family treasury increased as well. But until World War II with the active recruitment of married women into the labor force, most working-class wives ceded to their adolescent children primary responsibility for supplementary wage earning.

There was, however, in the early twentieth century a significant and growing minority of working wives who were employed in the interval between marriage and the birth of the first child. In Chicago in 1920, one-third of the working wives of unskilled workers were childless. Doubtless some of these women worked, as many wives do today, to enhance a family living standard that was modest but by no means impoverished. For these women, the desire to fill a conventional domestic role was clearly, if temporarily, less important than heightened material aspirations or enjoyment of the diversions of the workplace. As such, these women represent an important force for change, however incremental, in working-class family life.

But not only were women who worked of their own volition a minority among childless wives, they were very probably a minority even among childless wives at work. That a number of childless wives in the Chicago study were employed as servants and cleaning women suggests that many women, especially the foreign born, worked out of necessity before they became mothers. And a large number of childless wives in Chicago were employed only at keeping lodgers, which did not remove the wife from the home and her domestic responsibilities. The vast majority of employed childless wives, moreover, were conscious of being temporary workers. They normally retired to the home with the birth of the first child, which usually occurred relatively soon after marriage. And they expected to remain at home and to devote themselves principally to the considerable burdens of house-keeping and child care.[3]

Even in working-class families before 1930, then, employment for the wife was not the norm but generally a signal of family economic crisis. Most wives worked only when family need was acute, and only when the supplementary wages of older children were unavailable or insufficient. The mother's wage, especially, was a working-class family's final defense against destitution; her wages helped provide the family with the essentials of food, shelter, and medical care. Mothers rarely worked simply to increase a family's consumption of luxury goods.[4]

Married women, then, were atypical workers. Their employment reflected private cycles of fertility and family need. Most were intermittent workers; many worked for wages within the home. They were seriously limited in their choice of jobs. And married women, especially those with children, often sought work in the demoralizing atmosphere of family crisis: their very employment was a tacit admission of poverty, of defeat. Rather than publicly honoring the contributions she made to her family, some families contrived to keep secret a working mother.[5]

Married women at work were less often pioneering new roles for women than fulfilling—in times of economic crisis—essentially domestic obligations. Even as workers, most women clung to a primary identity as wife or mother; their work had meaning for them as it relieved family suffering. For these women, success normally meant their own "unemployment" and the resumption of uninterrupted domesticity. The very rhythm, the essential experience of married women's work differed from the work experience of single women and certainly from that of men.

"All 'Needed to Help a Little Out' ": Married Women's Work in a Family Context

The family poverty that forced wives into the labor force had various causes. Most critical to working-class poverty were the low wages of many unskilled men, low wages further depressed by the recurrent unemployment common to many industrial occupations. Prolonged unemployment or sudden emergency expenses often caused families of unskilled workers to fall into serious poverty. Sometimes short-term wage earning by the wife was essential to family survival, particularly when no children were of age to go to work. And an important minority of married women were employed because their husbands had ceased permanently to support the family—women who had been widowed, deserted, or divorced, and women whose husbands had suffered disabling injuries or illnesses. The poverty of mother-headed families—then as now—was the most severe in the nation.

The poverty that forced wives into the labor force was usually extreme, poverty that was beyond the normally stringent standards of life in unskilled workers' homes. In 1909 federal investigators interviewed in five major cities seventy-seven families with working wives. The weekly per capita income of these families, excluding the wife's earnings, was only $1.75. The low family incomes were due principally to seasonal unemployment of the husband and to the fact that these were families where the children were young and unable to earn.[6] In Chicago a Women's Bureau investigation of working mothers found in 1920 that a majority of families visited were headed by men whose annual wages fell well below subsistence levels.[7] Similarly, a 1918 study of married workers in Philadelphia found that even with the mother's wages, a majority of families studied earned less than the minimum income for a family of five as computed by the Philadelphia Bureau of Municipal Research—$1,633.79 per year, or $31.42 per week in 1918. In this group, 59% of the 728 families interviewed earned in total less than $30 a week, 37% were living on less than $20 per week, and 5% on less than $10 per week. Without the contribution of the working mother, a substantial number of these families would have been utterly destitute.[8]

Neither prolonged unemployment nor illness nor premature death of the primary wage earner were unusual occurrences in working-class communities before or during the Great Depression. And without the protections of the welfare state, families coped individually and privately with financial crisis. We might expect, then, that women and men who had grown to adulthood in working-class families would anticipate periodic crises and that wives and husbands would accept a married woman's intermittent employment as a normal if undesirable part of life. But the nonemployed wife was by the early twentieth century an important and emotionally charged symbol of respectability for many working-class families. Her unstinting labor was necessary to ensure a functioning household, minimally cared-for children, and a semblance of pleasant family life in the harsh urban world of the early twentieth century. Her work in the home allowed the family to present the appearance of stability and success to the world at large. Her domesticity was the complement to her husband's achievements as a worker and to the family loyalties of sons and daughters.

Thus, a married woman's employment usually meant more to the family than a temporary expedient in hard times. It symbolized defeat, a failure of family survival strategy in an intensely competitive society. And it meant a real and deeply felt decline in the quality of family life. Among families of skilled workers especially, a wife's wage earning in time of crisis might be deferred until the family was seriously in debt. Of one reluctant job seeker, the wife of a skilled and resourceful man, a Boston social worker wrote in 1915:

> Perhaps no one better than Mrs. R. gives a hint of the upheaval of plans the August panic spelt to many who had considered themselves perfectly secure. Mr. R. was a chauffeur, with two secondary trades—he could paint and he held an engineer's license. He had lost his place as a chauffeur early in the summer, but with his versatility it was easy for him to place himself soon at a temporary job of painting. When in autumn he tried again for a chauffeur's position, he found the market crowded with idle chauffeurs. Nor was he able to find other work. He had always maintained his wife and two little children in reasonable comfort, but months of idleness exhausted every resource. Even credit was no longer extended. They had

reached the terrifying point of possible eviction; they were not only afraid but ashamed. The little girl had been very ill, and her need for her mother's care was critical, yet there seemed no alternative to the mother's leaving her delicate child and looking for work.[9]

Even in very poor immigrant communities, where wives' wage earning at home or in the workplace was common, the work of married women was clearly understood to be the unhappy consequence of poverty. When Caroline Manning of the Women's Bureau interviewed immigrant women at work in Philadelphia in 1925, she noted that married women nearly always explained their employment in terms of family emergency. "All 'needed to help a little out'—husbands ill, husbands out of work or on part time, rent to pay and children to feed were indeed common to all."[10] And for these poorest of families as for the upper reaches of the working class, mobility meant for married women the assumption of a purely domestic role. Interviewing poor immigrant families on Manhattan's West Side in 1914, Katherine Anthony noted:

> [T]here is no local tradition favoring wage-earning by married women. The wife of the West Side workingman does not earn because she wishes to be independent. The idea is foreign to her experience. . . . Not to work is a mark of the middle class married woman, and the ambitious West Side family covets that mark.[11]

An impoverished immigrant husband and father in Philadelphia agreed: he wished that "things were so that men could earn enough to support a family, then women would not have to slave at two jobs."[12]

The "Married Woman's Job"

Most married women entered the labor force with especially severe constraints on job choice. Many married workers had young children and heavy household responsibilities; they needed work with relatively short or flexible hours, or they preferred part-time employment.[13] Women with children were even more likely than single women to choose work in the immediate neighborhood; proximity to home permitted them to return for lunch with children and to be accessible in an emergency.[14] And some married women, returning to work after years at home, believed themselves poorly equipped to perform jobs that required dexterity or learned skill or exposure to the public. Often, this lack of confidence was intensified by a deep sense of shame about the poverty that forced the return to work. Some women believed, as did some employers, that a married woman applying for work was a suppliant for charity; this tended to undermine the ability of married job seekers to negotiate decent wages and desirable job assignments.[15] Finally, older married women returning to work encountered overt age discrimination even in unskilled factory jobs and particularly in sales and clerical employment, where workers were usually expected to be youthful and attractive.[16]

Hampered by these disabilities, married women often chose jobs markedly different from the work done by most single women, and they generally chose jobs that bore no relation to the work they themselves had done before marriage.[17] Far more frequently than single women, married workers chose employment that could be done at home, and they were heavily concentrated in domestic and personal service occupations. Factory, sales, and clerical work, which accounted for most job choices of young, single, working-class women, were infrequently available on a part-time basis, had inflexible hours, and often required involuntary overtime. Married women often opted, of necessity, for jobs without industrial schedules. And when married women chose factory occupations, as they did increasingly in the years after the First World War, their desire for work close to home, plus employer discrimination, often limited them to the lowest-wage, most marginal industrial employment.

Most married workers, in short, inhabited their own separate labor market and found significantly fewer job opportunities than those normally available to the young and single. Married workers, indeed, generally inherited those occupations progressively abandoned by single women: they were especially likely, before the First World War, to be employed as servants, cleaning women, and industrial homeworkers, while single women, except perhaps some recent immigrants, preferred the greater freedom and sociability of the factory. In the 1920s, as better-educated working-class women increasingly chose clerical jobs, married women were found in larger and larger numbers in unskilled factory occupations. But even in 1920 the census estimated, probably conservatively, that from one-fourth to one-third of all married workers held jobs that were performed in the worker's own home. Very few young, single women were forced into such low-wage occupations.[18]

An examination of particular working-class populations in large cities illustrates the distinctive pattern of married women's employment. In a 1920 analysis of census data for Chicago, 1,134 wives of unskilled workers in the group studied were found to be contributing to family income. More than half, 668, earned money by keeping lodgers, and most of these women were not otherwise employed. One hundred eighty-three worked in industry, although this group included some homeworkers and laundresses employed outside the home. Only 38 of the 1,134 were clerical workers, and just 36 worked as saleswomen.[19]

Louise Odencrantz found a similar pattern in New York in 1913. She studied 544 Italian families with wage-earning daughters and discovered in these families 206 mothers who were gainfully employed. But a substantial majority worked at home: 94 were industrial homeworkers and 23 were janitors, while 89 worked outside the home as factory operatives. Sixty-one women kept boarders or lodgers. The daughters, however, were exclusively employed as factory operatives and retail clerks.[20]

Mary Van Kleeck, in her 1913 study of the artificial flower trade, found 76 mothers at work in 123 New York families where a daughter was a flower-maker. But only 17 of the mothers held jobs outside the home. Fifty did industrial homework, and 10 were janitors. Eleven families kept boarders or lodgers.[21] Similarly, in her 1913 study of the families of 120 single female bookbinders in New York, Van Kleeck found 45 married women at work, including 14 who kept boarders or lodgers. Seven were janitors, and 2 were industrial home-workers. Thirty-one mothers worked outside the home—18 were employed at domestic day work, 11 in factory work, 1 as a cook in a private family, and 1 in the laundry of a hospital.[22]

Even among working-class families in the textile mill districts of Philadelphia, where married women who worked traditionally took factory jobs—as indeed was the case in textile towns throughout the country—only 63% of the 723 married workers interviewed by Gwendolyn Hughes in 1918 were factory operatives. Thirty percent were employed in domestic and personal service, despite their living in a community where there were strong supports for industrial work for those wives who needed to earn.[23]

Their restricted job options condemned many married workers to exhausting work under clearly substandard conditions. Their work was often more physically taxing than the work of single women: heavy cleaning and laundering were more arduous, generally, than routine machine-tending. And married women worked more frequently than single women in jobs with completely unregulated conditions. Small neighborhood shops usually escaped even the cursory notice of the factory inspector.[24]

Katherine Anthony, investigating the work of mothers on Manhattan's West Side, documented the unusually oppressive work environments of these women. Most had accepted palpably inferior job conditions in order to work near home:

> The laundry on the block or the candy factory in the next street—almost automatically the women apply at these places for work. They may know conditions in the neighboring factory to be especially hard and conditions in a more distant factory to be more endurable, yet they will prefer the job in the nearer place.[25]

A majority of these small neighborhood factories and laundries were sweatshops, with work tables and machinery crowded into dark and poorly ventilated quarters never intended to support manufacturing. But for the married worker, the proximity of job to home more than justified her employment choice. She could be at work, yet not leave the area where her neighbors might be casually supervising her children. She could return home for lunch. She could experience some small comfort in knowing that she was not so very far away from the home and children who were her primary responsibility. And work in the neighborhood shop saved precious commuting time.

West Side married women were often employed at unusually heavy work, principally because domestic and personal service jobs had shorter, more stable hours than most industrial employments. Many West Side mothers worked in commercial laundries, which generally guaranteed an eight-hour day, with overtime no more than one rush day a week. But there were many strenuous jobs in the commercial laundry, and married women, because of their particular difficulty in bargaining with employers, were concentrated in these least desirable occupations. Married women were often "shakers," poorly paid workers who shook out the heavy garments and linens after they had been through the wringer. "Shaking" was the lowest-status job in a low-status industry. And even with relatively short hours, the work exhausted the strongest woman:

> Mrs. Kadowski is a comely Polish woman with black hair and eyes. On her tired face are many tired lines though she is not an old woman by any means. She is not particularly clean or neat in her dress. That is not strange, as she has just returned from her long day in the laundry. She has no sooner crossed her own threshold than she rolls up her sleeves and begins her family washing. A little must be done every night for they have few clothes and the baby necessarily soils a great many. Nor can she do this work uninterruptedly, for the baby clings to her skirts begging to be held and the mother drops everything to take him up. He is healthy and red-cheeked, but his little face and dress are very dirty.

Mrs. Kadowski shook towels in a neighborhood laundry at the rate of two per minute.[26]

Low wages were another important consequence of limited job choices for married women, as Katherine Anthony's West Side study documented. Domestic day work on New York's West Side paid an average weekly wage of $5.00 in 1913. This average wage included the pay of women who worked part-time, but many of these women worked no less than three or four full days a week. Public building cleaners, usually full-time but short-hour workers, earned a weekly average of $6.44. This employment was especially popular with married women because it was night work, and children could be left safely with a day-working husband. Laundry workers averaged $6.16 per week. Janitresses earned but an average weekly income of $3.52. None of these popular "married women's" jobs offered anything approximating a living wage; what they offered were relatively short or flexible hours, work near home, and enough supplementary income to make a difference to a family in poverty.[27]

Low wages were acceptable to many married women for precisely those reasons. Since married women went to work to alleviate unusual financial distress in a family, even a poverty-level wage meant a perceptible improvement in living standards. And since the work of married women was generally regarded as temporary, their wages were less a concern to family and worker than the wages of the male lifetime employee. Working-class husbands and fathers, noted Katherine Anthony, often refused work that was not "in their trade" or that paid a substandard wage, because as permanent breadwinners they had rights to dignified work and fair pay. A man's independence and prestige depended primarily on his job, and many working-class wives understood their husbands' reluctance "to take just anything."[28] But women were not entitled to such standards. When financial disaster threatened a family with young children, it was often the mother's responsibility to take whatever work she could find at whatever wage was offered. The wage was no reflection on her status, for her primary identity was not that of worker but of wife and mother. In the laundry or the factory, she was simply fulfilling a wifely and motherly obligation.

"The Long Day": Work in the Lives of Married Women

The married woman's experience of work can be fully understood only in the context of her life as wife and mother. The married woman who worked for wages endured a singularly long and exhausting workday, a day that included care of home and children as well as the hours spent on the job. Neither men nor adolescent workers commonly experienced lives so devoid of leisure. A 1918 Philadelphia study of working mothers described the reality of the married worker's long day, a day incapable of regulation by wage-and-hour laws:

> The mother's day begins with the preparation of an early breakfast. . . . Over 70% of all women who keep house and work a full day prepare breakfast alone. Before the mother leaves the house she must also see that there is something left for the children's lunch, if she cannot come home, and that their clothes are presentable for school. A mother who is no longer employed reports that "Sometimes I would wash and dress the children for school at night before they went to bed because I would be up and gone early in the morning." The mother may have the added responsibility of getting the baby ready to take to the nursery or to the home of a relative and sometimes she is obliged to do a little marketing before going to work. Her day in industry frequently begins at a quarter to seven or seven and it takes her at least ten or fifteen minutes to reach her place of employment. [29]

Nor were these Philadelphia women unusually burdened; other contemporary studies of married workers testified that women bore primary responsibility for housework and child care even when they worked full-time outside the home. There is little evidence to suggest that employment of the mother resulted in significant reapportionment of domestic labor in the working-class family. Married female workers were often the mothers of young children, children too small to help with housework but whose needs and activities added immeasurably to the mother's work load. And in a great many families, husbands were exempt from any serious contribution to domestic chores. Though the employed wife was clearly supplementing the husband's role as wage earner, the general understanding of a wife's work as temporary and extraordinary apparently justified for most husbands the maintenance of traditional domestic arrangements and robbed many wives of persuasive grounds for demanding change. [30] A Chicago investigator noticed this in 1918:

The burden that wage-earning mothers accept without comment comes out clearly from the simple matter-of-fact statement of an Italian mother. The father and mother both worked in a tailoring shop. The mother did all the housework aside from the washing, which was sent out, except that her husband dried the dishes for her "when he was not too tired."[31]

And housework was heavy physical labor for most working-class women. The poorest families, precisely those most likely to include working wives, lived in congested, poorly maintained housing that even in the 1920s often lacked hot running water, set laundry tubs, and private indoor toilets. Working-class neighborhoods were usually located in the dirtiest parts of the city, adjacent to mills and factories. Few working-class families could afford home appliances. Marketing in the working-class household was a daily activity, for iceboxes were small and inefficient. Laundering, without a washing machine, typically consumed several evenings a week. And where married women worked at home for wages, as many did, their paid work created additional housekeeping chores.[32]

Many employed wives, moreover, were diligent homemakers. Investigators commented on the orderly appearance of most married workers' homes, and some women continued to bake their own bread and preserve food when they worked for wages. Others sewed clothing for themselves and their children: " 'Men don't have to work as hard as women,' said a married woman who after a nine-hour day in a shop makes her children's dresses at home at night."[33] Clearly the status attached to competent housewifery in the working-class community was not diminished in value for women who worked outside the home; their need to meet community and personal standards of excellence in the domestic role testifies to the centrality of that role for working-class feminine identity. But competence as a housewife coupled with long hours on the job meant virtually ceaseless activity for many married workers, and the serious risk of damage to health through overwork. In Philadelphia Gwendolyn Hughes reported:

Most of the visits to the wage-earning mother were made in the late afternoon or evening when it was practically certain that she would be at home. Late afternoon calls found her just back from work, preparing supper; evening visits found her cooking, washing dishes, ironing, putting the children to bed. Saturday afternoons she was scrubbing the white marble steps, washing clothes, or marketing. It was only on Sunday, for a time in the afternoon, that there was any chance that she might be away from home.[34]

Another investigator of married women's work in Philadelphia echoed Miss Hughes:

Many of the interviews were made with the women while they peeled the potatoes, scrubbed the floors and steps, or bent over the washtub. . . . The brunt of the housework fell upon the wives and mothers, about a thousand of whom had practically no assistance with the housekeeping chores. . . . The family wash seemed to be the bugbear of these women.[35]

And in Chicago, Helen Wright of the Women's Bureau found an Irish mother of two small children whose demanding schedule permitted no leisure time:

She worked in one of the meat-packing companies, pasting labels from 7 a.m. to 3:30 p.m. She had entered the eldest child at school but sent her to the nursery for lunch and after school. The youngest was in the nursery all day. She kept her house "immaculately clean and in perfect order," but to do so worked until eleven o'clock every night in the week and on Saturday night she worked until five o'clock in the morning. She described her schedule as follows: on Tuesday, Wednesday, Thursday, and Friday she cleaned one room each night; Saturday afternoon she finished the cleaning and put the house in order; Saturday night she washed; Sunday she baked; Monday night she ironed.[36]

When a married woman worked a night shift, she was especially likely to be exhausted by the double burden of employment and domestic chores. Many married workers preferred night work because it left free the day's hours for housework and child care, but this arrangement usually meant very little sleep for mothers of young children. During the World War One employment boom in the Chicago stockyards district, Mary McDowell of the University of Chicago Settlement reported a significant increase in the numbers of married women working the night shift; nearly all of them were mothers of preschool children. None of these women had sufficient sleep during the workweek; they spent days doing housework and caring for children, and slept only during children's naps. Weekends, when the packinghouses were closed, were times for rest.[37]

Similarly, a Consumer's League study of working mothers in the textile mills of Passaic, New Jersey, noted that many young mothers preferred night work. Like the packinghouse night workers, these women slept little during the day. And in Passaic's poorest working-class districts, night work among mothers was apparently very common: "Knock on almost any door and you will find a weary, tousled woman, half-dressed, doing her housework, or trying to snatch an hour or two of sleep after her long night of work in the mill."[38]

Many night-working mothers were reported to be both physically and emotionally exhausted. "The results of their work are easily seen," wrote Mary McDowell. "The tired-looking faces and expressionless eyes cannot escape the observer's notice."[39] Officers of Chicago's Infant Welfare Society believed that in the stockyards district "the extensive employment of married women on night shifts has meant an enormous increase of undernourishment and other diseases among mothers as well as babies and young children in their families."[40] The emotional quality of family life often changed abruptly when a woman began to work at night; relationships with children and spouse were more tense, embittering.[41] Nor did night work generally offer the tired mother the supportive warmth of workroom friendships as partial reward for her sacrifice. A Consumer's League investigator noted the absence of conviviality on the night shift during a wartime inspection of a textile mill in Springfield, Massachusetts:

> [A] bundle of waste served as a pillow when the women threw themselves on the floor to sleep for more or less of the rest period. Some slept all the hour, and ate their lunch while going on with their work. Some used their neighbors as pillows. One or two retired to

dark corners or turned off their lights; others were tired enough to
sleep anywhere, they said.[42]

But poor health and nervous tension were characteristic as well of
married women on conventional work schedules. Generally drawn
from the poorest working-class families, most employed married
women suffered both from inadequate medical care and from overwork.[43] Katherine Anthony noted of working mothers on Manhattan's
West Side: "At the age of forty or fifty many of them are almost
toothless. To this is largely due the look of premature age which is
worn by women of forty in the tenements." Among older working
women, she continued, "varicose veins and hernia are familiar complaints."[44] Caroline Manning wrote of married immigrant wage
earners in Philadelphia: "They worked under such a strain while
young that they were prematurely old at forty."[45] And from Chicago,
the Women's Bureau reported in 1922:

> The situation in concrete instances is seen from the reports of the
> investigators:
> ". . . [M]other well but wearing out. Seemed languid and very
> tired."
> "Mother well and strong but very tired. Got up at 5 a.m. and left
> for work at 6."
> "Mother complained of being tired all the time."
> "Mother anemic—could not work steadily."
> "Mother nervous and overtired all the time."[46]

Married women on New York's West Side, according to Katherine
Anthony, often continued to work when they were ill, fearing that absence from work due to poor health would mean loss of a job. Many
married workers believed that employers discriminated against married
women in hiring and laying off. And many employers justified their
reluctance to hire "older women"—often, women over thirty-five—
on the grounds that only the young were reliably healthy and strong.
Survival for the older woman forced into work meant stoic endurance
of physical affliction. Thus, "Mrs. O'Brien, who was pantry girl in a
large hotel, working sixty-three hours a week, had suffered for years

from a chronic abscess on the leg. From time to time, when it was worse than usual, Mrs. O'Brien would say, 'My leg has been going against me lately.' ''[47] Mothers without husbands and employable children generally had no recourse but to work despite poor health. Among fifty New York working mothers, thirty-two of them widows, a 1915 investigation found evidence of serious sickness and disability in a majority, but ''in all cases the mother had had little time to attend a clinic, and had postponed hospital treatment as long as possible for fear of having to commit the children.''[48]

In the home, moreover, the married woman with young children rarely had an adequate substitute: ''When the mother of the family gives up and goes to bed,'' noted Miss Anthony, ''it usually means that she is seriously ill. She may be in a condition which urgently demands rest and medical attention, but with the habit of continuous exertion strongly fixed upon her, it requires the latter stages of an illness to confine her to bed.''[49] Working-class men were generally guaranteed some few hours of rest and relaxation each day. But for the working mother, leisure was simply not a right.[50]

Especially for the working woman with young children, then, the long day was physically and emotionally exhausting. Employment rarely meant escape from household responsibilities. To be sure, work friendships were sometimes a welcome alternative to the routine of household chores for the healthy older woman or the childless wife, although these less-burdened women too were normally fully occupied with domestic tasks.[51] But the many mothers of dependent children whom poverty forced temporarily, but perhaps repeatedly, into the labor force rarely found the diversions of work sufficient compensation for the sacrifices demanded of them.

Child Care and the Working Mother

The problem of child care was a serious one for many working mothers. In most working-class families, young children were the particular responsibility of the mother, and the responsibility did not diminish if the mother was forced to work, even if she worked full-time.[52] The employed mother, therefore, was the parent who made provision for care of the children during her absence, and it was she who was accountable for the consequences of this alternative care. And while some observers of working-class family life professed to see no strong emotional bond between mother and children, the behavior of working mothers themselves indicates that fear for the safety and well-being of children was often a disturbing personal consequence of a mother's wage earning.

Since many married women were employed because there were no adolescent wage earners in the family, a great many married workers were the mothers of young, including preschool, children. According to a 1920 Chicago study, the mother of very young children worked nearly as often as did the mother of older but not yet employable children in unbroken families. Slightly more than 16% of the wives of unskilled workers who had children under age fourteen were found in this study to be contributing to family income, although probably a majority of the mothers worked within the home. In two-parent Chicago families where there was a child at least sixteen years of age, however, the mother was less likely to be earning. And as the number of employable sons and daughters increased, the proportion of mothers at work continued to decline.[53]

In six working-class districts of Philadelphia in 1918, Gwendolyn Hughes found 1,430 children under legal working age in families where the wife was at work. Of these children, 308 were under five years of age, and another 511 were between five and ten years old. For these Philadelphia mothers, most of whom were employed outside the home, child care arrangements were often a difficult problem. Small children clearly required intensive supervision, yet the alternatives to the mother's personal attention were limited both by the low wages of most married workers and by a lack of formal child care institutions in working-class neighborhoods. Good day care cost money. Most working mothers could ill afford to buy the full-time services of neighbors as child-minders, and there were very few subsidized nurseries available even in large cities. When they could not rely on the free or very inexpensive services of relatives and friends, working mothers were often forced into wholly inadequate provisions for their children's care.

For preschool children, working mothers generally tried to provide substitute care in the home, either from a relative or a nonworking friend or a lodger who received room and board in exchange for this service. Among Gwendolyn Hughes's Philadelphia families, of the 308 children under the age of five, 208 were cared for by an adult in the child's own home, 34 by a neighbor in her home, 38 at a day nursery or charitable institution. But even among this group of very young children, 28 were cared for by a neighbor who "ran in" at intervals during the day.[54]

Caroline Manning reported the care of 441 children under the age of five of working mothers in Philadelphia and the nearby Lehigh Valley. Although the majority of these children were looked after in their own homes, Manning found evidence that much of this supervision was inadequate, certainly less attentive than regular care by the mother. Of these 441 children, a surprising 82 were left in the care of the father. But much of this paternal care was extremely casual: some of the fathers were craftsmen who worked at home and kept an intermittent eye on young children; others worked the night shift and slept the greater part of the mother's working day. Still other fathers were ill or disabled and their child-care capacities were often seriously impaired.

Manning found 40 children under five in the care of older brothers and sisters, some of whom presumably remained home from school for this purpose. An additional 123 young children were cared for in their own homes by relatives or family friends. Two children, toddlers aged two and three, were left in the house with no supervision.

One hundred seventy of the 441 children in the Manning study were taken daily to the homes of neighbors or relatives; 18 were delivered to a day nursery; 1 was in a kindergarten and not supervised outside of school hours; and 5 were boarded out and did not live with the working mother. In many of these cases the attention given the young child was probably no more than perfunctory, involving minimal physical care and protection. Many neighbors and relatives were generous in offering to care for a mother's young children—especially since most mothers could afford only a small payment in return—but neighbors and relatives did not always see themselves as true mother substitutes. One landlady told the investigator of her responsibility in "watching a little the children" of a working tenant; probably this describes the casual attitude of many neighborhood child-minders. Despite the concern of most working mothers for the care of their young children, Manning reported, "in too many families the arrangements made for the children were inadequate."[55]

Katherine Anthony echoed this concern in her investigation of working mothers on Manhattan's West Side. These mothers had a total of 221 children under school age, only 40 of whom were cared for in day nurseries. The remaining 181, Anthony explained, "were looked after by relatives or neighbors in a haphazard fashion." And for even this minimal supervision, many West Side mothers paid from $1.50 to $2.00 a week and provided the child's food. Only in some Italian families, according to the study, was warm, attentive child care available free of charge to the mother who worked away from home.[56]

Working widows and other employed mothers without husbands faced the most severe problems in caring for young children. The Massachusetts House of Representatives in 1913 commissioned a study of the children of the state's widowed mothers. In a sample population of 968 employed widows, 1,257 dependent children were found. Of these children, 59 attended day nurseries and 555 were in school. One hundred eighty-eight were cared for by other adults in the family, probably aunts and grandmothers; 121 were supervised by neighbors; 238 were in the charge of older brothers and sisters who were probably of school age; and for 75 of these children no apparent provisions had been made. Most of these working mothers were extremely poor; some could not afford even the most minimal charges for neighborhood child care. In the absence of a subsidized day nursery or helpful relatives, a female head-of-household might literally be unable to provide substitute care for small children. In such situations, some widowed working mothers lost children to foster homes.[57]

Working mothers often made less thoughtful provision for the care of school-age children during the workday than they did for the very young. With a child in school for even part of the day, many mothers relied on casual supervision by neighbors or older siblings for the after school hours. Indeed, once a child reached the age of six or seven, he could find his way about the streets, fix a simple lunch, and be trusted with a latch key, and some working mothers apparently believed that at that point the need for intensive maternal care ended.[58] This assumption worried sympathetic middle-class observers: "For one quarter of the children not twelve years old the time spent at school was the only period during which they were supervised," noted Caroline Manning, "and although the school session lasted only five or at most six hours, most of the mothers showed great relief that their children were in such good hands for even part of the day, and they trusted to luck and the neighbors for the rest of the time."[59] But concern came not only from the middle class. A 1918 Women's Bureau study of Chicago working mothers, stressing the prevalence and the potential hazards of leaving school-age children unattended, found that "the mothers themselves were in many cases quite aware of it and expressed themselves as much worried over the necessity of leaving their children in this way."[60] If, in a particular community, most mothers were not employed or if they worked in the home, then community standards for the care of older children might well emphasize the importance of maternal supervision, especially given the physical dangers of life in the streets and the powerful but—to parents— hazardous attractions of the peer group. Women whose work kept them away from home for long hours may well have experienced a diminished sense of competence and control as mothers, solely with reference to the standards endorsed by their neighbors and kin.

In the poorest working-class neighborhoods, where the largest numbers of working mothers were likely to be found, inadequate child care clearly contributed to the poor health of some children and certainly affected the school progress of older children who were kept out of school intermittently to care for younger siblings or whose school attendance was not enforced by a watchful parent.[61] Traveling through manufacturing towns and cities in the East, Midwest, and South in 1919 to investigate industrial day nurseries, Janet Geister of the Children's Bureau noted the striking lack of supervision of both young children and their school-age brothers and sisters:

> In the number of industrial communities visited the same scenes were witnessed over and over again. Half-grown children playing about, utterly neglecting the baby that had been entrusted to them, with babies sleeping everywhere but in their proper places, heads hanging grotesquely from go-carts, and half-empty nursing bottles covered with flies and exposed to the sun lying about. Many of the little packages of lunch hastily prepared by the mother before going to work at 6 or 7 am were noted. These were largely composed of hard dry sandwiches, fancy cookies, and tough, overdone meat. The meals that were left on the tables for the children to eat in their homes were equally unfit.[62]

Another Children's Bureau investigator in 1918 reported in one Chicago working-class neighborhood serious truancy problems that school officials attributed to a wartime increase in the employment of mothers. Older children were kept from school, not continuously, but sometimes two or three days a week, to care for younger siblings while the mother worked. As the investigator explained:

> A child can be kept out of school three days without an excuse from its mother. Where there are two children of school age, one child is kept out of school three days a week and the other child the two remaining school days to care for a young baby. This has been done so often that the teachers and principal believe that many children are getting behind in their work and getting disgusted and discouraged in trying to keep up with their classes.[63]

Nor was this problem caused solely by an abrupt increase in the employment of women during wartime. Ten years earlier, in the same city, a University of Chicago social settlement worker wrote with concern about the inadequate care afforded children of mothers employed in the stockyards:

> One eleven-year-old boy had entire charge all day of a fifteen-months-old baby ill with diarrhea. The Father could not get enough work in the yards to make the rent and the mother had to go to work. Another child, three years old, was on the street all day. The mother was a widow working in Armours blood room. The day neighborhood nursery was taking a vacation. Several babies were boarding with neighbors while their mothers worked.[64]

One might argue that standards of child care in working-class families in the early twentieth century were very different from those in middle-class families, and that employment of working-class mothers altered but little child-rearing practices characterized by brutal indifference to all but the most basic physical needs of the young. Some middle-class investigators of poor working mothers believed this.[65] Certainly the experience of many working-class children before the Second World War was harsh in some ways: the period of childhood dependency was relatively short; life was often lived as much on the streets as in crowded flats and four-room houses; tired parents—perpetually near poverty—were frequently quarrelsome and severe with children.

But it is not evident that the neglect of young children sometimes caused by employment of the mother was a normal part of working-class life. Too much in the behavior of working-class women indicates otherwise. Mothers of young children, believing their rightful place to be in the home as full-time mothers, worked only under pressure of poverty. Many of these women sacrificed wages in order to take work that could be done at home; others sacrificed rest and leisure, working nights so that they could be home with children during the daylight hours. Women earning six or seven dollars a week paid two dollars weekly to a neighbor to ensure that a young child was cared for. Mothers—not fathers—dealt with teachers, policemen, and charity workers when their children were in trouble, although "these apparently simple errands cost her a half or whole day's work besides carfare and inevitable worry"—cost more, in short, than comparable "errands" in the middle class.[66] And many mothers worked sixteen- and eighteen-hour days to cook, clean, and sew for their children, besides earning wages to ensure their survival.

The behavior of most working mothers, then, suggests that mothering was an extremely important activity for them. If their maternal behavior differed in significant ways from the behavior of their middle-class counterparts, this was due principally to the circumstances of poverty and not to a lack of commitment to child nurture and the maternal role on the part of the working-class woman. If anything, the working-class woman, with all other avenues of worldly success closed to her, depended more exclusively than the middle-class woman on the maternal role for a sense of achievement and self-worth.

If this is true, employment, because of the attendant problems of child care, may have been for many mothers of young children productive of severe anxiety, of feelings of inadequacy in the important domestic role. Wage earning for working-class women was indeed an extension of maternal responsibility, but wage earning could mean neglect of young children and certainly left little time to be a caring mother. If one's identity was bound up with successful mothering, work outside the home might well erode self-esteem and diminish a woman's status in the intimate community of neighbors and kin. For women, the persuasive rewards of life were so often other than monetary, and the clear avenues to self-esteem so firmly located in the domestic sphere, that much in their lives argued against deriving satisfaction and status from the job and its economic rewards. During her 1914 New York study, Katherine Anthony learned this from a widowed office cleaner:

> Mrs. Manley, who cleans the office in which this report is being written, works six days in the week for $6.00. Just after her husband's death she used to clean in a nearby theater seven days in the week for $9.00. "But I couldn't keep that up at no price," she said. "My Annie used to cry so about my going off on Sundays 'It's just as if I didn't have no father nor mother either,' she'd say."[67]

A Note on the Day Nursery

One important reason that adequate child care was a problem for the working mother was a lack of low-cost organized day care centers. There were no public day care facilities before the New Deal. There were relatively few charitable day nurseries in working-class neighborhoods of major cities—the Association of Day Nurseries recorded 450 centers nationwide in 1910.[68] Even during World War One, most major employers of female labor made no provision for child care.[69] And day care centers run for profit by working-class women were generally overcrowded, unsanitary, and virtually unregulated by state or city ordinance. The steady increase in the numbers of married women in the work force was not accompanied by a significant increase in adequate organized day care facilities. A transformed labor market encouraged the work of women outside the home, but no parallel institutional changes altered traditional family arrangements so that women might move in the world of work with the freedom enjoyed by men.

Significantly, many nurseries, both those run for profit and subsidized centers, did not provide more adequate care for young children than did casual neighborhood supervision. After 1917 both New York and Chicago passed laws requiring the licensing and regular inspection of day nurseries, but these laws were little enforced. Boston and Philadelphia before 1920 had no such laws.[70] Nor was the rare industrial day nursery, funded by a mill or factory with a substantial number of female employees, necessarily more sanitary, better equipped and staffed than its neighborhood counterpart.[71] There were, of course, excellent facilities sponsored by private charity and by industry, but there is evidence that the quality of care in most child-care centers was low. Though a working mother might count herself fortunate to secure a place for her child in a local day nursery—at the very least it cost less than arranging for individual care—the day nursery was no clear guarantee of decent and affectionate substitute mothering.

Many of the worst offenders in terms of sanitation and supervision were those nurseries run for profit, often by married women as paid employment within the home.[72] In Cleveland in 1918, a Children's Bureau fieldworker, distressed by the absence of effective regulation of these enterprises, listed for her superiors the very worst abuses that she found during her investigation:

> One woman occupying four dark, poorly ventilated rooms was crowding into them thirty and forty children each day; another was caring for twelve children in equally bad surroundings; a third who had less than a tenth vision was receiving fourteen children in her two rooms; and a fourth was caring for eight children whom she had the habit of shutting behind two locked doors on the second floor while she did her marketing. In all these places the food was sent by the mothers and was given cold.[73]

But even charitable nurseries not constrained by the need for profit were often seriously deficient in terms of sanitation, staff, and basic equipment. Children's Bureau investigators in Chicago found many of the subsidized nurseries overcrowded, in part because of the difficulty of denying service to needy mothers; they also found that in some of these institutions the most basic health precautions were neglected. "I have often observed," wrote one Bureau employee, "women attendants who not only looked ill and underfed, but who showed signs of skin diseases and other trouble. We all agreed that a great many of the nursery attendants, as well as the matrons, were put in because they were dependent upon some member of the board of directors. This habit was decryed [sic], but it is a constant problem in investigating day nurseries."[74] Nurseries frequently failed to provide clean bed linen for individual children—a serious omission in a population of poor children with inevitable skin and scalp conditions—and sometimes ignorant matrons failed to identify and isolate children with communicable diseases.[75] And even in charitable nurseries children were occasionally left unsupervised. Chicago's St. Elizabeth day nursery, for example, provided no adult substitute for the sisters absent at daily mass.[76]

In many subsidized nurseries where attention was paid to rudimentary hygiene and physical safety, toys, games, and space for play were often lacking. In some Chicago day nurseries, an experienced charity worker noted, "No playrooms were provided, no toys were given the children and no outlet was given for physical exercise or pleasure of any kind."[77] In an occasional center, the staff insisted on control of the children to the exclusion of all normal activity, perhaps reflecting the anxiety and hostility felt by middle-class directors toward the working-class clientele they ostensibly served. In other cases, lack of money or the ignorance of the matron resulted in a cold institutional atmosphere little responsive to the needs of active children. After an intensive but not unsympathetic investigation of Chicago's thirty-five charity day nurseries in the spring of 1917, Helen Brenton concluded:

> In a great many of the nurseries one encounters the typical institutional atmosphere, inimical to the whole idea of child culture and its inevitable resultant, the institution child, joyless, restrained, and sheep-like. Apathy and boredom would seem to have no place in the group life of normal children, yet they are to be found frequently among nursery groups.
>
> Some nurseries frankly recognize their failure in this respect. Others show inadvertently how little able they are to cope with the eager minds and spirits of their children. This inability shows itself in dangerously repressive measures, as in a nursery where the matron has trained the children to sit in a silent row against the wall whenever and for whatever length of time she desires. It is found in the nurseries where the old ideals of stereotyped manners, implicit obedience, and the ability to do certain performances, such as singing and marching in unison, are cherished. It is revealed in the nurseries where the children are invariably dull, quarrel frequently, appear defiant and about to perpetuate some malicious bit of mischief, and where they deface nursery property and carry it away.[78]

The rigid rules and inflexible policies of a number of day nurseries exacerbated inevitable tensions between middle-class directors and working-class clients, and some working mothers were reported to be unwilling to use the local charity nursery, even when it was substantially cheaper than private family child care.[79] Many nursery directors were apparently as interested in the control and reformation of working-class family life as they were in providing low-cost care to the children of working mothers. Some charitable day care centers were avowedly of missionary intent; funded and governed by particular religious denominations, they accepted only children of that faith, or they might require mothers to attend religious observances at the nursery regardless of individual belief.[80] Very likely Protestant institutions were sometimes involved in crude religious blackmail in heavily Catholic working-class neighborhoods. In other day nurseries, where there were no religious requirements, well-meaning staff persons often offended mothers by close questioning about family finances and morality; some social workers were genuinely convinced that offering nursery places to the children of unworthy parents only served to reward the antisocial behavior of the adults.[81] Logically, then, the conscientious charity worker punished the deviants' children: "One nursery which is particular about its admissions, accepting no children of able-bodied parents, both working, and investigating every application in true C.O.S. [Charity Organization Society] fashion," wrote Helen Brenton from Chicago to Julia Lathrop of the Children's Bureau, "is surrounded by the small commercial nurseries which take all comers for ten cents a day and where conditions are appalling."[82] Other charity workers, more tolerant, nevertheless considered it appropriate to investigate the family conditions of clients in order to offer advice and assistance.[83] And in some nurseries, strict rules governing the behavior of mothers as well as children testified to the suspicion with which charity workers often regarded working-class life. Katherine Anthony offered an illustration from her observation of subsidized child care centers on Manhattan's West Side:

It must be said that the attitude of the management too often shows the strain of autocracy with which we are prone to dilute our charity. At one nursery, the hotheaded Irish mothers were always getting their baby carriages mixed and then squabbling over them. Righteously indignant, the management finally forbade them to leave their go-carts at the nursery any longer. This severe ruling made it necessary for the mother either to carry a heavy child to the nursery in her arms or to let him walk too far on his unsteady legs, for it was impossible for her to return the go-cart and get to work on time.[84]

The difficulties that working-class women encountered in seeking alternative care for their children testify to the importance of their work in the home as housewives and mothers. Theirs was a world, indeed, where mothers were particularly without assistance. Not only did poverty limit the possibilities of alternative care, but schools in working-class districts often permitted or even encouraged truancy among older children. And the dangers to children of life on the streets were visibly greater in working-class than in middle-class neighborhoods.

No women, in short, were less able to move effectively in the world of work than these singularly overburdened mothers. The "day nursery problem" reminds us of the degree to which familial priorities necessarily governed their work choices and their work behavior.

The Female-Headed Household

A substantial minority of married women at work before 1930 were female heads of families. Of all widowed and divorced women in the United States in 1900, 32.5% were employed; 34.4% were at work in 1930.[85] Even in 1930, then, widowed and divorced women were roughly three times as likely to be employed as were married women who lived with their husbands. Local studies emphasize the importance of female heads of household in the married labor force. Katherine Anthony's 1914 survey of working mothers in a West Side Manhattan neighborhood revealed that over 43% of the 370 women interviewed were widows or deserted wives.[86] And when Gwendolyn Hughes conducted a house-by-house survey in six working-class districts in Philadelphia, she discovered 728 married women at work; among them there were 237 widows, 146 deserted wives, and 12 divorcees. Though only 14% the households in the survey contained no husband, 55% of the households of wage-earning mothers lacked a male head.[87]

Among a poorer population of fairly recent immigrants in Philadelphia and the Lehigh Valley in 1925, however, Caroline Manning found 1227 married women at work and only 364 working women who were widowed, separated, or divorced.[88] The percentage of female heads-of-household in a population of married workers thus depended on the economic status of particular working-class communities: the more affluent the community, the more likely were female family heads to figure prominently in the local married work force. Similarly, periods of economic recession probably had the effect of decreasing the relative importance of widowed, divorced, and deserted women in this population of workers. But absence of the husband was a powerful cause of married women's employment. A working-class woman without a husband and with children too young to earn was almost inevitably at work for wages.

Female heads-of-household were so often employed because in the early twentieth century the great majority of working-class families were too poor to make adequate provision against the premature death of the chief breadwinner. Most widows of working men were left with no savings. Investigations of widows' families in Massachusetts in 1912 and in Philadelphia in 1924 revealed that the vast majority had no money in the bank at the time of the husband's death.[89] Most working-class men carried industrial insurance—indeed, all family members were often insured—but the $150 to $300 typically yielded by such policies nearly always went to cover funeral expenses.[90] So common was this practice that morticians in some working-class neighborhoods first ascertained the amount of insurance carried and then arranged the funeral.[91] And if a man died after a long illness such as tuberculosis, there were usually unpaid medical bills plus debts for food and rent during the months when the man was unemployed and his wife was occupied at least part-time as his nurse.

Before the First World War, most families of men killed or permanently disabled on the job received little or no compensation from state or industry. At best, limited benefits were paid; this only deferred the inevitable financial crisis of the female-headed family. Katherine

Anthony found in a working-class community in Manhattan sixteen families whose chief breadwinner had been killed or injured in industrial accidents. Of these families, only two had received any compensation. One widow—on the advice of her husband's fellow workers—had sued the employer, but of the $1,000 she was awarded, $250 went to her lawyer. In the other case, a dying workman signed a company release for $100, and his wife was prevented from seeking further damages. This toll of neglect was recorded in a state that had in 1910 passed a workmen's compensation act.[92]

Indeed, by 1913, twenty-one states had passed workmen's compensation laws. Massachusetts and Pennsylvania were among them. By 1920, forty-three states had compensation programs. But compensation acts in virtually all states seriously limited the amount of relief granted a disabled worker or a surviving family. Waiting periods of at least two weeks after formal application were standard; maximum benefits were usually set at 50% of wages; and compensation for occupational disease was generally prohibited. The New Jersey act, for example, provided after amendment in 1913 a maximum payment of 50% of weekly wages in the event of total disability. The maximum benefit was limited to $10 weekly, with payment not to exceed four hundred weeks in cases of permanent total disability. The death benefit varied from 35% to 50% of wages but could not exceed $10 a week for three hundred weeks.[93] Nor is it clear how uniformly and effectively these laws covered those many workers isolated by language and culture from information about public welfare programs and their functioning. Probably many working-class families survived crises unassisted in the nascent welfare state of pre-New Deal America.

Certainly mothers' pension laws in most states assisted very limited numbers of female-headed families. Gwendolyn Hughes found 237 widows in her 1918 study of Philadelphia working-class communities. Although Pennsylvania had passed a Mother's Assistance Fund Law in 1913 to provide pensions for indigent widows and their families, only 38 of the 237 widows interviewed had applied for pensions, and only

9 were actually receiving them.[94] Similarly, a 1924 Philadelphia study found that the strict eligibility standards of the Pennsylvania law excluded from coverage perhaps as many as two-thirds of all potentially needy widows and their families. Further, of the eligible population at the end of a three and one-half year period of study, only about one-third had applied for and received the grant.[95]

Private charity was available to many female-headed families, especially in large cities, but most charitable agencies were willing and able only to supplement wages earned by an applicant or by her older children. Charity workers feared that full support would encourage dependency, and the resources of all urban charities were limited.[96] Despite popular belief that employment of mothers was detrimental to the welfare of children, greater loyalty to the ideology of "earning one's way" was necessary for charities to function even minimally as family-helping agencies:

> At a recent meeting of the District Secretaries of the Boston Associated Charities the employment of widows was discussed. Most of the secretaries felt that a day or two of work a week outside was really better for the mother than to keep her always at home, for life can be too dull sometimes, even in a tenement, and except where there is a young baby, this can be managed by putting the children below school age into a day nursery or in care of relatives or reliable neighbors. If the woman lives in a street where most of the women with husbands earn some money, or if the widow herself had earned before her husband's death, it becomes unnatural, in her eyes and those of her neighbors, to earn nothing. The widows known to the Associated Charities, even those with large families, are earning something.[97]

Since Boston's Overseers of the Poor in 1913 limited public assistance to widows' families to $2 to $3 per week in all but exceptional cases, and since private charities in Boston were not significantly more generous, many Boston widows with dependent children worked outside the home considerably more than a day or two each week.[98] Moreover, most mother-headed families were not assisted by charity. Women were often too proud to seek charity, unwilling the endure the extensive investigation of one's personal life that usually preceded a grant, and unwilling to accept the continued supervision of family life that a regular stipend often implied.[99] And though a woman's children could not legally be taken from her by private agencies, female heads-of-household often feared the charity worker as a potent threat to family integrity. Since charity workers had access to public agencies with the power to institutionalize the children of indigent mothers, and since these workers often presented themselves as critics of working-class life, women's fears about charity were not always without foundation.

Most fatherless working-class families were thus dependent for survival solely on the wage earning of family members, and unless there were children of working age, this meant full-time work for the mother. Generally this was work outside the home, for industrial home-work, domestic laundering and sewing, and keeping boarders paid too little to sustain a family at even a minimal level. If paid work was done in the home, it generally supplemented wages earned at an outside job by the mother or by older children. But although female heads-of-household were less likely than women with wage-earning husbands to perform paid work exclusively in the home, they nevertheless approximated the distinctive employment patterns of married workers in their choice of particularly low-wage, low-status occupations. Female family heads were employed primarily in domestic and service work and, especially after 1914, as factory operatives. Their job choices, like those of other working wives, were usually determined by the need for flexible or relatively short hours, by proximity of the workplace to home, and perhaps by a lack of self-confidence due to years away from the labor market.[100]

Most mother-headed working-class families were exceptionally poor. In 1914 Katherine Anthony investigated the families of fifty-five widows who had no children of working age. These women averaged $353.08 per year in wages and received from outside sources—lodgers, charity stipends, and contributions from relatives—an average of $42.12 annually. This meant an average weekly income of $7.60

for the support of a family usually of three to four persons; the New York State Factory Investigating Commission in the same year determined the subsistence wage for a single woman in New York City to be $9 per week. This bleak picture improved considerably once one or more children were of working age. In seventy mother-headed families with employed adolescent children, Miss Anthony found an average income of $785.20: $276.64 earned by the mother, $469.04 from wages of the children, and $39.52 from miscellaneous sources. Though in 1914 an annual income of $785 was below the generally accepted poverty line for an urban family of four, it was clearly an income on which a family might survive. A family income of under $400 a year, however, meant destitution, destructive both of health and emotional development.[101]

A 1915 investigation of fifty women—thirty-nine of them family heads—who had applied for assistance to New York's Charity Organization Society produced similar information. Among these poorest of working mothers, fully thirty-six earned less than $6 a week and fourteen earned from $6 to $10 per week. Twenty-three of these families lived in only two rooms; twenty-two lived in apartments of three rooms. The mother was reported to be in poor health in all but twelve families, and in only twelve families were the children described as "physically normal." Indeed, in nine families one or more of the children had died in the recent past.[102]

John Lovejoy Elliott, of New York's Hudson Guild, documented the wages of married women whom the guild aided through its employment office, probably in 1913. Again, the preference of many mothers for domestic work meant serious deprivation if a family was primarily dependent on a mother's earnings. Five hundred forty-two women had applied to the guild for work during one year, and of these 231 were widows. The average pay of all the various cleaning jobs channeled through the guild's office was $6.00 per week, and women with "steady employment," presumably full-time employment, received an average weekly wage of $6.31. Women who worked split shifts as office or factory cleaners—a few hours in the morning, a longer stint in the evening—earned an average of $5.60 per week, while women who worked for eight to ten hours a night as building cleaners earned an average of $6.35. "All of these women have children—most of them very young," testified Elliott, "and a part of their wages has to go for pay at day nurseries, leaving only a pittance for rent, food, and clothing for the family." A 1914 study of widows who were registered with private charities in major cities simply added the weight of numbers to the experience of the Hudson Guild: of 568 working widows questioned, only 6 earned more than $10 a week. The largest number, totalling 201, earned between $4 and $6 weekly.[103]

In Philadelphia and the Lehigh Valley in 1925, Caroline Manning of the Women's Bureau reported the weekly earnings of nearly one hundred working widows. Their median wage was just under $16, but one-fourth of the women earned less than $12 a week, and a few, some of whom were attempting to support families, actually made less than $10. Severe wartime inflation meant that these higher wage rates did not chart much economic progress for mother-headed families. In Philadelphia in 1919, according to the Bureau of Municipal Research, a working-class family needed $31.42 per week to sustain a minimally decent standard of living.[104]

Finally, a study of Philadelphia widows conducted in 1924 documented the economic insecurity of the female-headed family during a period of rising real wages and discernible gains in living standards for many working-class households. Of 101 working widows, 32 were at work in factories earning a customary weekly wage of $10 to $15. Seventeen women did domestic day work, generally part-time, earning $8 or $9 weekly. Thirteen women were engaged as regular houseworkers; their wages varied from $7 or $8 a week to $12 or $13. Seven women worked as waitresses and usually earned about $19 a week. Finally, 7 women did industrial home work, earning wages that varied from a low of $2 to a high of $6 weekly.[105]

Many of these families were subsidized by relatives; among a larger population of 225 Philadelphia widows' families, the same study found 86 receiving aid from kin. And the earnings of children were important: 66 children over the age of sixteen, and 18 children under age sixteen were at work for wages. Twenty-eight families received income from boarders and lodgers, and 16 were helped by private charity.[106] But these expedients were necessary in many cases precisely because the ability of most working-class women to earn a living wage had not improved substantially since early in the century. In the mid-1920s, the low wages of adult women still necessitated sacrifice of the occupational prospects of the younger generation.

Female-headed families survived wage poverty only through extreme deprivation, at least until children were of age to supplement family income. Female family heads practiced severe economy in housing, living in two or three rooms in the poorest tenements, even boarding with their children in the back bedroom of a flat or tiny house. They limited expenditures for essential foods, sometimes to the detriment of health. They rarely bought new clothing or household goods and seldom spent money for recreation.[107] Many women worked at more than one job, taking in washing or tending to the needs of lodgers after a long day at outside employment. During the Bureau of Labor study of the conditions of women's work between 1907 and 1910, one investigator found an exemplary "successful" widow, a woman supporting her only child. To do so, she found it necessary to work at three jobs, all low-wage occupations. In no one of these employments could this mother earn the freedom of minimal financial security:

> [She] worked in a bookbindery from 8:30 a.m. to 5:30 p.m. As janitress of the building where she lived she had to clean the halls before she went to work. In the evening after she had cooked and eaten her supper and cleared up her two small rooms, she worked at coloring post cards at the rate of 15 cents a hundred. She said that she often went to bed too tired to sleep and felt more tired when she got up in the morning than when she went to bed.[108]

There were, however, a small but significant minority of female family heads who were not successful. These were the women who lost their children to foster homes or public institutions because they could not support them or because they failed to function adequately as mothers. Often, in the reports of public child-helping agencies, these categories blur; it is impossible to know how many institutionalized children of "unfit mothers" were simply the children of mothers unable to provide them with minimal economic support. Certainly the vast majority of children taken from mother-headed families were institutionalized because of poverty, and the experience of these most helpless families demonstrated to a broad community audience how very essential for nearly all women was the economic protection of the two-parent family.

When a widowed, deserted, or divorced mother was truly destitute, she often had no practical alternatives to institutionalizing her children but aid from relatives, friends, or private charity. Assistance from kin and friends constituted an informal welfare system in most working-class communities, a welfare system funded, ironically, by those in the society least able to pay. But not all indigent women had close relatives or friends, and others had kin too poor to be of real assistance. And many women experienced the final crisis of family poverty without recourse to charitable agencies. A New York City survey of 980 families of widowed mothers, from which a total of 2,021 minor children had been committed to public institutions between 1912 and 1914, revealed that only 180 of these families were in receipt of any private charity. Moreover, the report added, "in these 180 families which were known to and being assisted by private charities, there was not enough relief available to prevent the commitment of some of the children and the consequent disruption of homelife."[109]

Some destitute mothers voluntarily committed their children to public care, either for the brief duration of unemployment or sickness or for longer periods of months and even years. With home representing hunger and maternal neglect during the long working day, some women considered foster care for their children the better alternative.[110] But other women lost their children to public care despite a determination to keep them at home. The example of New York State is illustrative: in counties outside New York City, a wide variety of officials possessed the right to institutionalize the children of destitute families. There was no hierarchy of authority in the procedure, no clear means of appeal, no central repository of responsibility. In this dense legal jungle, poor mothers found it extremely difficult to exercise the few rights they had. Within the city of New York, there was only one official legally able to order commitment of destitute children, but even this powerful authority had no alternative to commitment except the slender resources of private charity if children were clearly in need. Ironically, the New York City commissioner of charities possessed the power to spend public money in order to board destitute children with families other than their own, but he lacked the power to provide a children's allowance to a family in poverty.[111]

And though the percentage of poor children ever committed to public care was negligible, the actual numbers involved were probably not small. In New York City alone in the single year 1913, 956 children were committed to public care for the assigned cause "death of the father," and an additional 1,231 were committed because of "illness of the mother." Most of the latter were also fatherless.[112] And in Massachusetts in 1912, a mail poll of state social agencies revealed 754 children of widowed mothers in public care during the months between January and July; this was certainly an undercount.[113] In both New York and Massachusetts, the most important direct cause of commitment was family poverty.[114] And even in the mid-1920s, a study of widowed mothers in Philadelphia found some women, 19 of 312 interviewed, planning to board or institutionalize children while they themselves worked full-time outside the home. Investigators expressed surprise at this small number "in a community thoroughly accustomed to institutional care of children."[115]

The tiny minority of families separated by poverty and by arbitrary public assistance policies was a bitter symbol in at least some working-class communities of the vulnerability of the poor and especially of poor women.[116] Women especially were likely to note well the plight of the "poor widow" or the divorced or deserted wife and to find it particularly affecting. Regardless of how unsatisfactory she felt her marriage to be—no matter how genuinely she resented the restrictions of her life—the working-class wife could not help but learn from her less fortunate neighbor that, in the real world, women needed men.

The Domestic Role

Whether or not they worked for wages, married women in working-class families inevitably worked hard at housework and child care. This was the quintessential women's occupation, and one with very particular rewards. The slow pace of change in the lives of working-class women derives not only from the limited opportunities available to them outside the home: most working-class women clung to their domestic identities in part because the domestic occupation afforded them unique advantages.

Middle-class perspectives on family life in the working class were often negative, however. Even sympathetic observers were repelled by lives they considered spiritually impoverished, intellectually limited, and concerned alone with matters of physical survival. Observers noted a distinct separation in the worlds of working-class husbands and wives; they witnessed the cheerless aspects of family life in crowded quarters and heard frequent quarreling. Women in particular suffered from the bleak emotional climate of the home, these observers argued, for their lives revolved almost exclusively around domestic events.[117] From a middle-class point of view, their lives were at best limited and unfulfilling:

> The lives of these women are very narrow, and they have few interests outside their homes. A high grade of intelligence on national issues or industrial questions is occasionally found among the men, but the women have no time to read the papers, except the fashion or society notes, or some famous scandal or murder case. There is seldom any mental companionship between husband and wife. He rarely ill-treats her, but "restricted education and a narrow circle of activities hinders home life." Occasionally, one finds a very attrac-

tive, affectionate home life, but the common ideal of domestic felic-
ity was expressed by one woman who told the writer, "We've been
married fourteen years and he never said to me 'you're a liar,' nor I
to him."[118]

But if the family lives of working-class wives were affected by poverty, so too were their lives as wage earners. The realities of being
poor shaped the whole of working-class life, making this life different
indeed from that of the middle class. We must, therefore, understand
the domestic experience of the working-class wife not in contrast to a
middle-class standard of family life but in relation to those alternatives
available in her limited world. And the domestic role, its satisfactions
and frustrations, compares favorably in many ways to the female experience of wage earning.

Housework and child care was the occupation for which most
working-class women had effective vocational training. Though they
were usually equipped with no industrial skills, most adolescent girls
knew how to cook, clean, and tend young children, for they had
served a long apprenticeship within the family. And young women
understood clearly the criteria for success in the domestic role. As
unskilled workers, women were often described as timid, ignorant,
and easily manipulated. But in the home they worked with skill and
assurance, in control of the job and coequal with the judges of their
work—family members and other women in the neighborhood.

The role of housewife and mother, moreover, carried with it an inevitable respectability and the approval of family and neighbors. It entailed visibly necessary work, unlike so much routine industrial employment. The housewife's hard labors made family life possible in
the crowded, dirty world of the working-class neighborhood. Her very
presence in the home symbolized family cohesion and respectability.
Essentially no more a "woman's job" than most paid employment
open to the working-class female, housekeeping and mothering, if
done well, assured a woman high status in her small world.

Nor were working-class wives earlier in the century necessarily
the lonely and isolated workers who are today the popular ste-

reotype of the housewife. Most working-class families before the Second World War could not buy the privacy of a relatively large house or a suburban location. Families lived in small quarters, in congested city neighborhoods, where escape to the street in pleasant weather was a virtual necessity and where neighborhood sociability was easily integrated into the daily routine. ("All day long people streamed into our apartment as a matter of course," Alfred Kazin remembered of his working-class childhood.)[119] Marketing was a daily chore, bringing even the shy woman into the street and into contact with merchants and neighbors. And since men were largely absent from home and neighborhood for long hours each working day, women may have more readily established strong social networks than they do today, when much recreation, even among the working class, is exclusively a family affair.

Finally, and most important, the home represented the one area of life where working-class women could exercise real authority, over themselves and over others. The tendency of many working-class men to cede all things domestic to the wife's control meant that the home became her fief. She alone saw to its physical workings, she generally handled economic matters, she meted out discipline and affection to the children. The home was her workplace, her realm of authority, where she was assuredly a lifelong worker. In many working-class families early in the century, fathers possessed but the trappings of formal authority. Women, at the emotional center of the family, wielded much of the effective power in family life.[120]

The wife's authority in the home was symbolized by her special role in family economics. A great many working-class husbands were accustomed to giving the larger part of their wages to their wives each week, sometimes surrendering all their pay. In turn, men received a stipulated amount of "pocket money." This custom was noted in English, Irish, and German families, as well as Italian and Eastern European family groups.[121] The working-class wife was often the chief economic decision maker for the family; husbands earned the money and wives spent it, one informant said, and the task of budget management was a formidable and extremely important one. Living on a low income, always anticipating periods of short work or unemployment, the working-class wife sometimes displayed great skill in transforming her husband's scanty wages into a decent family living standard. And she made savings decisions too: it was often the wife who determined to put money away for a down payment on a house or for extended schooling for a bright child.[122]

But wives possessed more than economic power. The mother was the more authoritative parent in many working-class families and held the family together emotionally as well; ultimately, she made most of the decisions that governed child-rearing. Observers of working-class family life often commented on the father's lack of involvement with his small children; he did not lack affection for them but considered them the property of the mother. The mother was the parent primarily responsible for nurturing and disciplining young children, and when the children were older she remained the indulgent parent. Fathers often styled themselves aloof, stern disciplinarians of adolescent children.[123]

Working-class mothers were generally present in the home while men were away long hours at work, and their recreation was confined mainly to the home and the immediate neighborhood while husbands had recourse to the largely male world of the saloon and the athletic or political club. Women were with their children much more than men and were present in the home to make the countless daily decisions about discipline and child care that constitute true parental authority. Even when a mother worked outside the home, her contact with her children was very likely more extensive than her husband's.

Doubtless the physical and emotional burdens of mothering often wearied the working-class woman; certainly a world circumscribed by home and children could be limited. But the mothering role afforded the working-class woman personal power and substantial emotional rewards. In a world where families lived in perpetual danger of poverty, where individual fortunes were determined by distant economic and institutional forces, women—as mothers—were able to exercise some control, ordering life in the private domestic world. And they were generally recognized as particularly important people in the hierarchy of family and kin: it is mothers who loom largest in the lives of adolescent and young adult women in the social investigations of the period, and there is evidence too that in working-class communities it was the female relative bond that was the significant one underlying strong kinship networks.[124] In ceding the world of the family to their wives, working-class men gave up many of the rewards as well as the burdens of family life. Many working-class women, precisely because of the inegalitarian nature of marriage in the working class in the early twentieth century, possessed an unchallenged authority and importance in the home that might be diluted when both husband and wife shared responsibility for children and when hours of work and patterns of family recreation permitted men to spend more time with their sons and daughters.

As a woman's occupation, then, the domestic role possessed certain critical advantages. For most women, and especially for older women, the world of work rarely offered the status, the authority, and the sense of competence that the domestic role could provide. The latter, despite its intellectual limitations, offered to poor and unskilled women their richest opportunities to exercise authority, to develop a variety of skills, and to institute a job routine that avoided the monotony of the factory. And if the domestic role assumed a woman's absolute economic dependence on a man, with the social and psychological consequences this entailed, wage earning did not significantly alter this reality for most working-class women.

Conclusion

Most working-class women who grew to maturity between 1900 and 1930 worked outside the home for some years of their lives, most probably during adolescence. And many of them experienced and even anticipated employment as a means to heightened status and freedom in the parental home. The experience of wage earning, however, did not for most fundamentally alter the important choices made in adolescence and early adulthood: women normally moved through work to marriage and hoped for futures of uninterrupted domesticity. The reasons for this were, most critically, economic: because women were segregated in a low-wage labor market, relatively few employed women in the working-class could achieve economic independence. They needed the protection of family membership, and, for most women, the exchange of domestic services for economic protection remained a surer means to security than paid employment.

The actual experience of work, moreover, reinforced rather than challenged women's psychological dependence on family and on the domestic role. Most women found at work a world where their femininity meant a unique subordination, a powerlessness they were not likely to experience in the adult domestic role. The sexual hierarchy of the work world in its various manifestations eliminated for most women any ambiguities in the lessons of female socialization learned at home, at school, and in the community. And those lessons essentially directed women to the domestic role as the single sure and appropriate avenue to acceptance and authority.

It is true that many young women found at work a relatively unrestricted social environment and a peer group supportive of expanded social freedom for unmarried women. The vitality of group life at work was an important source of job satisfaction for most women and the principal reason that many young women found employment—at low wages and for long hours—more attractive than remaining at home as domestic helpers. But workroom sociability was an experience ultimately conservative in its effect on the lives of most working women. Young women at work confirmed for one another an understanding of femininity that centered a woman's identity in romance and marriage. Work group values gave expression to the rebelliousness of the young and to their desire for autonomy but served at the same time to support women in conventional life choices. The work community facilitated a degree of sexual emancipation for working-class women, but it failed to support a vision of adulthood where women could achieve individuality and autonomy in nonfamilial roles.

Work group values simply reflected the social realities of a larger working-class world. In this world, wives and mothers enjoyed considerable authority and status, primarily because sex-segregated roles in marriage gave women preeminence in domestic life. And in this world mothers were rarely as effective wage earners as were adolescent sons or even daughters. The heavy home responsibilities of working-class wives limited their freedom in the labor market. Their unusually low wages meant that it made economic sense in most working-class families to depend on children rather than wives as supplementary breadwinners.

It is well to consider, however, that a transition to contemporary patterns of women's work was underway in 1930, and that it accelerated rapidly thereafter—especially after the Second World War. The growing female labor force has aged significantly since 1930, working women have been increasingly better educated and concen-

trated in white-collar jobs, and—particularly since World War Two—
the typical female worker has been increasingly likely to be married.
Surely this indicates that paid employment has become a significantly
greater force for change in the lives of working-class women than it
was in the period we have studied. There is much to suggest that this
is so. Many women now work regularly outside the home despite marriage and motherhood. The shorter hours and vastly improved conditions of most women's work encourage this, as did a dramatic postwar
rise in real wages, which increased the earning power of wives as well
as single women. As long-term workers and effective contributors to
family support, wives apparently possess unprecedented ability to
modify domestic relationships, to achieve a more equal distribution of
physical and emotional labor within the home, to define their own
lives less exclusively in terms of family priorities. And there is research that indicates a movement toward a more equitable division of
domestic labor in working-class families where the wife is employed.[1]

Nevertheless, recent studies of working-class family life conclude
that most husbands share domestic burdens with their working wives
grudgingly, only when asked and reminded, and that their help leaves
the domestic division of labor far from equitable. Women still carry a
heavy double burden when they work outside the home.[2] We know,
also, that working-class women have continued to marry at ever-
younger ages, which indicates that increased earning power has not
been sufficient inducement to delay marriage for a period devoted to
broadening social and sexual experience. And we know that women
have remained disadvantaged in the labor market. Indeed, in the past
two decades, women's wages have declined relative to men's wages as
more and more women compete for jobs in a labor market sharply
segregated by sex. Relatively fewer women today belong to unions
than in 1950. Evidently, most women continue to regard equality at
work as a goal too chimerical or costly to pursue. Indeed, like their
counterparts in the early twentieth century, many women today apparently feel little aggrieved by continued inequities in wages and job
opportunities.[3]

This is true in large part because women are still very much hyphenated workers: they are wives and mothers (or potential wives and mothers), and they make work choices that accommodate and reflect family needs or the rewards and demands of an anticipated family. Their greater education and the relative ease of white-collar work have not seriously eroded the familial commitments of most working-class women. Education and white-collar employment have failed to generate greater change in these women's lives, I would argue, because the work open to them is still principally work that is rigidly segregated by sex. Sex-segregated work means significantly lower wages for women than for men. The experience of sex-segregated work has a decided impact on a woman's sense of who she is and what is possible in the life she leads. Indeed, in an era of articulate public feminism, it is possible that employment is important for many women as a chastening experience, a sober corrective to heady notions of autonomy and freedom from limiting roles. This is especially likely to be true for working-class women, who find today few opportunities beyond the jobs traditionally assigned to women, and whose jobs are even today not likely to offer intrinsically interesting work.

Feminists have, then, rightly understood the enormous importance for women of a direct assault on the conventions that govern the segregated workplace. No battle is more critical if a greater equality between the sexes is to be achieved. But is this a battle that most women wish to join? In the past many women appear to have found what satisfaction and meaning was possible in their lives quite apart from work. Most women today do not behave in ways that suggest deep dissatisfaction with their palpably inferior situation as workers. We must ask whether the continued disadvantage nearly all women experience as workers really matters to them. Are concerns about greater job opportunities for women relevant largely to upper-middle-class professionals? Indeed, might it not be good social policy to subsidize female heads-of-household from public funds, and assume that most women who live with their husbands are content to function as supplementary breadwinners or to remain out of the labor force entirely?

These questions cannot be easily dismissed. Feminists are ever in danger of prescribing remedies for patients who do not feel pain. Contemporary feminism is particularly prone to devalue the domestic role and to underestimate the rewards it affords many women. Middle-class feminists have especial difficulty appreciating the monotony that defines many of the jobs actually or potentially open to working-class women. And most of us are wont to assume that higher pay means greater job satisfaction, although this is not invariably the case.

To argue that continued inequality in wages and job opportunities is acceptable, however, is to argue that it is acceptable for the majority of women and their children to be dependent for an adequate livelihood on stable marriages and healthy husbands, or—failing that—on the state. But it is precisely this dependence that accounts for the large population of women and children who are today numbered among the "officially" poor. One would wish that family and communal loyalties were sufficiently strong that the economic weakness of a large social group was not a problem. But they are not sufficiently strong, nor have they ever been. Women need, for their own protection, access to broad job opportunities and to the highest wages their skills and abilities can secure.

It is the unacceptability of women's economic dependence that justifies the efforts of the state to end sex discrimination in the workplace. For this reason alone, feminists must continue to press for serious, intensive enforcement of equal employment opportunities, regardless of how insensitive to the values and expectations of many women feminist concerns may sometimes appear. This pressure is, moreover, especially necessary today, for the role that adult women play in the economy has changed greatly since the early twentieth century. A majority of women now work outside the home; wives today are in many families the only source of supplementary income. And when women are themselves economic heads-of-household, they can no longer depend on their teenaged children to assume the major burden of family support. The segregated world of low-wage work, and the attitudes and values that world represents and perpetuates, are thus wholly inappropriate to the expanded economic role women fill today.

The young employed daughters and the overburdened working wives who are the subjects of this study are—most of them—now dead. But important features of the work world they knew are alive for many women today. In the clean, quiet office, the file clerk does her routine work with other women in an environment where men alone normally possess high status, and she earns a low women's wage. Although she may be far more aware than her grandmother of feminist ideology, she is nonetheless likely to find in her work strong support for early marriage, unassertive job behavior, and a lack of self-confidence in any but the most familiar roles. "It's good wages for a girl," a young worker told Sophonisba Breckinridge in 1906. Many women today still explain the inequities of their jobs in these terms, with all that this implies for their lives as women and as workers.

Notes

INTRODUCTION

1. William E. Leuchtenburg, *The Perils of Prosperity, 1914–1932* (Chicago and London: University of Chicago Press, 1954), p. 160.
2. Clarence D. Long, *The Labor Force Under Changing Income and Employment* (Princeton: Princeton University Press, 1958), pp. 287–288.
3. On this point see, Herbert J. Gans, *The Urban Villagers: Group and Class in the Life of Italian-Americans* (New York: Free Press, 1962), Chapter 11, pp. 229–263.
4. Lillian Breslow Rubin, *Worlds of Pain: Life in the Working-Class Family* (New York: Basic Books, 1976), p. 95.

CHAPTER I

1. Long, *Labor Force Under Changing Income and Employment*, p. 299.

Labor force as percent of female population fourteen and older in Boston, Chicago, New York, and Philadelphia, 1900–1930

City	1900	1920	1930
Boston	31.9	37.4	36.4
Chicago	23.7	31.8	31.5
New York	27.9	33.0	32.0
Philadelphia	29.4	32.2	33.4

In thirty-eight large cities, including the above, 26.7% of females fourteen and older were employed in 1900, 31.6% in 1920, and 31.9% in 1930.

Using national census data, economist Valerie Oppenheimer has estimated that the great majority of women gainfully employed since 1900 have been so in disproportionately female occupations (an occupation being considered "disproportionately female" when women form a higher proportion of workers in a given occupation than they do in the labor force as a whole):

Year	Percent of female labor force observed in these occupations
1900	74
1910	83
1920	86
1930	89
1940	89
1950	86

Because occupational classifications in the census are necessarily broad, and because traditionally "male" and "female" occupations have sometimes been observed to vary from locality to locality, these figures certainly underestimate the degree of actual labor market sex segregation. Additionally, no positive trend toward increasing sex segregation can safely be read into the table:

> I do not think it is wise to try to use these data for a trend analysis. The tables were not designed with this in mind. It is unlikely that the data, though adjusted, are sufficiently comparable to allow us to trust anything but very large differences. The more detailed the classification, the more likely were "men's" and "women's" jobs to be distinguished. I have always used the most detailed classification available. Thus, the data are not quite comparable, and changes could easily be the result of a more or less refined set of occupational categories. In general, the trend appears to have been toward a more detailed classification.

Valerie Kincade Oppenheimer, *The Female Labor Force in The United States, Demographic and Economic Factors Governing its Growth and Changing Composition,* University of California at Berkeley Population Monograph Studies No. 5 (Berkeley, 1970), pp. 68–69.

Contemporary studies of specific industries and localities indicate how very extensively sex segregation was enforced within occupations by employers and sometimes by male-dominated trade unions. Thus, the extensive Senate-sponsored investigation of women's work conducted between 1907 and 1909 found relatively few women performing the same jobs as men:

> Even when men and women were nominally engaged in the same occupation there was frequently a difference in the kind and quality of work undertaken by them. Thus in gilding pottery, the simplest form, lining, is done almost wholly by women, while the more difficult form, filling in designs, is done by both sexes.
>
> But there is no competition between them, as the men do the artistic work which requires long preliminary training, while the women do those parts which may be learned in a few months. The men receive the higher wages and are said to be displacing the women, partly because they do better work and partly because they can move their ware about without assistance.

U.S., Department of Labor, Bureau of Labor Statistics, *Summary of the Report on Condition of Woman and Child Wage-Earners in the United States,* Bulletin of the Bureau of Labor Statistics No. 175 (Washington, D.C.: Government Printing Office, 1915), p. 23. *See also* Barbara Bergmann and Irma Adelson, "The 1973 Report of the President's Council of Economic Advisors: The Economic Role of Women," *American Economic Review,* LXIII (Sept. 1973), pp. 509–511, and Edward Gross, "Plus ça Change . . . ? The Sexual Structure of Occupations over Time," *Social Problems,* XVI (Fall 1968), pp. 198–208.

2. Leo Wolman, *The Growth of American Trade Unions, 1880–1923,* Publications of the National Bureau of Economic Research, No. 6 (New York: National Bureau of Economic Research, Inc., 1924), pp. 88, 104–108. *See also* Leo Wolman, "Extent of Labor Organization in the United States in 1910," *Quarterly Journal of Economics,* XXX (May 1916).

3. Robert W. Smuts, *Women and Work in America* (New York: Schocken Books, 1971), pp. 110–142; Roy Lubove, *The Struggle for Social Security, 1900–1935* (Cambridge: Harvard University Press, 1968), pp. 99–100, 107–109.

4. U.S., Department of Labor, Women's Bureau, *State Laws Affecting Working Women,* Bulletin of the Women's Bureau No. 16 (Washington, D.C.: Government Printing Office, 1921), chart IX. For a survey of early minimum wage legislation for women see, John R. Commons et al, eds., *History of Labor in the United States, 1896–1932,* Vol. 3 (New York: The Macmillan Company, 1935), pp. 501–539.

5. New York, Factory Investigating Commission, *Fourth Report of the Factory Investigating Commission,* Vol. 1 (Albany, 1915), p. 793.
6. Connecticut, Bureau of Labor Statistics, *Report of the Bureau of Labor on the Conditions of Wage-Earning Women and Girls* (Hartford, 1914), p. 97.
7. Caroline Manning, *The Immigrant Woman and Her Job,* U.S., Department of Labor, Women's Bureau, Bulletin of the Women's Bureau No. 74 (Washington, D.C., Government Printing Office, 1930), p. 117. *See also* Louise Odencrantz, *Italian Women in Industry: A Study of Conditions in New York City* (New York: Russell Sage Foundation, 1919), p. 317.
8. New York, Factory Investigating Commission, *Fourth Report of the Factory Investigating Commission,* Vol. 2, (Albany, 1915), p. 149.
9. U.S., Department of Labor, Bureau of Labor Statistics, *Summary of the Report on Condition of Woman and Child Wage-Earners,* p. 24.
10. Appended are wage statistics from the three most extensive investigations of women's wages for the period 1900 to 1915. All have reference to the minimum subsistence budget—quite a conservative estimate—computed by the New York State Factory Investigating Commission in 1914 and accepted as reasonable by a number of other

Wages in the men's clothing industry: New York, Philadelphia, Chicago, 1908

Percent of female shop workers sixteen years of age and over earning classified amounts in a representative week:

	Under $2	$2 to $3.99	$4 to $5.99	$6 to $7.99	$8 to $9.99	$10 to $11.99	$12 and over
Chicago (n: 3582)	2.8	10.6	24.1	23.7	19.0	10.4	9.4
New York (n: 2506)	2.2	18.4	31.8	25.1	13.2	5.4	3.9
Philadelphia (n: 969)	2.6	22.2	33.1	22.5	11.0	5.7	2.9

Note: Assume: $8–9 minimum subsistence wage for single woman living alone.

Source: U.S., Congress, Senate, *Report on Condition of Woman and Child Wage-Earners in the United States,* Vol. 2: *Men's Ready-Made Clothing,* S. Doc. 645, 61st Cong., 2nd sess. (Washington, D.C.: Government Printing Office, 1911), p. 140.

61.2% of Chicago workers surveyed, 77.5% of New York workers surveyed, and 80.4% of Philadelphia workers surveyed earned less than $8 in a representative week.

investigators and social workers. No comparably broad wage investigations exist for the politically conservative 1920s, but state department of labor studies confirm a continuing poverty wage problem for working-class women during this decade. *See,* for example, New York, Department of Labor, Bureau of Women in Industry, *Hours and Earnings of Women in Five Industries,* Department of Labor Special Bulletin No. 121 (Albany, 1923), p. 24; idem., *Hours and Earnings of Women Employed in Power Laundries in New York State,* Department of Labor Special Bulletin No. 153 (Albany, 1927), pp. 26–30; idem., *The Paper Box Industry in New York City,* Department of Labor Special Bulletin No. 154 (Albany, 1928), pp. 32–39.

Wage-earning women in stores and factories: Boston, New York, Philadelphia, Chicago, 1908

Percent of female wage earners in department and other retail stores, by those living at home and not living at home and by average weekly earnings:

	n.	Under $4	$4 to $5.99	$6 to $7.99	$8 to $9.99	$10 to $11.99	$12 and over
Boston							
Living at home	243	6.6	29.2	33.7	15.2	9.5	5.8
Not living at home	84	1.2	17.9	33.3	27.4	5.9	14.3
Total	327	5.2	26.3	33.6	18.3	8.6	8.0
New York							
Living at home	343	14.8	36.2	27.7	12.8	4.4	4.1
Not living at home	24	4.2	29.1	37.5	16.7	8.3	4.2
Total	367	14.2	35.7	28.3	13.1	4.6	4.1
Philadelphia							
Living at home	269	5.2	18.6	40.2	19.3	10.0	6.7
Not living at home	64	3.1	20.3	39.1	15.6	6.3	15.6
Total	333	4.8	18.9	40.0	18.6	9.3	8.4
Chicago							
Living at home	185	1.1	12.4	42.7	19.5	11.9	12.4
Not living at home	127	—	9.4	43.3	25.2	9.5	12.6
Total	312	.6	11.2	43.0	21.8	10.9	12.5

Note: Assume: $8–9 minimum subsistence wage for single woman living alone.

Source: U.S., Congress, Senate, *Report on Condition of Woman and Child Wage-Earners in the United States,* Vol. 5: *Wage-Earning Women in Stores and Factories,* S. Doc. 645, 61st Cong., 2nd sess. (Washington, D.C.: Government Printing Office, 1910), p. 348.

Wage-earning women in stores and factories: Boston, New York, Philadelphia, Chicago, 1908

Percent of female wage earners in factories, by those living at home and not living at home and by average weekly wages:

	n.	Under $4	$4 to $5.99	$6 to $7.99	$8 to $9.99	$10 to $11.99	$12 and over
Boston							
Living at home	489	5.7	26.6	45.0	16.7	3.5	2.5
Not living at home	130	7.7	24.6	45.4	13.1	6.9	2.3
Total	619	6.1	26.2	45.1	16.0	4.2	2.4
New York							
Living at home	1540	10.8	38.5	28.5	13.5	6.0	2.7
Not living at home	209	11.5	37.3	30.6	12.9	5.3	2.4
Total	1749	10.9	38.4	28.7	13.4	5.9	2.7
Philadelphia							
Living at home	752	7.1	26.3	38.6	15.4	8.6	4.0
Not living at home	171	9.9	27.5	36.8	19.9	4.1	1.8
Total	923	7.6	26.5	38.2	16.3	7.8	3.6
Chicago							
Living at home	192	13.0	17.2	30.7	20.3	11.5	7.3
Not living at home	116	8.6	19.8	31.0	21.6	15.5	3.5
Total	308	11.4	18.2	30.8	20.8	13.0	5.8

Note: Assume $8–9 minimum subsistence wage for single woman living alone.

Source: Ibid., pp. 348–349.

Earnings of women in retail stores in Boston, 1911

Cumulative percent of women wage earners investigated in the Boston stores, classified by weekly earnings and occupations:

Occupation	n.	Under $3	Under $4	Under $5	Under $6	Under $7	Under $8	Under $9	$9 & over
Cashiers, bundle girls, examiners	527	8.2	56.9	77.7	92.0	97.9	99.8	100.0	—
Saleswomen	1086	0.2	2.5	7.1	33.9	65.4	88.0	95.2	4.8

Occupation	n.	Under $3	Under $4	Under $5	Under $6	Under $7	Under $8	Under $9	$9 & over
Assistant buyers, milliners, alteration hands, hairdressers, floor clerks, etc.	198	3.0	15.7	34.3	60.6	75.8	96.5	100.0	—

Note: Assume: $9 minimum subsistence wage for single woman living alone.

Note: The above table excluded miscellaneous store workers who routinely received wages or salaries of more than $8 per week: buyers, certain millinery, and alteration workers, and some hairdressers. As a percentage of the total store work force, however, these workers were negligible.

Source: Massachusetts, Commission on Minimum Wage Boards, *Report of the Commission on Minimum Wage Boards* (Boston, 1912), p. 116.

For further wage data for female employees of retail stores in Boston, see especially: U.S., Department of Labor, Bureau of Labor Statistics, *Unemployment Among Women in Department and Other Retail Stores of Boston*, Bureau of Labor Statistics Bulletin No. 182 (Washington, D.C.: Government Printing Office, 1916), p. 26.

Wages in stores and factories in New York City, 1914

Cumulative percent of female employees, classified according to actual weekly earnings by trade, retail stores, men's shirt factories, paper box factories, New York City, 1914:

Earnings	Dept. stores, stock and sales*	Neighborhood stores, stock and sales*	5 & 10¢ stores, stock & sales	Men's shirts, factories	Paper boxes, factories
Less than $3	.01	—	3.2	5.6	2.8
$3 to $3.49	1.4	1.7	4.3	10.4	5.5
$3.50 to $3.99	5.1	5.3	5.4	15.3	8.8
$4 to $4.49	12.7	13.8	9.7	21.9	14.4
$4.50 to $4.99	16.6	17.2	19.5	28.5	21.0
$5 to $5.49	22.2	25.6	41.9	37.0	30.5
$5.50 to $5.99	24.1	27.8	45.2	43.2	38.0
$6 to $6.49	34.1	46.8	72.3	51.6	47.1
$6.50 to $6.99	35.8	48.5	81.2	58.1	52.3
$7 to $7.49	48.9	62.5	88.0	65.7	60.0
$7.50 to $7.99	49.8	63.3	91.8	71.3	64.2
$8 to $8.99	62.7	71.8	95.4	81.5	75.4
$9 to $9.99	71.9	85.0	97.0	88.3	85.5
$10 to $10.99	78.8	91.8	98.1	93.3	92.0
$11 to $11.99	81.9	92.6	99.1	95.3	95.5

Wages in stores and factories in New York City, 1914

Cumulative percent of female employees, classified according to actual weekly earnings by trade, retail stores, men's shirt factories, paper box factories, New York City, 1914:

Earnings	Dept. stores, stock and sales*	Neighborhood stores, stock and sales*	5 & 10¢ stores, stock & sales	Men's shirts, factories	Paper boxes, factories
$12 to $12.99	88.0	95.5	99.2	97.4	98.0
$13 to $13.99	89.3	96.7	99.6	98.3	99.0
$14 to $14.99	91.5	98.0	—	98.8	99.5
$15 to $15.99	93.8	99.0	99.8	99.4	99.7
$16 to $17.99	95.7	99.2	100.0	99.7	99.9
$18 to $19.99	97.2	99.6	—	99.8	100.0
$20 to $24.99	98.7	99.8	—	99.9	—
$25 to $29.99	99.4	99.9	—	100.0	—
$30 to $34.99	99.6	100.0	—	—	—
$35 to $39.99	99.9	—	—	—	—
$40 and over	100.0	—	—	—	—
	n: 12,898	n: 1,318	n: 554	n: 4,691	n: 5,522

Note: Assume: $10 minimum subsistence wage for a single woman living alone.

Source: New York, Factory Investigating Commission, *Fourth Report of the Factory Investigating Commission,* Vol. 3 (Albany, 1915), pp. 990, 1022, 1039, 1049, 1073.

* designates scheduled weekly wages

11. New York, Factory Investigating Commission, *Fourth Report of the Factory Investigating Commission,* Vol. 4 (Albany, 1915), pp. 1593–1594.
12. Massachusetts, *Report of the Commission on Minimum Wage Boards,* p. 222.
13. See note 10 above.
14. New York, *Fourth Report of the Factory Investigating Commission,* Vol. 4, pp. 1565, 1598–1599.
15. *Ibid.,* p. 1565.
16. See note 10 above.
17. U.S., Congress, Senate, *Report on the Condition of Woman and Child Wage-Earners,* Vol. 2, p. 133.
18. New York, Department of Labor, *Employment and Earnings of Men and Women in New York Factories,* Department of Labor Special Bulletin No. 145 (Albany, 1926), p. 21. *See also* Elizabeth Beardsley Butler, *Women and the Trades: Pittsburgh, 1907–1908,* The Pittsburgh

Survey, ed. Paul Underwood Kellogg Vol. 1 (New York: Russell Sage Foundation, Charities Publication Committee, 1909), p. 213; Mary Van Kleeck, *Artificial Flower Makers* (New York: Russell Sage Foundation, Survey Associates, 1913), p. 63; U.S., Department of Labor, Bureau of Labor Statistics, *Summary of Report on Condition of Woman and Child Wage-Earners*, p. 23; May Allinson, *Dressmaking as a Trade for Women in Massachusetts*, U.S., Department of Labor, Bureau of Labor Statistics, Bulletin of the Bureau of Labor Statistics No. 193 (Washington, D.C.: Government Printing Office, 1916), p. 129; New York, Department of Labor, Division of Women in Industry. *The Employment of Women in Five and Ten Cent Stores*, Department of Labor Special Bulletin No. 109 (Albany, 1921), pp. 44–45; New York, Department of Labor, *The Paper Box Industry in New York City*, p. 9.

19. In New York City's paper box industry in 1915, a study by the New York State Factory Investigating Commission revealed that while 85.5% of women surveyed earned less than $10 in an average week, 46.8% of men in the industry earned less than this amount. In the manufacture of men's shirts in New York City, 88.3% of women earned less than $10 a week, while only 47.8% of men surveyed earned less than $10. And 71% of women in department store stock and sales occupations in New York City in 1915 earned less than $10 weekly; 24% of men surveyed in these occupations earned less than this amount.

20. Butler, *Women and the Trades*, p. 340.

21. Charles E. Persons, "Women's Work and Wages in the United States," *Quarterly Journal of Economics*, XXIX (February 1915), p. 210.

22. Taking paper boxes as a fairly representative seasonal industry, the New York State Factory Investigating Commission argued that overtime in the trade did not compensate women for wages lost in slow periods: ". . . the average weekly wage of nearly 200 women operatives, questioned as to seasonal wages, rose only 10 percent above the usual earnings, but dropped 23 percent below." And, the report continued, "taking the entire year into account, the slack time is spread out over a much longer period than the rush. The proportions are approximately 30 to 20 weeks."
    New York, *Fourth Report of the Factory Investigating Commission*, Vol. 2, p. 544.

23. Van Kleeck, *Artificial Flower Makers*, pp. 72–73, 88; New York, Factory Investigating Commission, *Fourth Report of the Factory Investigating Commission*, Vol. 5, (Albany, 1915), p. 2638; Elizabeth Hasanovitz, *One of*

Them: Chapters from a Passionate Autobiography (Boston and New York: Houghton Mifflin Company, 1918), p. 116.

24. Van Kleeck, *Artificial Flower Makers,* p. 88; Hasanovitz, *One of Them,* p. 116.

25. New York, *Fourth Report of the Factory Investigating Commission,* Vol. 2, pp. 156–157; Mary Van Kleeck, *A Seasonal Industry: A Study of the Millinery Trade in New York* (New York: Russell Sage Foundation, Survey Associates, 1917), p. 137.

26. Massachusetts, *Report of the Commission on Minimum Wage Boards,* p. 102; Ernest L. Talbert, *Opportunities in School and Industry for Children of the Stockyards District,* A Study of Chicago's Stockyards Community, Vol. 1 (Chicago: University of Chicago Press, 1912), p. 31; New York, *Fourth Report of the Factory Investigating Commission,* Vol. 2, pp. 156–157, ibid., Vol. 4, p. 1590.

27. Chicago School of Civics and Philanthropy, Department of Social Investigation, *Finding Employment for Children who Leave the Grade Schools to Go to Work* (Chicago: n. pub., 1911), p. 21; Anna Charlotte Hedges, *Wage-Worth of School Training: An Analytical Study of Six Hundred Women Workers in Textile Factories,* Teachers College, Columbia University, Contributions to Education No. 71 (New York: Teachers College, Columbia University, 1915), p. 57.

28. New York, *Fourth Report of the Factory Investigating Commission,* Vol. 1, p. 665.

29. Van Kleeck, *A Seasonal Industry,* p. 147. *See also* Massachusetts, Commission on Industrial and Technical Education, *Report of the Commission on Industrial and Technical Education,* Teachers College, Columbia University, Educational Reprints No. 1 (New York: Teachers College, Columbia University, 1906), pp. 72–73; Chicago School of Civics and Philanthropy, *Finding Employment for Children,* pp. 23–24; Allinson, *Dressmaking as a Trade for Women,* pp. 147–150; Lorinda Perry, *The Millinery Trade in Boston and Philadelphia: A Study of Women in Industry* (Binghamton, New York: The Vail-Ballou Company, 1916), p. 113.

30. Mary Van Kleeck and Alice P. Barrows, "How Girls Learn the Millinery Trade," *The Survey,* XXIV (April 16, 1910), p. 108.

31. U.S., Congress, Senate, *Report on Condition of Woman and Child Wage-Earners,* Vol. 2, pp. 139, 228–229; New York, Factory Investigating Commission, *Second Report of the Factory Investigating Commission,* Vol. 1 (Albany, 1913), pp. 109–111; Women's Educational and Industrial Union, Department of Research, *Industrial Home Work in Massachusetts,* Amy

Hewes, director (Boston: Women's Educational and Industrial Union, 1915), p. 39; Pennsylvania, Department of Labor and Industry, *Industrial Home Work in Pennsylvania,* by Agnes Mary Hadden Byrnes, Department of Labor and Industry Special Bulletin No. 3 (Harrisburg, 1921), p. 59; New York, Department of Labor, Bureau of Women in Industry, *Some Social and Economic Aspects of Homework,* Department of Labor Special Bulletin No. 158 (Albany, 1929), pp. 24–25; U.S., Department of Labor, Women's Bureau, *Industrial Home Work,* Bulletin of the Women's Bureau No. 79 (Washington D.C.: Government Printing Office, 1930), p. 7.

32. As late as 1926, the New York State Department of Labor estimated that 13% of all workers in the men's clothing industry in New York City were homeworkers.

    New York, Department of Labor, Bureau of Women in Industry, *Homework in the Men's Clothing Industry in New York and Rochester,* Department of Labor Special Bulletin No. 147 (Albany, 1926), p. 14. *See also* U.S., Congress, Senate, *Report on Condition of Women and Child Wage-Earners,* Vol. 2, p. 134; New York, Factory Investigating Commission, *Second Report of the Factory Investigating Commission,* Vol. 2 (Albany, 1913), pp. 677–679; Women's Educational and Industrial Union, *Industrial Home Work in Massachusetts,* pp. 12–13, 19–20; Odencrantz, *Italian Women,* p. 257; New York, Department of Labor, *Some Social and Economic Aspects of Homework,* pp. 27–28; U.S., Department of Labor, Women's Bureau, *Industrial Home Work,* pp. 2–3.

33. Nellie Mason Auten, "Some Phases of the Sweating System in the Garment Trades of Chicago," *American Journal of Sociology,* VI (March 1901), p. 199; Mabel Hurd Willett, *The Employment of Women in the Clothing Trade,* Columbia University Studies in History, Economics and Public Law (New York: Columbia University Press, 1902), p. 199; U.S., Congress, Senate, *Report on Conditions of Woman and Child Wage-Earners,* Vol. 2, p. 300; Women's Educational and Industrial Union, *Industrial Home Work in Massachusetts,* p. 64; Pennsylvania, Department of Labor and Industry, *Industrial Home Work,* pp. 84–85; New York, Department of Labor, *Some Social and Economic Aspects of Homework,* p. 31.

34. Caroline F. Ware, *Greenwich Village, 1920–1930: A Comment on American Civilization in the Post-War Years* (Boston: Houghton Mifflin Company, 1935), p. 49.

35. Annie Marion MacLean, *Wage-Earning Women* (New York: Macmillan Company, 1910), p. 58.

36. Odencrantz, *Italian Women,* p. 158.

37. U.S., Department of Labor, Women's Bureau, *Women in the Candy Industry in Chicago and St. Louis: A Study of Hours, Wages, and Working Conditions in 1920–1921*, by Mary V. Robinson, Bulletin of the Women's Bureau No. 25 (Washington D.C.: Government Printing Office, 1923), p. 50; idem, *A Survey of Laundries and their Women Workers in Twenty-Three Cities*, by Ethel L. Best and Ethel Erickson, Bulletin of the Women's Bureau No. 78 (Washington D.C.: Government Printing Office, 1930), p. 30; idem, *The Employment of Women in Slaughtering and Meatpacking*, by Mary Elizabeth Pidgeon, Bulletin of the Women's Bureau No. 88 (Washington D.C.: Government Printing Office, 1932), p. 40.

38. Agnes Nestor, *Woman's Labor Leader: An Autobiography of Agnes Nestor* (Rockford, Ill.: Bellevue Books Publishing Company, 1954), p. 157.

39. Rose Schneiderman, "A Cap Maker's Story," *The Independent*, LVIII (April 27, 1905), p. 936.

40. U.S., Congress, Senate, *Report on Condition of Woman and Child Wage-Earners*, Vol. 2, p. 195; Massachusetts, *Report of the Commission on Minimum Wage Boards*, p. 11–12; U.S., Congress, Senate, *Report on Condition of Woman and Child Wage-Earners in the United States*, Vol. 18: *Employment of Women and Children in Selected Industries*, S. Doc. 645, 61st Cong., 2nd sess. (Washington D.C.: Government Printing Office, 1913), p. 24; Massachusetts, Department of Labor and Industries, Division of Minimum Wage, *Statement and Decree Concerning the Wages of Women in the Brush Industry in Massachusetts*, Bulletin of the Minimum Wage Division No. 3 (Boston, 1914), pp. 7–8; New York, Factory Investigating Commission, *Third Report of the Factory Investigating Commission* (Albany, 1914), pp. 80–81; Massachusetts, Department of Labor and Industries, Division of Minimum Wage, *Wages of Women in the Paper-Box Factories in Massachusetts*, Bulletin of the Minimum Wage Division No. 8 (Boston, 1915), p. 22; New York, *Fourth Report of the Factory Investigating Commission*, Vol. 2, p. 149; ibid., Vol. 5, p. 2785; U.S., Department of Labor, Woman in Industry Service, *Wages of Candy Makers in Philadelphia in 1919*, Bulletin of the Woman in Industry Service No. 4, (Washington D.C.: Government Printing Office, 1919), pp. 19–20; Women's Educational and Industrial Union, Department of Research, *Training for Store Service: The Vocational Experiences and Training of Retail Department, Dry Goods, and Clothing Stores in Boston*, Lucille Eaves, director (Boston: Richard G. Badger, The Gorham Press, 1920), pp. 92–93.

41. Massachusetts, *Report of the Commission on Minimum Wage Boards*, p.

61, U.S., Department of Labor, Women's Bureau, *Women in the Candy Industry in Chicago and St. Louis,* p. 34.

CHAPTER II

1. Edith Abbott and Sophonisba P. Breckinridge, "Women in Industry: The Chicago Stockyards," *Journal of Political Economy,* XIX (October 1911), pp. 653–654; Sue Ainslie Clark and Edith Wyatt, *Making Both Ends Meet: The Income and Outlay of Working Girls* (New York: Macmillan Company, 1911), p. 95; Elizabeth Beardsley Butler, *Saleswomen in Mercantile Stores: Baltimore, 1909* (New York: Russell Sage Foundation, Charities Publication Committee, 1912), p. 87; Talbert, *Opportunities in School and Industry,* p. 31; Consumers' League of Eastern Pennsylvania, *Occupations for Philadelphia Girls: Paper Box Making* (Philadelphia, n.pub.), pp. 19–20; Mary Van Kleeck, *Women in the Bookbinding Trade* (New York: Russell Sage Foundation, Survey Associates, 1913), pp. 211–212; Edna Bryner, *The Garment Trades,* Cleveland Education Survey (Cleveland: Cleveland Foundation, Survey Committee, 1916), pp. 36–37, 43, 120; R. R. Lutz, *Wage-Earning and Education,* Cleveland Education Survey (Cleveland: Cleveland Foundation, Survey Committee, 1916), p. 197; Odencrantz, *Italian Women,* pp. 51, 265; U.S., Department of Labor, Women's Bureau, *Women in the Candy Industry in Chicago and St. Louis,* pp. 6, 54.

2. New York, *Fourth Report of the Factory Investigating Commission,* Vol. 5, pp. 2720–2721.

3. Gwendolyn Salisbury Hughes, *Mothers in Industry: Wage-Earning by Mothers in Philadelphia* (New York: New Republic, 1925), p. 158.

4. Josephine Goldmark, "The Necessary Sequel of Child Labor Laws," *American Journal of Sociology,* XI (November 1905), p. 314.

5. New York, Factory Investigating Commission, *Preliminary Report of the Factory Investigating Commission,* Vol. 1 (Albany, 1912), p. 295; Ethel M. Johnson, "Employment of Women in Laundries in Massachusetts: Summary of Investigation Made by the Department of Labor and Industries in 1920–1921," May 1921, typewritten (Ethel M. Johnson Papers, Schlesinger Library, Radcliffe College), p. 9.

6. New York, *Third Report of the Factory Investigating Commission,* p. 118.

7. U.S., Congress, Senate, *Report on Condition of Woman and Child Wage-Earners in the United States,* Vol. 18, pp. 18, 83.

8. Butler, *Women and the Trades,* pp. 365–366.

9. U.S., Congress, Senate, *Report on Condition of Woman and Child Wage-Earners in the United States,* Vol. 18, p. 124.

10. Responses from 516 northeastern textile workers, all of them women, in 1913 to the question, "How long did it take you to learn your present occupation?":

No. of days	No. of respondents
1	97
2	31
6	178
12	123
24	34
"no response"	101

Hodges, *Wage Worth of School Training,* p. 60. *See also* Margaret Hodgen, *Factory Work for Girls* (New York: The Woman's Press, 1920), p. 69.

11. Manning, *Immigrant Woman and Her Job,* p. 121.

12. Odencrantz, *Italian Women,* p. 265.

13. New York, *Fourth Report of the Factory Investigating Commission,* Vol. 4, p. 1359.

The millinery trade provided skilled jobs for women, but opportunities in this prestigious trade were limited. At the height of the busy season in both Boston and Philadelphia, Lorinda Perry found in 1916 that only 14% of the millinery work force surveyed were designers and trimmers. Fully 86% were makers and apprentices, all low-wage employees with minimal job security. Perry, *The Millinery Trade in Boston and Philadelphia,* p. 23.

On the limited opportunities for advancement in women's occupations, *see also* Belva Mary Herron, *The Progress of Labor Organization Among Women, Together with Some Considerations Concerning Their Place in Industry,* The University Studies, Vol. 1 (Urbana, Ill.: University of Illinois Press, 1905), p. 31; Massachusetts, *Report of the Commission on Industrial and Technical Education,* p. 51; Abbott and Breckinridge, "Women in Industry: The Chicago Stockyards," pp. 653–654; Clark and Wyatt, *Making Both Ends Meet,* p. 88; U.S., Congress, Senate, *Report on Condition of Woman and Child Wage-Earners in the United States,* Vol. 2, pp. 188–189, 199; ibid., Vol. 18, pp. 151, 181–182, 288; Massachusetts, Department of Labor and Industries, Division of Minimum Wage, *Wages of Women in the Candy Factories in Massachusetts,* Bulletin of the Minimum Wage Division No. 4 (Boston, 1914), p. 17; idem, *Wages of Women in Women's Clothing Factories in Massachusetts*, Bulletin of the Minimum Wage Division No. 9 (Boston, 1915), pp. 15–16; New York, *Fourth Report of the Factory Investigating Commission*, Vol. 2, p. 180; ibid., Vol. 4, p. 1335; Bryner, *The Garment Trades*, pp. 48, 52; Consumers' League of New York City, *Behind the Scenes in a Restaurant: A Study of 1917 Women Restaurant Employees* (New York: n.pub., 1916), p. 26; Massachusetts, Department of Labor and Industries, Division of Minimum Wage, *Wages of Women in Muslin Underwear, Petticoat, Apron, Kimono, Women's Neckwear, and Children's Clothing Factories in Massachusetts*, Bulletin of the Minimum Wage Division No. 14 (Boston, 1917), p. 19; idem, *Wages of Women in Shirt, Workingmen's Garment, and Furnishing Goods Factories in Massachusetts*, Bulletin of the Minimum Wage Division No. 15 (Boston, 1917), p. 26; Odencrantz, *Italian Women*, pp. 265, 270; Hodgen, *Factory Work for Girls*, pp. 68–69; Consumer's League of New York, *Behind the Scenes in a Hotel*, (New York: n.pub., 1922), p. 15; U.S., Department of Labor, Women's Bureau, *Domestic Workers and Their Employment Relations: A Study Based on the Records of the Domestic Efficiency Association of Baltimore, Md.*, by Mary V. Robinson, Bulletin of the Women's Bureau No. 39 (Washington D.C.: Government Printing Office, 1924), p. 53.

14. Willett, *The Employment of Women in the Clothing Trade*, pp. 136–137.

15. Elizabeth Beardsley Butler, "The Stogy Industry in Pittsburgh," *The Survey*, XX (July 4, 1908), pp. 445–446; U.S., Congress, Senate, *Report on Condition of Woman and Child Wage-Earners*, Vol. 18, p. 91.

16. Abbott and Breckinridge, "Women in Industry: the Chicago Stockyards," p. 653; U.S., Congress, Senate, *Report on Condition of Woman and Child Wage-Earners*, Vol. 18, pp. 41–42, 121, 123, 165; Massachusetts, Department of Labor and Industries, Division of Minimum Wage, *Wages of Women in the Candy Factories in Massachusetts*, pp. 13, 19; U.S., Department of Labor, Women's Bureau, *Women in the Candy Industry in Chicago and St. Louis*, pp. 4, 5.

17. Butler, *Saleswomen in Mercantile Stores*, p. 60; Massachusetts, Department of Labor and Industries, Division of Minimum Wage, *Wages of Women in Retail Stores in Massachusetts*, Bulletin of the Minimum Wage Division No. 6 (Boston, 1915), pp. 10–12; Women's Educational and Industrial Union, *Training for Store Service*, pp. 32–33; New York, Department of Labor, *The Employment of Women in Five and Ten Cent Stores*, pp. 21, 26.

18. Bryner, *The Garment Trades*, p. 48; U.S., Department of Commerce,

Bureau of the Census, *Women in Gainful Occupations, 1870–1920,* by Joseph Hill (Washington, D.C.: Government Printing Office, 1929), p. 57; Janet M. Hooks, *Women's Occupations Through Seven Decades,* U.S., Department of Labor, Women's Bureau, Bulletin of the Women's Bureau No. 218 (Washington, D.C.: Government Printing Office, 1947), pp. 196–197.

19. Van Kleeck, *Women in the Bookbinding Trade,* pp. 211–212.
20. Ibid., p. 69.
21. Massachusetts, Department of Labor and Industries, Division of Minimum Wage, *Wages of Women in Retail Stores in Massachusetts,* p. 19; New York, *Fourth Report of the Factory Investigating Commission,* Vol. 2, pp. 215, 345, 349, 571–572, 590–591, 612.
22. New York, *Fourth Report of the Factory Investigating Commission,* Vol. 2, pp. 411, 594–595; Perry, *The Millinery Trade in Boston and Philadelphia,* pp. 14–15, 53, 58; Van Kleeck, *A Seasonal Industry,* p. 80; Massachusetts, Department of Labor and Industries, Division of Minimum Wage, *Report on the Wages of Women in the Millinery Industry in Massachusetts,* Bulletin of the Minimum Wage Division No. 20 (Boston, 1919), p. 10.
23. Chicago School of Civics and Philanthropy, *Finding Employment for Children,* p. 33; Butler, *Saleswomen in Mercantile Stores,* p. 96; Consumers' League of Eastern Pennsylvania, *Occupations for Philadelphia Girls: Paper Box Making,* p. 14; Van Kleeck, *Artificial Flower Makers,* p. 43; Massachusetts, Department of Labor and Industries, Division of Minimum Wage, *Wages of Women in the Candy Factories in Massachusetts,* p. 25; New York, *Fourth Report of the Factory Investigating Commission,* Vol. 2, pp. 528–529, 569; Allinson, *Dressmaking as a Trade for Women,* pp. 94–95; Massachusetts, Department of Labor and Industries, Division of Minimum Wage, *Supplementary Report on the Wages of Women in Candy Factories in Massachusetts,* Bulletin of the Minimum Wage Division No. 18 (Boston, 1919), pp. 9–10; U.S., Department of Labor, Woman in Industry Service, *Wages of Candy Makers in Philadelphia in 1919,* pp. 30–31; Consumers' League of New York, *Behind the Scenes in Candy Factories,* Lillian Symes, investigator (New York: Consumers' League of New York, 1928), pp. 34–36; New York, Department of Labor, *The Paper Box Industry in New York City,* pp. 22–23.
24. U.S., Department of Labor, Women's Bureau, *The Employment of Women in Slaughtering and Meatpacking,* pp. 94, 96.
25. Van Kleeck, *Women in the Bookbinding Trade,* p. 120; New York, *Third*

Report of the Factory Investigating Commission, p. 129; Odencrantz, *Italian Women,* pp. 119–120.

26. Katherine Anthony, *Mothers Who Must Earn* (New York: Russell Sage Foundation, Survey Research Associates, 1914), p. 106.

27. Van Kleeck, *Women in the Bookbinding Trade,* p. 126; Hasanovitz, *One of Them,* pp. 62–63; Odencrantz, *Italian Women,* pp. 119–120.

28. Louise C. Odencrantz, "The Irregularity of Employment of Women Factory Workers," *The Survey,* XXII (May 1, 1909), p. 210.

29. Odencrantz, *Italian Women,* p. 68.

30. MacLean, *Wage-Earning Women,* pp. 36–39, 63; New York, *Preliminary Report of the Factory Investigating Commission,* Vol. 1, p. 339; U.S., Congress, Senate, *Report on Condition of Woman and Child Wage-Earners,* Vol. 18, p. 90; Van Kleeck, *Women in the Bookbinding Trade,* pp. 147–148; New York, *Fourth Report of the Factory Investigating Commission,* Vol. 2, p. 427; Van Kleeck, *A Seasonal Industry,* p. 143; Odencrantz, *Italian Women,* p. 68.

31. Auten, "Some Phases of the Sweating System," pp. 635–636; U.S., Congress, Senate, *Report on Condition of Woman and Child Wage-Earners in the United States,* Vol. 12: *Employment of Women in Laundries,* S. Doc. 645, 61st Cong., 2nd sess. (Washington, D.C.: Government Printing Office, 1911), p. 12; New York, *Fourth Report of the Factory Investigating Commission,* Vol. 2, pp. 123, 427; Van Kleeck, *A Seasonal Industry,* p. 143; Odencrantz, *Italian Women,* p. 66; Consumers' League of New York, *Candy Factories,* pp. 54–55.

32. New York, *Preliminary Report of the Factory Investigating Commission,* Vol. 1, p. 129.

33. Abbott and Breckenridge, "Women in Industry: The Chicago Stockyards," pp. 652–653.

34. The worst of such conditions was recorded in a 1910 letter from Rose McHugh, superintendent of the South Central District, United Charities of Chicago, to Mary McDowell of the University of Chicago Settlement:

> I wonder if you will be interested in learning of the condition under which one of our girls has been working in the Stock Yards. She has been employed in the canning department of Libby, McNeil, and Libby. I do not think I can describe her work accurately, but as near as I can learn from her, she handles the cans as she feeds them to the machinery. If there was any water in them she was obliged to empty it, and as there was no place to pour it, except on the floor, she stood constantly in a pool of water. She says she was paid $6.00 a week for this because they never could get any of the girls who had been there any length of time to

do the work and only the new and inexperienced hands would do this work. The girl had been ill as a result of standing in the water. She is Katie Stetz, 3227 Paulina St.

Jan. 15, 1910. (Mary McDowell Papers, Chicago Historical Society.)

35. New York, *Preliminary Report of the Factory Investigating Commission,* Vol. 1, p. 277; New York, *Second Report of the Factory Investigating Commission,* Vol. 2, pp. 418, 425; New York, Department of Labor, *A Study of Hygienic Conditions in Steam Laundries and Their Effect upon the Health of Workers,* Department of Labor Special Bulletin No. 130 (Albany, 1924), p. 10.

36. Florence Kelley, "Wage-Earning Women in War-Time: The Textile Industry," reprinted from *The Journal of Industrial Hygiene,* Oct. 1919 (National Consumers' League, n.d.), p. 6.

37. New York, Factory Investigating Commission, *Preliminary Report of the Factory Investigating Commission,* Vol. 2 (Albany, 1912), p. 119; Van Kleeck, *Women in the Bookbinding Trade,* p. 148; Massachusetts, Department of Labor and Industries, Division of Minimum Wage, *Wages of Women in Retail Stores in Massachusetts,* p. 19; Odencrantz, *Italian Women,* p. 67; New York, Department of Labor, *A Study of Hygienic Conditions in Steam Laundries,* p. 43; U.S., Department of Labor, Women's Bureau, *Women in Illinois Industries: A Study of Hours and Working Conditions,* Bulletin of the Women's Bureau No. 51 (Washington, D.C.: Government Printing Office, 1926), p. 8; idem, *The Employment of Women in Slaughtering and Meatpacking,* p. 36.

38. "Working Girl" to the New York Women's Trade Union League, Nov. 24, 1912 (Leonora O'Reilly Papers, Schlesinger Library, Radcliffe College.)

39. New York, Department of Labor, *A Study of Hygienic Conditions in Steam Laundries,* p. 43. *See also* U.S., Congress, House, *Conditions in the Chicago Stockyards,* by James B. Reynolds and Charles P. Neill, H. Doc. 873, 59th Cong., 1st sess. (Washington, D.C.: Government Printing Office, 1906), pp. 4–5; New York, *Preliminary Report of the Factory Investigating Commission,* Vol. 2, pp. 111–115, 120, 722–725, 727; New York, *Second Report of the Factory Investigating Commission,* Vol. 2, p. 418; Kelley, "Wage-Earning Women in War-Time," pp. 6–7; Odencrantz, *Italian Women,* p. 71. U.S., Department of Labor, Women's Bureau, *Women in the Candy Industry in Chicago and St. Louis,* pp. 42–43; Consumers' League of New York, *Candy Factories,* pp. 54–55; New York, Department of Labor, *The Paper Box Industry in New York City,* p. 15.

40. New York, *Preliminary Report of the Factory Investigating Commission,* Vol. 1, p. 71.

41. "S.B." to the New York Women's Trade Union League, March 28, 1911 (Leonora O'Reilly Papers).

42. U.S., Congress, House, *Conditions in the Chicago Stockyards,* p. 4; New York, *Preliminary Report of the Factory Investigating Commission,* Vol. 1, pp. 131, 275; Van Kleeck, *Women in the Bookbinding Trade,* p. 148; New York, *Third Report of the Factory Investigating Commission,* p. 1952; Van Kleeck, *A Seasonal Industry,* p. 143; Odencrantz, *Italian Women,* p. 69; U.S., Department of Labor, Women's Bureau, *Women in Illinois Industries,* p. 8.

43. "Your sisters, the Employees of Cohen Brothers" to the New York Women's Trade Union League, March 30, 1911 (Leonora O'Reilly Papers).

44. Auten, "Some Phases of the Sweating System," p. 619.

45. New York, *Second Report of the Factory Investigating Commission,* Vol. 2, p. 431; *See also* U.S., Congress, House, *Conditions in the Chicago Stockyards,* p. 4; MacLean, *Wage-Earning Women,* p. 60; U.S., Congress, Senate, *Report on Condition of Woman and Child Wage-Earners,* Vol. 12, p. 11; New York, *Preliminary Report of the Factory Investigating Commission,* Vol. 1, pp. 72, 275, 277, 347; New York, *Second Report of the Factory Investigating Commission,* Vol. 2, p. 418; Van Kleeck, *Artificial Flower Makers,* p. 131; Van Kleeck, *Women in the Bookbinding Trade,* p. 148; Odencrantz, *Italian Women,* p. 69.

46. New York, Factory Investigating Commission, *Preliminary Report of the Factory Investigating Commission,* Vol. 3 (Albany, 1912), p. 1951; ibid., Vol. 1, p. 282.

47. Ibid., Vol. 3, p. 1951.

48. Women's Educational and Industrial Union, "What are the Opportunities and Demand for Girls in the Manufacture of Paper Boxes?" n.d., typewritten. (Women's Educational and Industrial Union Papers, Schlesinger Library, Radcliffe College), p. 5.

49. U.S., Department of Labor, Bureau of Labor Statistics, *Employment of Women in Power Laundries in Milwaukee: A Study of the Physical Demands of the Various Laundry Occupations,* by Marie L. Obenauer, Bureau of Labor Statistics Bulletin No. 122 (Washington, D.C.: Government Printing Office, 1913), p. 23. *See also* New York, *Preliminary Report of the Factory Investigating Commission,* Vol. 1, pp. 283, 343.

50. Ibid., p. 348; U.S., Congress, Senate, *Report on Condition of Woman and Child Wage-Earners,* Vol. 18, p. 122; U.S., Department of Labor,

Women's Bureau, *Women in the Candy Industry in Chicago and St. Louis,* p. 10; Consumers' League of New York, *Candy Factories,* pp. 19, 48–49; U.S., Department of Labor, Women's Bureau, *Employment of Women in Slaughtering and Meatpacking,* p. 36.

51. Mrs. John Van Vorst and Marie Van Vorst, *The Woman Who Toils: Being the Experiences of Two Gentlewomen as Factory Girls* (New York: Doubleday, Page, and Company, 1903), p. 137; Clark and Wyatt, *Making Both Ends Meet,* p. 47; U.S., Congress, Senate, *Report on Condition of Woman and Child Wage-Earners,* Vol. 18, pp. 149, 183, 287; Bryner, *The Garment Trades,* pp. 41–42.

52. Odencrantz, *Italian Women,* p. 72.

53. Manning, *Immigrant Woman and Her Job,* p. 121.

54. Sylvia Zwirn, "A Dress Shop," in *Echoes,* 2nd issue, Bryn Mawr Summer School for Women Workers, 1927, mimeographed. (Hilda Smith Papers, Schlesinger Library, Radcliffe College), p. 1.

55. "My Clothing Shop," in *I am a Woman Worker: A Scrapbook of Autobiographies;* ed. Andria Taylor Hourwich and Gladys L. Palmer (New York: The Affiliated Schools for Workers, 1936), p. 30.

56. Anna Segal, "All Through the Day," in a collection of student poetry from the Bryn Mawr Summer School for Women Workers, n.d. mimeographed (Hilda Smith Papers).

57. U.S., Department of Labor, Women's Bureau, *The Employment of Women in Hazardous Industries in the United States: Summary of State and Federal Laws Regulating the Employment of Women in Hazardous Occupations: 1919,* Bulletin of the Women's Bureau No. 6 (Washington, D.C.: Government Printing Office, 1921), pp. 3–4; Kazin, Alfred, *A Walker in the City* (New York: Harcourt, Brace, and World, 1959), pp. 67–68.

58. "Conditions in Triangle Shop," *The Survey,* XXVI (April 8, 1911), p. 86.

59. "Seyferlich finds Sixty-Nine Buildings Unsafe; 15,417, Mostly Women, in Fire Peril," unidentified Chicago newspaper, n.d., but c. 1911 (Chicago Women's Trade Union League Collection, Chicago Circle Campus Library, University of Illinois, Chicago Circle Campus); "Shocking Conditions Found," *Chicago Examiner,* April 13, 1911 (Chicago Women's Trade Union League Collection); New York, *Preliminary Report of the Factory Investigating Commission,* Vol. 1, p. 278; ibid., Vol. 2, pp. 18–19, 99; New York, *Second Report of the Factory Investigating Commission,* Vol. 2, p. 425; Massachusetts, House, *Report of the Special Committee Appointed by the House of Representatives of 1913 to Inves-*

tigate the Conditions under Which Women and Children Labor in the Various Industries and Occupations, H. Doc. 2126 (Boston, 1914), p. 21; New York, *Third Report of the Factory Investigating Commission,* pp. 56–57, 604–605.

60. Letters: "Your sisters, the Employees of Cohen Brothers" to New York Women's Trade Union League, March 30, 1911; "an employee" to the New York Women's Trade Union League, March 27, 1911; "a working girl" to the New York Women's Trade Union League, no date, but 1911; "employee" to the New York Women's Trade Union League, no date, but 1911; Hattie Rosofsky to the New York Women's Trade Union League, March 27, 1911. Letters and questionnaires are in the Leonora O'Reilly Papers.

61. New York, *Preliminary Report of the Factory Investigating Commission,* Vol. 1, p. 312; New York, *Fourth Report of the Factory Investigating Commission,* Vol. 2, p. 523.

62. Nestor, *Woman's Labor Leader,* p. 29.

63. Katherine Coman, "Official Report of the Strike Committee, Chicago Garment Workers' Strike, Oct. 29, 1910–Feb. 28, 1911," 1911 mimeographed (National Women's Trade Union League Collection, Schlesinger Library, Radcliffe College), p. 8; Woods Hutchinson, M.D., "The Hygienic Aspects of the Shirtwaist Strike," *The Survey,* XXIII (January 22, 1910), p. 547; Illinois, Senate, *Report of the Senate Vice Committee, Created Under the Authority of the Senate of the 49th General Assembly* (n. pub., 1916), p. 396.

64. "Grievances of Basters, Shop II, Van Buren and Market Streets," n.d. typewritten. (National Women's Trade Union League Collection.), no pagination.

65. U.S., Congress, Senate, *Report on Condition of Woman and Child Wage-Earners,* Vol. 5, pp. 34, 109; Louise DeKoven Bowen, *The Department Store Girl: Based Upon Interviews with Two Hundred Girls* (Chicago: Juvenile Protective League of Chicago, 1911), no pagination; Butler, *Saleswomen in Mercantile Stores,* p. 30; New York, *Preliminary Report of the Factory Investigating Commission,* Vol. 1, pp. 325, 348–349; ibid., Vol. 2, p. 112; ibid., Vol. 3, p. 1637; New York, *Second Report of the Factory Investigating Commission,* Vol. 2, pp. 1217, 1220; Van Kleeck, *Women in the Bookbinding Trade,* p. 148; Kelley, "Wage-Earning Women in War-Time," p. 9; Odencrantz, *Italian Women,* pp. 73–74. U.S., Department of Labor, Women in Industry Service, *Wages of Candy Makers in Philadelphia,* pp. 36–37; U.S., Department of Labor, Women's Bureau, *Women in the Candy Industry in Chicago and St. Louis,* p.

10; New York, Department of Labor, *A Study of Hygienic Conditions in Steam Laundries,* p. 50; Pennsylvania, Department of Labor and Industry, *Conference on Women in Industry, Dec. 8–9, 1925,* Department of Labor Special Bulletin No. 10 (Harrisburg, 1926), p. 85; Consumers' League of New York, *Candy Factories,* pp. 21, 47; U.S., Department of Labor, Women's Bureau, *Employment of Women in Slaughtering and Meatpacking,* p. 36.

66. New York, *Preliminary Report of the Factory Investigating Commission,* Vol. 1, p. 294.

67. U.S., Congress, Senate, *Report on Condition of Woman and Child Wage-Earners,* Vol. 5, pp. 109–110.

68. "Grievances of Basters," no pagination; *See also* MacLean, *Wage-Earning Women,* p. 37; Butler, *Saleswomen in Mercantile Stores,* p. 132; Massachusetts, *Report of the Commission on Minimum Wage Boards,* pp. 49–50, 106; New York, *Second Report of the Factory Investigating Commission,* Vol. 2, p. 1237; Van Kleeck, *Women in the Bookbinding Trade,* pp. 83–84; New York, *Fourth Report of the Factory Investigating Commission,* Vol. 2, p. 426; Odencrantz, *Italian Women,* p. 155; U.S., Department of Labor, Women in Industry Service, *Wages of Candy Makers in Philadelphia,* p. 32; U.S., Department of Labor, Women's Bureau, *A Survey of Laundries and Their Women Workers in Twenty-Three Cities,* p. 86.

69. Willett, *The Employment of Women in the Clothing Trade,* p. 140.

70. Maud Nathan to the *New York Times,* Nov. 26, 1900 (Maud Nathan Papers, Schlesinger Library, Radcliffe College).

71. New York, *Fourth Report of the Factory Investigating Commission,* Vol. 2, p. 85.

72. Coman, "Official Report of the Strike Committee," p. 8; Butler, *Saleswomen in Mercantile Stores,* p. 132; MacLean, *Wage-Earning Women,* p. 62; Massachusetts, *Report of the Commission on Minimum Wage Boards,* pp. 106–107; New York, *Second Report of the Factory Investigating Commission,* Vol. 1, p. 269; New York, *Fourth Report of the Factory Investigating Commission,* p. 161; Odencrantz, *Italian Women,* pp. 159–160.

73. Butler, *Saleswomen in Mercantile Stores,* pp. 133–134; Massachusetts, *Report of the Commission on Minimum Wage Boards,* p. 107; Connecticut, Bureau of Labor Statistics, *Report of the Bureau of Labor,* pp. 92–93; Odencrantz, *Italian Women,* p. 159.

74. "Grievances of Basters," no pagination.

75. New York, *Fourth Report of the Factory Investigating Commission*, Vol. 2, p. 140.
76. Odencrantz, *Italian Women*, pp. 156–157; MacLean, *Wage-Earning Women*, p. 58.
77. Constance D. Leupp, "Shirtwaist Makers' Strike," *The Survey*, XXIII (Dec. 18, 1909), p. 386.
78. MacLean, *Wage-Earning Women*, p. 59; *see also* Hutchinson, "The Hygienic Aspects of the Shirtwaist Strike," p. 547.
79. U.S., Congress, House, *Conditions in the Chicago Stockyards*, p. 9. See also Butler, *Saleswomen in Mercantile Stores*, p. 37.
80. U.S., Department of Labor, Woman in Industry Service, *Wages of Candy Makers in Philadelphia*, pp. 34–35; U.S., Department of Labor, Women's Bureau, *Women in Illinois Industries*, p. 51; Consumers' League of New York, *Candy Factories*, p. 32.
81. U.S., Department of Labor, Women's Bureau, *Women in the Candy Industry in Chicago and St. Louis*, pp. 42–43.
82. U.S., Department of Labor, Woman in Industry Service, *Wages of Candy Makers in Philadelphia*, p. 35.
83. Van Vorst and Van Vorst, *The Woman Who Toils*, pp. 33–34.
84. Ibid., p. 35.
85. ". . . the firm where long hours are worked is not capable of developing a permanent working force to the same extent as the short-hour firm.

    "The group working 61 hours or more per week shows the lowest proportion of employees who have been in their positions one year or over of any of the hour groups in Chicago or in the remainder of the State."

    Illinois, Industrial Survey, *Hours and Health of Women Workers: Report of the Illinois Industrial Survey*, Dec. 1918 (Springfield, 1919), p. 16.

    See also New York, *Preliminary Report of the Factory Investigating Commission*, Vol. 1, p. 295; New York, Department of Labor, *Employment of Women in Five and Ten Cent Stores*, p. 38.
86. U.S., Department of Labor, Women's Bureau, *Women in Illinois Industries*, pp. 9–10.
87. U.S., Congress, Senate, *Report on Condition of Woman and Child Wage-Earners*, Vol. 2, pp. 106–107; ibid., Vol. 5, pp. 161, 204, 208; ibid., Vol. 12, pp. 15–16; ibid., Vol. 18, pp. 145, 158–159, 176–177; Massachusetts, *Report of the Commission on Minimum Wage Boards*, pp. 42, 92–93; New York, *Preliminary Report of the Factory Investigating Com-*

mission, Vol. 1, pp. 295–297; New York, *Third Report of the Factory Investigating Commission*, pp. 86–88, 127–129; Manning, *Immigrant Woman and Her Job*, p. 97; U.S., Department of Labor, Women's Bureau, *Women in Illinois Industries*, pp. 7–8.

88. New York, *Preliminary Report of the Factory Investigating Commission*, Vol. 1, p. 296.

89. Leonora O'Reilly, "Plea for the Fifty-Four Hour Bill," May 1911, typewritten (Leonora O'Reilly Papers), pp. 2–4; "Summary of the Reports on Hotels," n.d., but c. 1912, typewritten (Juvenile Protective League of Chicago Papers, Chicago Circle Campus Library, University of Illinois, Chicago Circle Campus), p. 7.

90. Allinson, *Dressmaking as a Trade for Women*, pp. 115–116.

91. Ibid., p. 116.

92. "Josephine" to Agnes Nestor, April 26, 1911 (Agnes Nestor Papers, Chicago Historical Society).

93. MacLean, *Wage-Earning Women*, p. 66; U.S., Congress, Senate, *Report on Condition of Woman and Child Wage-Earners*, Vol. 5, pp. 89, 208, 210; Bowen, *The Department Store Girl*, no pagination; Butler, *Saleswomen in Mercantile Stores*, pp. 125–126; New York, *Fourth Report of the Factory Investigating Commission*, Vol. 2, pp. 88, 154, 515, 613; Nestor, *Woman's Labor Leader*, pp. 11–12.

94. U.S., Congress, Senate, *Report on Condition of Woman and Child Wage-Earners*, Vol. 5, p. 90; Clark and Wyatt, *Making Both Ends Meet*, p. 191; Consumers' League of Eastern Pennsylvania, *Occupations for Philadelphia Girls: Paper Box Making*, p. 13; Allinson, *Dressmaking as a Trade for Women*, p. 123; Van Kleeck, *A Seasonal Industry*, pp. 140–141; Odencrantz, *Italian Women*, pp. 92–93; Consumers' League of New York, *Candy Factories*, p. 44.

95. Consumers' League of New York, *Candy Factories*, p. 44; Odencrantz, *Italian Women*, p. 94.

96. Allison, *Dressmaking as a Trade for Women*, p. 116; Odencrantz, "Irregularity of Employment for Women Factory Workers," p. 207; Van Kleeck, *Women in the Bookbinding Trade*, p. 173; Odencrantz, *Italian Women*, pp. 107, 160.

97. Quoted in Alice Kessler-Harris, "Organizing the Unorganizable: Three Jewish Women and Their Union," *Labor History*, XVII (Winter 1976), p. 7.

CHAPTER III

1. U.S., Department of Commerce, Bureau of the Census, *Women in Gainful Occupations, 1870–1920,* by Joseph Hill (Washington, D.C.: Government Printing Office, 1929), p. 14.

Percentage of women engaged in gainful occupations, classified by age, race and nativity, for cities of 100,000 or over, 1920

Race and Nativity	16 years and over	16–24 years	25–44 years	45 years and over
All classes	32.5%	55.3%	29.8%	18.3%
Native white, native parentage	33.2	51.5	30.6	18.6
Native white, foreign or mixed parentage	37.4	61.9	31.3	19.0
Foreign-born white	22.4	50.7	21.4	13.6
Negro	53.7	53.2	55.0	50.9

"While these figures clearly establish the fact that in each generation the percentage of women gainfully employed diminishes very materially as they grow older, the age groups are too comprehensive to show how rapidly or how gradually the change takes place in the successive years of life. It is probable, however, that if we had figures for each year of age, we should find that the percentage of women in gainful occupations decreases rapidly in the period between 20 and 30 years of age, this being the decade of life in which there is a rapid increase in the percentage of married women and a corresponding decrease in the percentage remaining single. Thus, in this interval of 10 years the percentage married increases from 38.4% for women who are 20 years of age to 78.4% for those 29 years of age, while the percentage single declines from 60.0% to 17.5%.

"In the census report on women at work, published in 1907, there is an attempt to obtain through an analysis of age statistics some indication of the extent to which young women on account of marriage or for other reasons give up their occupations as they grow older. On the basis of figures there presented it seems, in the language of the report, to be 'a very conservative conclusion that not less than one-half of the native white women 15 to 24 years of age who were breadwinners in 1890 and were still living in 1900 (being then 25 to 34 years of age) had given up their gainful occupation in the interval.' No similar computation can be made for a later decade, either 1900 to 1910 or 1910 to 1920, since the requisite age detail for women gainfully employed was not tabulated in the census of 1910."

U.S., Department of Commerce, Bureau of the Census, *Women in Gainful Occupations*, pp. 68–69.

2. On adolescent male groups in working-class neighborhoods, *see* Robert A. Woods, ed., *The City Wilderness: A Settlement Study by Residents and Associates of the South End House* (Boston and New York: Houghton Mifflin Company, 1898), pp. 114–122; Jane Addams, *The Spirit of Youth and the City Streets* (New York: Macmillan Company, 1909), pp. 10–11; Ware, *Greenwich Village*, pp. 355–363.

3. Diary of Agnes Nestor, entries for Jan. 17, 19, 23; April 1, 12, 18; May 2, 9, 16; June 13, 1901 (Agnes Nestor Papers); Willett, *The Employment of Women in the Clothing Trade*, p. 91; Van Vorst and Van Vorst, *The Woman Who Toils*, pp. 31–32; Annie Marion MacLean, "The Sweat-Shop in Summer," *American Journal of Sociology*, IX (November 1903), p. 304; Richardson, *The Long Day*, pp. 64–91, 94–107, 188–189; Clark and Wyatt, *Making Both Ends Meet*, pp. 187–188; U.S., Congress, Senate, *Report on Condition of Woman and Child Wage-Earners*, Vol. 12, p. 113; ibid., Vol. 18, pp. 93–94; Hasanovitz, *One of Them*, p. 83; Frances Donovan, *The Woman Who Waits* (Boston: Richard G. Badger, The Gorham Press, 1920), p. 94; Hughes, *Mothers in Industry*, pp. 23–24, 136–137; Zwirn, "A Dress Shop"; Frances Donovan, *The Saleslady* (Chicago: University of Chicago Press, 1929), pp. 41, 95, 242; O. Latham Hatcher, *Rural Girls in the City for Work: A Study Made for the Southern Woman's Educational Alliance* (Richmond, Va.: Garrett and Massie, 1930), p. 65; Mary Anderson with Mary N. Winslow, *Woman at Work: The Autobiography of Mary Anderson* (Minneapolis: University of Minnesota Press, 1951), p. 27; Nestor, *Woman's Labor Leader*, pp. 8, 28.

4. Nestor, *Woman's Labor Leader*, p. 28.

5. Louise Montgomery, *The American Girl in the Stockyards District*, A Study of Chicago's Stockyards Community, Vol. 2 (Chicago: University of Chicago Press, 1913), p. 29; U.S., Congress, Senate, *Report on Condition of Woman and Child Wage-Earners*, Vol. 18, pp. 93–94; Van Kleeck, *Women in the Bookbinding Trade*, p. 83; Nestor, *Woman's Labor Leader*, p. 9.

6. Ruth S. True, *The Neglected Girl*, West Side Studies (New York: Russell Sage Foundation, Survey Associates, 1914), p. 46.

7. Van Vorst and Van Vorst, *The Woman Who Toils*, p. 33.

8. Diary of Agnes Nestor.

9. Goldie Share, "My First Job," *Bryn Mawr Diary*, Vol. 2, July 8, 1922, mimeographed (Hilda Smith Papers), no pagination.

10. "My Clothing Shop," *I am A Woman Worker*, ed. Hourwich and Palmer, pp. 30–31.

11. Massachusetts, House, *Report of the Special Committee Appointed by the House of Representatives of 1913 to Investigate the Conditions under Which Women and Children Labor in the Various Industries and Occupations*, H. Doc. 2126 (Boston, 1914), p. 92.

12. Hazel Grant Ormsbee, *The Young Employed Girl* (New York: The Woman's Press, 1927), pp. 45–46.

13. Hasanovitz, *One of Them*, pp. 45–46.

14. Dorothy Richardson, *The Long Day: The Story of a New York Working Girl as Told by Herself*, in William O'Neill, ed., *Women at Work* (Chicago: Quadrangle Books, 1972), pp. 281–282. MacLean, *Wage-Earning Women*, p. 38; Robert A. Woods and Albert J. Kennedy, *Young Working Girls: A Summary of Evidence from Two Thousand Social Workers* (Boston and New York: Houghton Mifflin Company, 1913), p. 23; True, *The Neglected Girl*, p. 43; Anthony, *Mothers Who Must Earn*, p. 51; Donovan, *The Woman Who Waits*, pp. 145, 224; Pennsylvania, Department of Labor and Industry, *Conference on Women in Industry*, p. 12.

15. Anzia Yezierska, *Breadgivers* (New York: Venture/George Braziller, 1975), p. 156.

16. Lena Gragnam to Leonora O'Reilly, Oct. 26, 1906 (Leonora O'Reilly Papers).

17. Anderson, *Woman at Work*, pp. 16–17.

18. Clark and Wyatt, *Making Both Ends Meet*, p. 187.

19. Richardson, *The Long Day*, pp. 75–86.

20. Hortense Powdermaker, "From the Diary of a Girl Organizer," *The Amalgamated Illustrated Almanac*, prepared by the Education Department of the Amalgamated Clothing Workers of America (New York: n. pub., 1924), p. 46.

21. Butler, *Women and the Trades*, p. 62; Elias Tobenkin, "The Immigrant Girl in Chicago," *The Survey*, XXIII (Nov. 6, 1909), p. 190; U.S., Congress, Senate, *Report on Condition of Woman and Child Wage-Earners*, Vol. 2, pp. 51–52.

22. New York, *Preliminary Report of the Factory Investigating Commission*, Vol. 3, p. 1635.

23. Ibid., Vol. 1, p. 309.

24. Butler, *Women and the Trades*, p. 224; Clark and Wyatt, *Making Both*

Ends Meet, p. 188; Mary McDowell, "Our Proxies in Industry," n.d., mimeographed (Mary McDowell Papers), p. 5.

25. Richardson, *The Long Day,* pp. 235, 247, 250.

26. Ibid., p. 190; Butler, *Women and the Trades,* p. 188; Hasanovitz, *One of Them,* p. 157; Consumers' League of New York, *Candy Factories,* pp. 18–19, 29; Nestor, *Woman's Labor Leader,* p. 35.

27. Clark and Wyatt, *Making Both Ends Meet,* pp. 187–188.

28. Van Vorst and Van Vorst, *The Woman Who Toils,* pp. 24–25, 35, 38; Richardson, *The Long Day,* pp. 70–71, 73, 99, 100, 107; Amy E. Tanner, "Glimpses at the Mind of a Waitress," *American Journal of Sociology,* XIII (July 1907), p. 52; Hasanovitz, *One of Them,* pp. 229–230; Donovan, *The Woman Who Waits,* p. 135; Donovan, *The Saleslady,* p. 95; Powdermaker, "From the Diary of a Girl Organizer," p. 27.

29. Van Vorst and Van Vorst, *The Woman Who Toils,* pp. 132–133.

30. Lillian Greensweig, "A Worker's Life," *Bryn Mawr Light,* Vol. 2, Summer 1926, mimeographed (Hilda Smith Papers), no pagination.

31. ". . . it would not be found easy to organize the wage-earning women to better their economic conditions. The workers are young—they dream of marriage, of giving up the world of wages to make a home for 'that not impossible he, wrapped up in mystery.' The girls do not differ from the young in any walk of life. They no more consider the welfare of that mysterious future than does the daughter of their boss."

Mary McDowell, "Our Proxies in Industry," p. 11. *See also* Woods and Kennedy, *Young Working Girls,* pp. 161–162; Alice Henry, *The Trade Union Woman* (New York and London: D. Appleton and Company, 1915), pp. 217–218; New York, *Fourth Report of the Factory Investigating Commission,* Vol. 1, p. 778; Donovan, *The Woman Who Waits,* p. 222.

32. Richardson, *The Long Day,* pp. 73, 96.

33. Donovan, *The Woman Who Waits,* p. 219.

34. Lillian D. Wald, "Organization Amongst Working Women," *The Annals of the American Academy of Political and Social Science,* XXVII (June 1906), p. 641; Butler, *Women and the Trades,* p. 372; New York, *Third Report of the Factory Investigating Commission,* p. 146; Henry, *The Trade Union Woman,* p. 82; New York, *Fourth Report of the Factory Investigating Commission,* Vol. 4, pp. 1577–1579; Perry, *The Millinery Trade in Boston and Philadelphia,* p. 17; Hasanovitz, *One of Them,* pp. 247, 300; Emilie Josephine Hutchinson, "Women's Wages: a Study of the Wages of Industrial Women and Measures Suggested to Increase Them" (Ph.D. dissertation, Columbia University, 1919), p. 62; Odencrantz, *Italian*

Women, p. 273; Mollie Ray Carroll, "Women and the Labor Movement in America," Report of the Women in Industry Committee, National League of Women Voters, 1923, mimeographed (National Woman's Trade Union League Collection), p. 11; Consumers' League of New York, *Candy Factories*, p. 29; Alice Henry, *Memoirs of Alice Henry*, ed. Nettie Palmer (Melbourne: n. pub., 1944), p. 49; Anderson, *Woman at Work*, p. 65.

35. True, *The Neglected Girl*, p. 73.
36. Mary McDowell, "The Young Girl in Industry," n.d., typewritten (Mary McDowell papers), pp. 1–3; Woods, *The City Wilderness*, pp. 195–196; Addams, *The Spirit of Youth*, pp. 4–5; U.S., Congress, Senate, *Report on Condition of Woman and Child Wage-Earners*, Vol. 5, p. 75; Montgomery, *The American Girl in the Stockyards District*, p. 68; Woods and Kennedy, *Young Working Girls*, pp. 105–107; Donovan, *The Woman Who Waits*, pp. 138, 184.
37. Richardson, *The Long Day*, pp. 73, 106, 107; Massachusetts, *Report of the Commission on Minimum Wage Boards*, pp. 89–90; Donovan, *The Woman Who Waits*, p. 135.
38. Odencrantz, *Italian Women*, pp. 228–229.
39. McDowell, "Our Proxies in Industry," p. 1.
40. Woods, *The City Wilderness*, p. 107; *see also* Hutchins Hapgood, *Types from City Streets* (New York and London: Funk and Wagnalls Company, 1910), pp. 126–127; MacLean, *Wage-Earning Women*, p. 65.
41. Montgomery, *The American Girl in the Stockyards District*, p. 60; Ormsbee, *The Young Employed Girl*, p. 49; McDowell, "The Young Girl in Industry," pp. 2, 3.
42. National Women's Trade Union League, "How to Organize: A Problem: Resume of Findings, One Day Institute on Trade Union Organization," 1929 (Mary Van Kleeck Papers, Sophia Smith Collection, Smith College Library), p. 30.
43. Ormsbee, *The Young Employed Girl*, pp. 45–48.
44. National Women's Trade Union League, "How to Organize: A Problem," p. 27.
45. Richardson, *The Long Day*, p. 213; Montgomery, *The American Girl in the Stockyards District*, p. 31.
46. Bryner, *The Garment Trades*, p. 100; U.S., Department of Labor, Women's Bureau, *The Employment of Women in Slaughtering and Meatpacking*, p. 56.
47. Van Kleeck, *Artificial Flower Makers*, p. 38.
48. Richardson, *The Long Day*, p. 243; Van Kleeck, *Women in the Bookbinding Trade*, pp. 67–68.

49. Sophonisba P. Breckinridge, "Political Equality for Women and Women's Wages," *The Annals of the American Academy of Political and Social Science*, LVI (November, 1914), p. 132. *See also* Fania M. Cohn, "Are Women Organizable?" reprinted from *Labor Age*, March 1927, (National Women's Trade Union League Collection), no pagination.

50. New York, *Fourth Report of the Factory Investigating Commission*, Vol. 4, p. 1708; Esther Malamud, "A Worker's Life," *Bryn Mawr Light*, Vol. 2, Summer 1926, mimeographed (Hilda Smith Papers), no pagination; Consumers' League of New York, *Candy Factories*, p. 7; "The 1909 Strike," *I am a Woman Worker*, ed. Hourwich and Palmer, p. 112.

51. True, *The Neglected Girl*, pp. 46–47.

52. For a fuller discussion of the importance of the foreman in workers' perceptions of their jobs, *see* Peter N. Stearns, *Lives of Labor: Work in a Maturing Industrial Society* (New York: Holmes and Meier Publishers, 1975), pp. 177–178.

53. ". . . it is almost universally true that, during the course of a year, for one position, a succession of persons are hired and discharged, or leave for some reason. The State Factory Investigating Commission's investigation in New York City showed that in the confectionery industry 45% and in the paper-box industry 40% stayed four weeks or less in the same factory. Miss Van Kleeck showed that in millinery 52% stayed only eight weeks or less. In the manufacture of men's clothing, a more steady trade, an investigation of conditions in the five leading cities in the trade, 1907–1908, showed that 28% of the women worked less than five weeks in the same place. Among salesgirls the conditions are similar. In a large Boston store 20.8% remained less than five weeks, while a Washington D.C. investigation showed that 25% remained three months or less . . .

"In laundries, too, a very great shifting of workers is constantly taking place. One Massachusetts establishment reported that 57% remained less than three months; while a Washington employer stated that 'sixty to ninety days eliminate a crew completely.' "

New York, *Fourth Report of the Factory Investigating Commission*, Vol. 2, pp. 521–522.

On the high job turnover in women's industries, *see also* Massachusetts, *Report of the Commission on Industrial and Technical Education*, p. 50; Butler, *Women and the Trades*, pp. 42, 202, 219, 267–268; Henry, *The Trade Union Woman*, pp. 148–149; New York, *Fourth Report of the Factory Investigating Commission*, Vol. 2, pp. 532, 555, 610; ibid., Vol. 4, p. 1352; Van Kleeck, *A Seasonal Industry*, p. 91; Odencrantz, *Italian Women*, pp. 153, 270, 280; Donovan, *The Woman Who*

Waits, p. 124; Consumers' League of New York, *Candy Factories,* p. 22. On the job behavior of unskilled and semi-skilled women, *see* U.S. Industrial Commission, *Report of the Industrial Commission on the Relations and Conditions of Capital and Labor Employed in Manufacturing and General Business,* Vol. 7. (Washington, D.C.: Government Printing Office, 1901), p. 61; Richardson, *The Long Day,* pp. 278–279; Tanner, "Glimpses at the Mind of a Waitress," pp. 50, 52; MacLean, *Wage-Earning Women,* p. 57; Women's Educational and Industrial Union, Department of Research, "Industrial Opportunities for Women in Somerville, 1910–1911," n.d., typewritten (Women's Educational and Industrial Union Papers), p. 19; Massachusetts, *Report of the Commission on Minimum Wage Boards,* pp. 53, 169–170; Montgomery, *The American Girl in the Stockyards District,* pp. 30, 33; Van Kleeck, *Artificial Flower Makers,* pp. 37–39; New York, *Fourth Report of the Factory Investigating Commission,* Vol. 1, p. 806; ibid., Vol. 2, p. 523; ibid., Vol. 4, p. 1707; Perry, *The Millinery Trade in Boston and Philadelphia,* p. 17; Van Kleeck, *A Seasonal Industry,* p. 68; U.S., Department of Labor, Woman in Industry Service, *Wages of Candy Makers in Phildelphia in 1919,* p. 32; Donovan, *The Woman Who Waits,* p. 114; New York, Department of Labor, *The Employment of Women in Five and Ten Cent Stores,* pp. 18–19; National Consumers' League, *The Unstandardized Industry Hotels* (n. pub., 1922) p. 3; Carroll, "Women and the Labor Movement in America," p. 12; Consumers' League of New York, *Candy Factories,* p. 25–26; U.S., Department of Labor, Women's Bureau, *The Effects on Women of Changing Conditions in the Cigar and Cigarette Industry,* by Caroline Manning and Harriet A. Byrne, Bulletin of the Women's Bureau No. 100 (Washington, D.C.: Government Printing Office, 1932), p. 27.

54. Wald, "Organization Amongst Working Women," p. 643; Leonora O'Reilly to Mme. Irene of Mme. Irene Corsetiere, New York, n.d., but c. July 1910 (Leonora O'Reilly Papers); Massachusetts, *Report of the Commission on Minimum Wage Boards,* p. 42; Mary McDowell, untitled report on conditions in the stockyards district, n.d., but c. 1916, typewritten (Mary McDowell Papers), no pagination; Manning, *Immigrant Woman and Her Job,* pp. 120–121; Nestor, *Woman's Labor Leader,* pp. 6, 30; Rose Schneiderman with Lucy Goldthwaite, *All for One* (New York: Paul A. Erickson, Inc., 1967), p. 89; McDowell, "Our Proxies in Industry," p. 2; Mary McDowell, "Labor: the Great Strike," n.d., typewritten (Mary McDowell Papers), p. 10.

55. Charles J. Bushnell, "Some Social Aspects of the Chicago Stock Yards: The Stock Yard Community at Chicago," *American Journal of Sociol-*

ogy, VII (November 1901), p. 469; Odencrantz, *Italian Women*, p. 99; Cornelia Stratton Parker, *Working with the Working Woman* (New York: Harper and Brothers, 1922), pp. 134–135.

56. Diary of Agnes Nestor.
57. Goldie Share, "My First Job."
58. Parker, *Working with the Working Woman*, pp. 38–39.
59. MacLean, *Wage-Earning Women*, p. 45.

PART TWO

1. Jane Addams, *Democracy and Social Ethics* (New York: Macmillan Company, 1902), p. 196.

CHAPTER IV

1. Day Monroe, *Chicago Families: A Study of Unpublished Census Data* (Chicago: University of Chicago Press, 1932), pp. 173–174.
2. W. Jett Lauck and Edgar Sydenstricker, *Conditions of Labor in American Industries: A Summarization of the Results of Recent Investigations* (New York and London: Funk and Wagnalls Company, 1917), pp. 138–139.
3. Crystal Eastman, "The Temper of the Workers Under Trial," *Charities and the Commons*, XXI (January 2, 1909), p. 563.
4. Lauck and Sydenstricker, *Conditions of Labor*, p. 248.

Average annual income of workingmen's families in the United States, summary from contemporary wage investigations

Year of investigation and nature of investigation		Number of families included in data	Average annual income
1901	Bureau of Labor, cost of living study, all sections of U.S., all races & ethnic groups	25,440	$749
1903–4	Louise B. More, budgetary study of families in Greenwich Village, NYC	200	851
1907	Robert Chapin, budgetary study of families of varied ethnicity and occupation, NYC	391	838
1907	N.Y. State Conference of Charities and Corrections, studies of families of varied ethnicity and occupation, Rochester, N.Y.	100	600

Year of investigation and nature of investigation		Number of families included in data	Average annual income
1908	Margaret Byington, study of steel workers' families in Homestead, Pa.	99	349
1908–9	Bureau of Labor, studies of silk, cotton, men's clothing, and glass workers' families with wage-earning women and/or children	8,741	883
1908–9	Immigration Commission; data for families of all races and ethnic groups in 38 principal industries in all Eastern and Southern sections	15,725	721
1909–10	University of Chicago Settlement, families of Chicago stockyards workers, principally recent immigrants	184	442

5. Robert Coit Chapin, *The Standard of Living Among Workingmen's Families in New York City* (New York: Russell Sage Foundation, Charities Publication Committee, 1909), pp. 245–247; Louise Bolard More, *Wage-Earners' Budgets: A Study of Standards and Costs of Living in New York City* (New York: Henry Holt and Company, 1907), pp. 269–70; Margaret F. Byington, *Homestead: The Households of a Mill Town*, The Pittsburgh Survey, Vol. 4, ed. Paul Underwood Kellogg (New York: Russell Sage Foundation, Charities Publication Committee, 1910), p. 105; Montgomery, *The American Girl in the Stockyards District*, p. 7; J. C. Kennedy, *Wages and Family Budgets in the Chicago Stockyards District, with Wage Statistics from Other Industries Employing Unskilled Labor*, A Study of Chicago's Stockyards Community, Vol. 3 (Chicago; University of Chicago Press, 1914), pp. 7–8; New York *Fourth Report of the Factory Investigating Commission*, Vol. 4, pp. 1625, 1668, 1671; Dorothy W. Douglas, "The Cost of Living for Working Women: A Criticism of Current Theories," *Quarterly Journal of Economics*, XXXIV (February 1920) p. 247; Esther Louise Little and William Joseph Henry Cotton, "Budgets of Families and Individuals of Kensington, Philadelphia" (Ph.D. dissertation, University of Pennsylvania, 1920), p. 145.

6. Douglas, "Cost of Living for Working Women," p. 247.

7. Ormsbee, *The Young Employed Girl*, pp. 56–57, 63, 103.

8. Chapin, *The Standard of Living*, pp. 55–57.

9. U.S., Congress, Senate, *Reports of the Immigration Commission,* Vol. 19: *Immigrants in Industries, Part 23: Summary Report on Immigrants in Manufacturing and Mining,* Vol. 1, S. Doc. 633, 61st Cong., 2nd sess. (Washington, D.C.: Government Printing Office, 1911), pp. 129–130.

Sources of entire family income in 15,704 workingmen's families in the principal industries, 1908–1909

Sources of Entire Family Income	Percent of families		
	Native born (white)	Foreign born	Total
Husband	58.4	38.0	40.7
Husband and wife	3.1	3.9	3.8
Husband and children	14.0	12.8	12.7
Husband, wife and children	0.5	0.5	0.5
Husband and boarders or lodgers	6.7	25.5	23.2
Wife	0.3	0.2	0.2
Wife and children	1.0	0.2	0.5
Wife and boarders or lodgers	0.2	0.1	0.1
Children	1.6	1.4	1.4
Children and boarders or lodgers	0.2	0.6	0.5
Boarders or lodgers	0.0	0.3	0.3
Other sources and combinations of sources	14.0	16.2	15.9

See also Van Kleeck, *Artificial Flower Makers,* p. 76; Van Kleeck, *Women in the Bookbinding Trade,* pp. 89–90; Kennedy, *Wages and Family Budgets,* p. 66; Van Kleeck, *Working Girls in Evening Schools,* p. 112; Van Kleeck, *A Seasonal Industry,* p. 60; Odencrantz, *Italian Women,* p. 17; Little and Cotton, "Budgets of Families," p. 147; U.S., Department of Labor, Women's Bureau, *The Share of Wage-Earning Women in Family Support,* Bulletin of the Women's Bureau No. 30 (Washington, D.C.: Government Printing Office, 1923), pp. 74–75; Leila Houghteling, *The Income and Standard of Living of Unskilled Laborers in Chicago* (Chicago: University of Chicago Press, 1927), p. 86; Monroe, *Chicago Families,* p. 150.

10. Van Kleeck, *Artificial Flower Makers*, pp. 79–80; Anthony, *Mothers Who Must Earn*, pp. 129–130; Monroe, *Chicago Families*, p. 157.

11. F. W. Taussig, "Minimum Wages for Women," *Quarterly Journal of Economics*, XXX (May 1916), pp. 417–418.

12. Robert A. Woods, ed., *Americans in Process: A Settlement Study by Residents and Associates of the South End House* (Boston and New York: Houghton Mifflin Company, 1903), p. 125; More, *Wage-Earners' Budgets*, p. 87; Byington, *Homestead*, p. 126; Talbert, *Opportunities in School and Industry*, pp. 16, 40; Odencrantz, *Italian Women*, pp. 168, 205; Little and Cotton, "Budgets of Families," p. 146.

13. Montgomery, *The American Girl in the Stockyards District*, pp. 11, 20; True, *The Neglected Girl*, p. 41; R. R. Lutz, *Wage-Earning and Education*, p. 34; Ormsbee, *The Young Employed Girl*, p. 30.

14. Addams, *The Spirit of Youth and the City Streets*, pp. 125–126; Talbert, *Opportunities in School and Industry*, p. 14; Van Kleeck, *Artificial Flower Makers*, p. 204; New York, *Fourth Report of the Factory Investigating Commission*, Vol. 4, p. 1485; Odencrantz, *Italian Women*, pp. 251–253.

15. Addams, *Democracy and Social Ethics*, p. 46; Jane Sheldrick Howe, *All Work and No Play: A Plea for Saturday Afternoon: Stories Told by Two Hundred Department Store Girls* (Chicago: Juvenile Protective Association of Chicago, 1910), no pagination; MacLean, *Wage-Earning Women*, p. 82; U.S., Congress, Senate, *Report on Condition of Woman and Child Wage-Earners*, Vol. 5, pp. 21–22, 106; Massachusetts, *Report of the Commission on Minimum Wage Boards*, pp. 7, 140; Montgomery, *The American Girl in the Stockyards District*, p. 57; Van Kleeck, *Artificial Flower Makers*, pp. 84–87; Van Kleeck, *Women in the Bookbinding Trade*, p. 100; Woods and Kennedy, *Young Working Girls*, p. 55; Anthony, *Mothers Who Must Earn*, p. 46; True, *The Neglected Girl*, pp. 19, 20, 104; New York, *Third Report of the Factory Investigating Commission*, pp. 150–153; New York, *Fourth Report of the Factory Investigating Commission*, Vol. 4, p. 1538; U.S., Department of Labor, Woman's Bureau, *Summary of the Report on Condition of Woman and Child Wage-Earners*, p. 20; Annie Marion MacLean, *Women Workers and Society* (Chicago: A. C. McClurg Company, 1916), pp. 41–42; Odencrantz, *Italian Women*, p. 21; Little and Cotton, "Budgets of Families," p. 2; U.S. Department of Labor, Women's Bureau, *Women in Illinois Industries*, p. 7; Ormsbee, *The Young Employed Girl*, pp. 49–50; Consumers' League of New York, *Candy Factories*, p. 2.

16. Montgomery, *The American Girl in the Stockyards District*, pp. 57–58.

17. Addams, *Democracy and Social Ethics,* pp. 45–46.
18. Talbert, *Opportunities in School and Industry,* p. 23; Woods and Kennedy, *Young Working Girls,* pp. 46–47.
19. Josephine Roche, "The Italian Girl," in True, *The Neglected Girl,* p. 109; Amy Hewes, *Women as Munition Workers: A Study of Conditions in Bridgeport, Connecticut* (New York: Russell Sage Foundation, 1917), p. 165; Odencrantz, *Italian Women,* p. 254; Manning, *Immigrant Woman and Her Job,* p. 58.
20. Odencrantz, *Italian Women,* p. 176.
21. Woods and Kennedy, *Young Working Girls,* p. 55.
22. Edythe Greth, "The Open Door," *Bryn Mawr Light,* Vol. 2, Summer 1926, mimeographed (Hilda Smith Papers), no pagination.
23. Odencrantz, *Italian Women,* p. 179.
24. U.S., Congress, Senate, *Report on Condition of Woman and Child Wage-Earners,* Vol. 5, p. 148.
25. Ware, *Greenwich Village,* p. 416.
26. "Statements of Six Garment Strikers," n.d., but c. 1910, typewritten (National Women's Trade Union League Collection, Schlesinger Library, Radcliffe College), p. 2.
27. New York, *Fourth Report of the Factory Investigating Commission,* Vol. 4, p. 1484.
28. U.S., Department of Commerce, Bureau of the Census, *Fourteenth Census of the United States,* 1920, Vol. II: *Population: General Report and Analytical Tables* (Washington, D.C.: Government Printing Office, 1922), pp. 1091, 1099, 1111; idem, *Fifteenth Census of the United States,* 1920, Vol. II: *Population: General Report: Statistics by Subjects* (Washington, D.C.: Government Printing Office, 1933), pp. 1145–1146.
29. U.S., Congress, Senate, *Reports of the Immigration Commission,* Vol. 14: *Children of Immigrants in Schools,* Vol. 2, pp. 190–193, 564–568; ibid., Vol. 16: *Children of Immigrants in Schools,* Vol. 4, pp. 626—627, 786–790.
30. Chicago School of Civics and Philanthropy, *Finding Employment for Children,* p. 18.
31. Ware, *Greenwich Village,* p. 329; Massachusetts, *Report of the Commission on Industrial and Technical Education,* pp. 5, 87; Talbert, *Opportunities in School and Industry,* p. 18; Montgomery, *The American Girl in the Stockyards District,* pp. 12–13; Perry, *The Millinery Trade in Boston and Philadelphia,* p. 99; Ormsbee, *The Young Employed Girl,* p. 35.
32. Montgomery, *The American Girl in the Stockyards District,* p. 16; Van Kleeck, *Working Girls in Evening Schools,* pp. 32–33; New York, *Fourth*

Report of the Factory Investigating Commission, Vol. 5, pp. 2910–2911; Pennsylvania, State Department of Public Instruction, *Report of the Survey of the Public Schools of Philadelphia,* Book II: *Organization and Administration: Pupils* (Philadelphia: The Public Education and Child Labor Association of Pennsylvania, 1922), pp. 183–187; Ormsbee, *The Young Employed Girl,* pp. 16–17, 19, 20; George D. Strayer, *Report of the Survey of the Schools of Chicago, Illinois,* Vol. V: *Summary of Findings and Recommendations* (New York: Bureau of Publications, Teachers College, Columbia University, 1932), pp. 75–76, 79–80.

33. Joseph King Van Denburg, *Causes of the Elimination of Students in Public Secondary Schools of New York City* (New York: Teachers College, Columbia University, 1911), p. 185.

34. Chicago, Board of Education, *Fifty-Eighth Annual Report of the Board of Education,* 1912, in Montgomery, *The American Girl in the Stockyards District,* p. 27.

35. Bryner, *The Garment Trades,* p. 137; Ormsbee, *The Young Employed Girl,* p. 37.

36. Ware, *Greenwich Village,* p. 69.

37. Women's Educational and Industrial Union, "Industrial Opportunities for Women in Somerville," pp. 14–15; Talbert, *Opportunities in School and Industry,* pp. 43–44; Montgomery, *American Girl in the Stockyards District,* p. 6; Anthony, *Mothers Who Must Earn,* pp. 4, 47.

38. More, *Wage-Earners' Budgets,* p. 148.

39. Talbert, *Opportunities in School and Industry,* p. 15; Montgomery, *American Girl in the Stockyards District,* p. 3.

40. Montgomery, *American Girl in the Stockyards District,* p. 3; Odencrantz, *Italian Women,* pp. 255–256.

41. Edith Abbott and Sophonisba P. Breckinridge, *Truancy and Non-Attendance in the Chicago Schools* (Chicago: University of Chicago Press, 1917), p. 142; Elizabeth Beardsley Butler, "Sharpsburg: A Waste of Childhood," in *Wage-Earning Pittsburgh,* ed. Paul Underwood Kellogg, The Pittsburgh Survey, Vol. 6 (New York: Russell Sage Foundation, Charities Publication Committee, 1911), p. 285; Montgomery, *The American Girl in the Stockyards District,* pp. 3, 6.

42. Byington, *Homestead,* p. 160; Talbert, *Opportunities in School and Industry,* p. 15; Montgomery, *The American Girl in the Stockyards District,* p. 15.

43. Woods, *Americans in Process,* pp. 296–297; Montgomery, *The American Girl in the Stockyards District,* pp. 7, 16–17.

44. Lillian Wolfe, "How and Why I Chose My First Job," *The Bryn Mawr*

Daisy, July 8, 1922, mimeographed (Hilda Smith Papers), no pagination.

45. Elsa G. Herzfeld, *Family Monographs: The History of Twenty-Four Families Living in the Middle-West Side of New York City* (New York: James Kempster Printing Company, 1905), pp. 55–56, 142–143; True, *The Neglected Girl*, p. 35; Elizabeth A. Irwin, *Truancy: A Study of the Mental, Physical, and Social Factors of the Problem of Non-Attendance at School* (New York: n. pub., 1915), pp. 26–27.

46. Roche, "The Italian Girl," in True, *The Neglected Girl*, p. 102.

47. Ware, *Greenwich Village*, p. 69.

48. Montgomery, *The American Girl in the Stockyards District*, pp. 7, 8; Van Kleeck, *Artificial Flower Makers*, p. 85.

49. Van Kleeck, *Artificial Flower Makers*, p. 86.

50. On the relationship between economic opportunity and the schooling level of working-class girls, *see* Miriam Cohen, "Italian-American Women in New York City, 1900–1950: Work and School," *Class, Sex, and the Woman Worker*, ed. Milton Cantor and Bruce Laurie, Contributions in Labor History, No. 1 (Westport, Conn.: Greenwood Press, 1977), pp. 120–143.

51. Montgomery, *American Girl in the Stockyards District*, pp. 18, 50.

52. Woods and Kennedy, *Young Working Girls*, p. 59.

53. Talbert, *Opportunities in School and Industry*, p. 42; Lillian Wald, *The House on Henry Street* (New York: Dover Publications, 1971), p. 196.

54. Montgomery, *The American Girl in the Stockyards District*, p. 58.

55. Women's Educational and Industrial Union, "Industrial Opportunities for Women in Somerville," p. 17; Clara E. Laughlin, *The Work-a-Day Girl: A Study of Some Present-Day Conditions* (New York: Fleming H. Revell, 1913), pp. 216–217; Montgomery, *The American Girl in the Stockyards District*, p. 19; Van Kleeck, *Women in the Bookbinding Trade*, pp. 196–197; MacLean, *Women Workers and Society*, p. 105.

56. Butler, *Women and the Trades*, pp. 306–307; Ethel M. Johnson, "Some of the Industrial Opportunities for Women in Massachusetts," n.d., mimeographed (Ethel M. Johnson Papers), p. 5.

57. U.S., Congress, Senate, *Report on Condition of Woman and Child Wage-Earners*, Vol. 5, p. 81; Talbert, *Opportunities in School and Industry*, p. 22; Montgomery, *The American Girl in the Stockyards District*, p. 19; Van Kleeck, *Artificial Flower Makers*, p. 74; Van Kleeck, *Women in the Bookbinding Trade*, p. 126; Woods and Kennedy, *Young Working Girls*, pp. 17–18; Van Kleeck, *A Seasonal Industry*, p. 153; Odencrantz, *Italian Women*, pp. 34, 272–273, 315.

58. Montgomery, *The American Girl in the Stockyards District*, p. 31.

59. Abbott and Breckinridge, "Women in Industry: The Chicago Stockyards," p. 651.

60. Butler, *Women and the Trades*, p. 225; MacLean, *Wage-Earning Women*, p. 44; Chicago School of Civics and Philanthropy, *Finding Employment for Children Who Leave the Grade Schools*, p. 16; Montgomery, *The American Girl in the Stockyards District*, pp. 37–38; Van Kleeck, *Artificial Flower Makers*, pp. 37–39, 211; Roche, "The Italian Girl," in True, *The Neglected Girl*, p. 111; Lutz, *Wage-Earning and Education*, p. 2; Odencrantz, *Italian Women*, pp. 272–273; Consumers' League of New York, *Candy Factories*, pp. 25–26.

61. On this point *see* Stearns, *Lives of Labor*, pp. 60–61, 76.

62. Woods and Kennedy, *Young Working Girls*, pp. 29–30.

63. U.S., Congress, Senate, *Report on Condition of Woman and Child Wage-Earners*, Vol. 12, p. 99. *See also* More, *Wage-Earners' Budgets*, p. 87; Addams, *The Spirit of Youth and the City Streets*, pp. 54–55; Montgomery, *The American Girl in the Stockyards District*, p. 58; Woods and Kennedy, *Young Working Girls*, p. 53; Anthony, *Mothers Who Must Earn*, p. 45; Odencrantz, *Italian Women*, pp. 21, 176, 204; U.S., Department of Labor, Women's Bureau, *Share of Wage-Earning Women in Family Support*, pp. 60, 80, 163; Hughes, *Mothers in Industry*, pp. 205.

64. Woods and Kennedy, *Young Working Girls*, pp. 53–54; Anthony, *Mothers Who Must Earn*, p. 123; True, *The Neglected Girl*, p. 51; Odencrantz, *Italian Women*, p. 179.

65. Montgomery, *American Girl in the Stockyards District*, p. 58; Little and Cotton, "Budgets of Families," p. 76.

66. Odencrantz, *Italian Women*, p. 176.

67. Montgomery, *The American Girl in the Stockyards District*, pp. 59–60; Woods and Kennedy, *Young Working Girls*, pp. 36–37; True, *The Neglected Girl*, p. 51; New York, *Fourth Report of the Factory Investigating Commission*, Vol. 4, p. 1543; Hewes, *Women as Munitions Workers*, p. 65; Mary McDowell, "The Foreign Born," n.d., typewritten (Mary McDowell Papers), p. 5–6; McDowell, "The Young Girl in Industry," p. 3.

68. Montgomery, *The American Girl in the Stockyards District*, p. 32.

69. McDowell, "The Young Girl in Industry," p. 1.

70. Addams, *Spirit of Youth and the City Streets*, p. 91. On the social lives of working-class girls, *see also* John M. Gillette, "The Cultural Agencies of a Typical Manufacturing Group: South Chicago," *American Journal of Sociology*, VII (September 1901), p. 207; Bushnell, "Some Social Aspects of the Chicago Stockyards: The Stock Yard Community at Chi-

cago," p. 306; Albert Benedict Wolfe, *The Lodging House Problem in Boston*, Harvard Economic Studies, Vol. 2 (Boston and New York: Houghton Mifflin Company, 1906), pp. 30–31; Addams, *The Spirit of Youth and the City Streets*, pp. 18–19, 46, 84, 86–87; Margaret F. Byington, "The Family in a Typical Mill Town," *American Journal of Sociology*, XIV (March 1909), p. 657; Belle Lindner Israels, "The Way of the Girl," *The Survey*, XXII (July 3, 1909), pp. 486–497; Louise DeKoven Bowen, *The Public Dance Halls of Chicago* (Chicago: Juvenile Protective League of Chicago, 1910), no pagination; Hapgood, *Types from City Streets*, pp. 131–136. U.S., Congress, Senate, *Report on Condition of Woman and Child Wage-Earners*, Vol. 5, p. 120; Montgomery, *The American Girl in the Stockyards District*, pp. 32, 59, 68; Woods and Kennedy, *Young Working Girls*, pp. 106–107; MacLean, *Women Workers and Society*, pp. 109–110; Illinois, Senate, *Report of the Senate Vice Committee, Created Under the Authority of the Senate of the 49th General Assembly* (n. pub., 1916), p. 495; Leroy E. Bowman and Maria Ward Lambin, "Evidence of Social Relations as Seen in Types of New York City Dance Halls," *Journal of Social Forces*, III (January 1925), p. 286; Ormsbee, *The Young Employed Girl*, pp. 6–7; William J. Blackburn, "A Brief Report of a Study Made of the Organization, Program and Services of the University of Chicago Settlement, 1927–1928," n.d., typewritten (Mary McDowell Papers), pp. 5–6.

71. MacLean, *Wage-Earning Women*, pp. 44–45.
72. Woods, *The City Wilderness*, pp. 101–102; Emily W. Dinwiddie, *Housing Conditions in Philadelphia* (Philadelphia: Octavia Hill Association, 1904), pp. 19–20, 26; More, *Wage-Earners' Budgets*, pp. 130–131; U.S., Congress, Senate, *Reports of the Immigration Commission*, Vol. 26: *Immigrants in Cities*, Vol. 1, S. Doc. 338, 61st Cong., 2nd sess. (Washington, D.C.: Government Printing Office, 1911), pp. 184, 197; Van Kleeck, *Artificial Flower Makers*, p. 83; Lauck and Sydenstricker, *Conditions of Labor*, pp. 291–293; Odencrantz, *Italian Women*, pp. 15, 197; Mary McDowell, "Housing," 1921, typewritten (Mary McDowell Papers), p. 1; Hughes, *Mothers in Industry*, p. 185; Houghteling, *Income and Standard of Living*, pp. 106–107; National Industrial Conference Board, *The Cost of Living in Twelve Industrial Cities* (New York: National Industrial Conference Board, Inc., 1928), pp. 23–24.
73. McDowell, "Our Proxies in Industry," p. 1.
74. Ware, *Greenwich Village*, p. 368.
75. Mary Kingsbury Simkhovitch, "A New Social Adjustment," in *Proceedings of the Academy of Political Science in the City of New York: The*

Economic Position of Women, Academy of Political Science, Columbia University (New York: Columbia University, 1910), p. 87.

76. Ware, *Greenwich Village,* p. 405.
77. Addams, *The Spirit of Youth and the City Streets,* pp. 44–45.
78. Ware, *Greenwich Village,* p. 187.

CHAPTER V

1. MacLean, *Wage-Earning Women,* pp. 29, 54, 72, 82; U.S., Congress, Senate, *Report on Condition of Woman and Child Wage-Earners,* Vol. 5, p. 15; Butler, *Saleswomen in Mercantile Stores,* p. 146; New York, *Fourth Report of the Factory Investigating Commission,* Vol. 4, p. 1492; Perry, *The Millinery Trade in Boston and Philadelphia,* p. 14; Van Kleeck, *A Seasonal Industry,* p. 127; Women's Educational and Industrial Union, Department of Research, in cooperation with the Massachusetts Department of Health, *The Food of Working Women in Boston,* Lucille Eaves, director (Boston: Women's Educational and Industrial Union, 1917), pp. 66–67; U.S., Department of Labor, Women's Bureau, *Women in Five and Ten-Cent Stores and Limited-Price Stores,* by Mary Elizabeth Pidgeon, Bulletin of the Women's Bureau No. 76 (Washington, D.C.: Government Printing Office, 1930), pp. 9–10.
2. Willett, *The Employment of Women in the Clothing Trade,* p. 93.
3. Ware, *Greenwich Village,* p. 111.
4. Persons, "Women's Work and Wages," p. 223.
5. U.S., Congress, Senate, *Report on Condition of Woman and Child Wage-Earners,* Vol. 5, p. 59; New York, *Third Report of the Factory Investigating Commission,* p. 156; New York, *Fourth Report of the Factory Investigating Commission,* Vol. 4, p. 1700; Van Kleeck, *A Seasonal Industry,* p. 127; Odencrantz, *Italian Women,* p. 221.
6. Chapin, *The Standard of Living,* p. 55; U.S., Congress, Senate, *Report on Condition of Woman and Child Wage-Earners,* Vol. 5, p. 151; New York, *Fourth Report of the Factory Investigating Commission,* Vol. 4, pp. 1552, 1556, 1560; Hasanovitz, *One of Them,* pp. 165–166; Little and Cotton, "Budgets of Families," p. 146; Ormsbee, *The Young Employed Girl,* p. 63; Florence Kelley, "Congestion and Sweated Labor," n.d., typewritten (Consumers' League of Massachusetts Papers, Schlesinger Library, Radcliffe College), pp. 2, 3.
7. Isola Forrester, "A New York Girl Who Lives on $2.50 a Week—and How She Does It," unidentified newspaper, n.d., but c. 1906 (Maud Nathan Papers).

8. New York, *Fourth Report of the Factory Investigating Commission*, Vol. 4, p. 1701.

9. Louise Marion Bosworth, "The Living Wage of Women Workers: A Study of Incomes and Expenditures of Four Hundred and Fifty Women Workers in the City of Boston," *Supplement to The Annals of the American Academy of Political and Social Science*, XXXVII (Philadelphia: The American Academy of Political and Social Science, May 1911), p. 31; Odencrantz, *Italian Women*, pp. 217–218.

10. New York, *Fourth Report of the Factory Investigating Commission*, Vol. 4, pp. 1700–1701.

11. Ibid., p. 1505; Van Kleeck, *A Seasonal Industry*, p. 129; Odencrantz, *Italian Women*, pp. 224–225; National Civic Federation, New England Section, *Report on Unemployment Among Boston Women in 1915*, by Eleanor H. Woods, (n.d., n.pub.) no pagination.

12. Odencrantz, *Italian Women*, p. 224.

13. U.S., Congress, Senate, *Report on Condition of Woman and Child Wage-Earners*, Vol. 5, p. 62.

14. U.S., Bureau of Labor, *Boarding Homes and Clubs for Working Women*, by Mary S. Fergusson, Bulletin of the U.S. Bureau of Labor No. 15 (Washington, D.C.: Government Printing Office, 1898), p. 142; Woods, *The City Wilderness*, p. 64; Richardson, *The Long Day*, p. 52; Wolfe, *The Lodging House Problem*, pp. 35–37; Hasanovitz, *One of Them*, p. 181; Bureau of Social Hygiene, *Housing Conditions of Employed Women in the Borough of Manhattan* (New York: n. pub., 1922), p. 32.

15. Hasanovitz, *One of Them*, pp. 4–5.

16. Wolfe, *The Lodging House Problem*, pp. 103–104.

17. Illinois, *Report of the Senate Vice Committee*, p. 338.

18. Bureau of Social Hygiene, *Housing Conditions of Employed Women*, pp. 30–31; Franklin Kline Fretz, "The Furnished Room Problem in Philadelphia" (Ph.D. dissertation, University of Pennsylvania, 1912), p. 27.

19. Fretz, "The Furnished Room Problem," p. 41.

20. Wolfe, *The Lodging House Problem*, p. 110; Fretz, "The Furnished Room Problem," p. 26.

21. Fretz, "The Furnished Room Problem," p. 155.

22. Wolfe, *The Lodging House Problem*, p. 109.

23. Harvey Warren Zorbaugh, *The Gold Coast and the Slum: A Sociological Study of Chicago's Near North Side* (Chicago: University of Chicago Press, 1929), p. 75.

24. Women's Educational and Industrial Union, *The Food of Working Women*, p. 83.
25. Fretz, "The Furnished Room Problem," p. 41.
26. U.S., Congress, Senate, *Report on Condition of Woman and Child Wage-Earners*, Vol. 5, p. 93; New York, *Fourth Report of the Factory Investigating Commission*, Vol. 4, p. 1702.
27. Wolfe, *The Lodging House Problem*, p. 66; Connecticut, *Report of the Bureau of Labor*, p. 42; Illinois, *Report of the Senate Vice Committee*, p. 338.
28. U.S., Congress, Senate, *Report on Condition of Woman and Child Wage-Earners*, Vol. 5, pp. 65–66.
29. 'Wolfe, *The Lodging House Problem*, pp. 100, 112; Women's Educational and Industrial Union, *The Food of Working Women*, p. 78.
30. Ibid., pp. 68–69.
31. New York, *Fourth Report of the Factory Investigating Commission*, Vol. 4, p. 1679.
32. The New York State Factory Investigating Commission estimated in 1915 that about 3000 women lived in subsidized boarding and lodging houses in New York City. The Bureau of Social Hygiene placed the figure for Manhattan at 4417 in 1921. A Chicago newspaper report in 1908 listed only five subsidized homes for working women in that city.

    New York, *Fourth Report of the Factory Investigating Commission*, Vol. 4, p. 1564; Bureau of Social Hygiene, *Housing Conditions of Employed Women*, p. 7; "What is Living Wage for Girls?" *Chicago Inter-Ocean*, n.d., but 1908 (Chicago Women's Trade Union League Papers).
33. U.S., Bureau of Labor, *Boarding Homes and Clubs*, pp. 145, 183; U.S., Congress, Senate, *Report on Condition of Woman and Child Wage-Earners*, Vol. 5, p. 70
34. Frances A. Kellor, "Immigrant Woman," *Atlantic*, 100 (Sept. 1907), reprinted in Edna D. Bullock, ed., *Selected Articles on the Employment of Women* (New York: H. Wilson Company, 1920), p. 53.
35. Hasanovitz, *One of Them*, p. 304.
36. U.S., Bureau of Labor, *Boarding Homes and Clubs*, pp. 146–147; New York, *Fourth Report of the Factory Investigating Commission*, Vol. 4, pp. 1680–1681; Women's Educational and Industrial Union, *Food of Working Women*, p. 123; Bureau of Social Hygiene, *Housing Conditions of Employed Women*, p. 65.
37. U.S., Bureau of Labor, *Boarding Homes and Clubs*, pp. 146–147;

New York, *Fourth Report of the Factory Investigating Commission*, Vol. 4, p. 1564.
38. U.S., Congress, Senate, *Report on Condition of Woman and Child Wage-Earners*, Vol. 5, p. 151.
39. New York, *Fourth Report of the Factory Investigating Commission*, Vol. 4, pp. 1696, 1699.
40. Richardson, *The Long Day*, pp. 157–179; New York, *Fourth Report of the Factory Investigating Commission*, Vol. 4, pp. 1681, 1696–1697.
41. U.S., Congress, Senate, *Report on Condition of Woman and Child Wage-Earners*, Vol. 5, p. 70.
42. New York, *Fourth Report of the Factory Investigating Commission*, Vol. 4, p. 1680.
43. U.S., Congress, Senate, *Report on Condition of Woman and Child Wage-Earners*, Vol. 5, p. 151; Douglas, "The Cost of Living for Working Women," p. 232; Bureau of Social Hygiene, *Housing Conditions of Employed Women*, p. 10.
44. New York, *Third Report of the Factory Investigating Commission*, p. 157; New York, *Fourth Report of the Factory Investigating Commission*, Vol. 4, p. 1688; ibid., Vol. 5, pp. 2810, 2812; Hasanovitz, *One of Them*, p. 193; U.S., Department of Labor, Woman in Industry Service, *Wages of Candy Makers in Philadelphia*, pp. 26–27; Douglas, "The Cost of Living for Working Women," pp. 231–232; Little and Cotton, "Budgets of Families," p. 188; U.S. Department of Labor, Women's Bureau, *Women in the Candy Industry in Chicago and St. Louis*, pp. 56–57.
45. Women's Educational and Industrial Union, *Food of Working Women*, p. 172.
46. U.S., Congress, Senate, *Report on Condition of Woman and Child Wage-Earners*, Vol. 5, pp. 17–18; New York, *Third Report of the Factory Investigating Commission*, p. 156; New York, *Fourth Report of the Factory Investigating Commission*, Vol. 4, pp. 1675–1677.
47. New York, *Fourth Report of the Factory Investigating Commission*, Vol. 4., p. 1544.
48. U.S., Congress, Senate, *Report on Condition of Woman and Child Wage-Earners*, Vol. 5, p. 149.
49. Hasanovitz, *One of Them*, pp. 192–193.
50. Massachusetts, *Report of Commission on Minimum Wage Boards*, p. 224.
51. MacLean, *Wage-Earning Women*, p. 61; Clark and Wyatt, *Making Both Ends Meet*, p. 7; Massachusetts, *Report of Commission on Minimum Wage Boards*, p. 187; New York, *Fourth Report of the Factory Investigating Commission*, Vol. 4, p. 1704.

52. New York, *Fourth Report of the Factory Investigating Commission,* Vol, 4, pp. 1686–1688, 1690, 1706; Van Kleeck, *A Seasonal Industry,* p. 169; Consumers' League of New York, *Candy Factories,* p. 40.

53. New York, *Fourth Report of the Factory Investigating Commission,* Vol. 4, p. 1686.

54. Ibid., p. 1687.

55. Lubove, *The Struggle for Social Security,* p. 57.

56. New York, *Fourth Report of the Factory Investigating Commission,* Vol. 4, p. 1682. *See also* Women's Educational and Industrial Union, *Food of Working Women,* p. 81.

57. Bosworth, *Living Wage of Women Workers,* p. 67; New York, *Fourth Report of the Factory Investigating Commission,* Vol. 4, pp. 1682–1683; Odencrantz, *Italian Women,* p. 233.

58. U.S., Congress, Senate, *Report on Condition of Woman and Child Wage-Earners,* Vol. 5, p. 18; New York, *Fourth Report of the Factory Investigating Commission,* Vol. 4, pp. 1681–1682, 1707; ibid., Vol. 5, p. 2809; Odencrantz, *Italian Women,* p. 229.

59. New York, *Fourth Report of the Factory Investigating Commission,* Vol. 4, p. 1683.

60. Little and Cotton, "Budgets of Families," pp. 187–188.

61. Bosworth, *Living Wage of Women Workers,* p. 80; Clark and Wyatt, *Making Both Ends Meet,* p. 7; New York, *Fourth Report of the Factory Investigating Commission,* Vol. 4, p. 1686; Odencrantz, *Italian Women,* pp. 238–239.

62. Women's Educational and Industrial Union, *Food of Working Women,* p. 88; New York, *Fourth Report of the Factory Investigating Commission,* Vol. 4, p. 1505; Van Kleeck, *A Seasonal Industry,* pp. 129, 171.

63. U.S., Congress, Senate, *Report on Condition of Woman and Child Wage-Earners,* Vol. 5, p. 65; Bureau of Social Hygiene, *Housing Conditions of Employed Women,* p. 10.

64. U.S., Department of Labor, Bureau of Labor Statistics, *Summary of Report on Condition of Woman and Child Wage-Earners,* p. 25.

65. Massachusetts, *Report of Commission on Minimum Wage Boards,* p. 187; New York, *Fourth Report of the Factory Investigating Commission,* Vol. 4, p. 1687; Women's Educational and Industrial Union, *Food of Working Women,* pp. 69–70, 88–89.

66. U.S., Congress, Senate, *Report on Condition of Woman and Child Wage-Earners,* Vol. 5, pp. 64–65.

67. Clark and Wyatt, *Making Both Ends Meet,* p. 93.

68. U.S., Department of Labor, Women's Bureau, "Immigrant Woman and

Her Job,'' study records, Schedule 7/10/3, n.d. (Records of the Women's Bureau, Record Group 86, National Archives, Washington, D.C.). *See also* Clark and Wyatt, *Making Both Ends Meet,* p. 94; U.S., Congress, Senate, *Report on Condition of Woman and Child Wage-Earners,* Vol. 5, pp. 64–65; Massachusetts, *Report of Commission on Minimum Wage Boards,* pp. 187–188; New York, *Fourth Report of the Factory Investigating Commission,* Vol. 5, pp. 2811–2812.

69. Massachusetts, *Report of Commission on Minimum Wage Boards,* p. 187; New York, *Fourth Report of the Factory Investigating Commission,* Vol. 4, pp. 1688–1689.

70. Clark and Wyatt, *Making Both Ends Meet,* p. 94; New York, *Fourth Report of the Factory Investigating Commission,* Vol. 5, p. 2813.

71. New York, *Fourth Report of the Factory Investigating Commission,* Vol. 4, pp. 1686–1687.

72. U.S., Congress, Senate, *Report on Condition of Woman and Child Wage-Earners,* Vol. 5, p. 58.

73. New York, *Fourth Report of the Factory Investigating Commission,* Vol. 4, p. 1689.

74. Douglas, ''The Cost of Living for Working Women,'' p. 231.

75. Women's Educational and Industrial Union, *Food of Working Women,* p. 70.

76. National Civic Federation, *Unemployment Among Boston Women,* no pagination.

CHAPTER VI

1. Bureau of the Census, *Women in Gainful Occupations,* p. 269.

Percent married women in gainful occupations in Boston, Chicago, New York, Philadelphia, 1900–1920

	Year		
City	1900	1910	1920
Boston	6.0	10.6	9.9
Chicago	3.5	7.1	10.4
New York	4.9	9.4	9.6
Philadelphia	5.1	9.8	10.0

2. U.S., Congress, Senate, *Reports of the Immigration Commission*, Vol. 26: *Immigrants in Cities*, Vol. 1, pp. 232, 319, 405, 485, 578, 660.
3. Monroe, *Chicago Families*, pp. 212, 216.
4. More, *Wage-Earners' Budgets*, pp. 5–6; Anthony, *Mothers Who Must Earn*, p. 56; National Consumers' League and the Consumers' League of New Jersey, *Night-Working Mothers in Textile Mills*, by Agnes de Lima (n.pub., 1920), p. 8; Parker, *Working with the Working Woman*, p. 38; U.S., Department of Labor, Women's Bureau, *The Share of Wage-Earning Women in Family Support*, pp. 60, 84; Hughes, *Mothers in Industry*, pp. 6, 22, 79; U.S., Department of Labor, Women's Bureau, *Family Status of Breadwinning Women in Four Selected Cities*, Bulletin of the Women's Bureau No. 41 (Washington, D.C.: Government Printing Office, 1925), p. 10; Manning, *Immigrant Woman and Her Job*, pp. 52, 56; U.S., Department of Labor, Women's Bureau, *The Employment of Women in Slaughtering and Meatpacking*, pp. 126–127.
5. Anthony, *Mothers Who Must Earn*, p. 16.
6. U.S., Congress, Senate, *Report on Condition of Woman and Child Wage-Earners*, Vol. 2, p. 380.
7. U.S. Department of Labor, Children's Bureau, *Children of Wage-Earning Mothers: A Study of a Selected Group in Chicago*, by Helen Russell Wright, Children's Bureau Publication No. 102 (Washington, D.C.: Government Printing Office, 1922), p. 13.
8. Hughes, *Mothers in Industry*, pp. 107, 126–127.
9. National Civic Federation, *Report on Unemployment Among Boston Women*.
10. Manning, *Immigrant Woman and Her Job*, p. 50.
11. Anthony, *Mothers Who Must Earn*, pp. 15–16.
12. Manning, *Immigrant Woman and Her Job*, p. 56.
13. Bureau of the Census, *Women in Gainful Occupations*, p. 79.
14. Van Kleeck, *Women in the Bookbinding Trade*, pp. 91–92; Manning, *Immigrant Woman and Her Job*, p. 43.
15. V. G. Weatherly, "How Does the Access of Women to Industrial Occupations React on the Family?" *American Journal of Sociology*, XLV (May 1909), pp. 744–745.
16. Manning, *Immigrant Woman and Her Job*, p. 111.
17. Wright, *Children of Wage-Earning Mothers*, p. 7.
18. Bureau of the Census, *Women in Gainful Occupations*, pp. 80–83.
19. Monroe, *Chicago Families*, pp. 186, 194, 200, 202, 203, 205.
20. Odencrantz, *Italian Women*, p. 20.

21. Van Kleeck, *Artificial Flower Makers*, p. 77.
22. Van Kleeck, *Women in the Bookbinding Trade*, p. 93.
23. Hughes, *Mothers in Industry*, p. 129.
24. Van Kleeck, *Artificial Flower Makers*, pp. 116–117; Van Kleeck, *Women in the Bookbinding Trade*, p. 94; Wright, *Children of Wage-Earning Mothers*, pp. 31, 34; Hughes, *Mothers in Industry*, p. 142; U.S., Department of Labor, Children's Bureau, *Children of Working Mothers in Philadelphia*, Part I, by Clara Mortenson Beyer, Children's Bureau Publication No. 204 (Washington, D.C.: Government Printing Office, 1931), pp. 26–27.
25. Anthony, *Mothers Who Must Earn*, p. 58.
26. Ibid., p. 76–78.
27. Ibid., pp. 118–119.
28. Ibid., p. 84.
29. Hughes, *Mothers in Industry*, p. 177.
30. U.S., Congress, Senate, *Report on Condition of Woman and Child Wage-Earners*, Vol. 2, p. 378; New York, *Second Report of the Factory Investigating Commission*, Vol. 1, p. 193; Anthony, *Mothers Who Must Earn*, p. 144; Odencrantz, *Italian Women*, p. 196; Wright, *Children of Wage-Earning Mothers*, pp. 38–41; Hughes, *Mothers in Industry*, pp. 167, 178–179, 181; U.S., Department of Labor, Women's Bureau, *Family Status of Breadwinning Women in Four Selected Cities*, p. 17; Massachusetts, Senate, Committee on Labor and Industry, *Report of Hearing Before the Committee on Labor and Industry of the Massachusetts Legislature, re Senate Bill 149 and Senate Bill 191* (Boston: Associated Industries of Massachusetts, 1928), p. 74; Manning, *Immigrant Woman and Her Job*, pp. 60–61; U.S., Department of Labor, Women's Bureau, *The Employment of Women in Slaughtering and Meatpacking*, p. 131; New York, Department of Labor, Bureau of Labor Statistics, *Annual Report* (1900), p. 69, quoted in Louis D. Brandeis and Josephine Goldmark, *Women in Industry: Decision of the United States Supreme Court in Curt Muller vs. State of Oregon Upholding the Constitutionality of the Oregon Ten-Hour Law for Women, and Brief for the State of Oregon* (New York: National Consumers' League, n.d.), p. 58.

Only in families where the mother worked regularly outside the home for long periods have I found much evidence of routine sharing of household tasks by older children and husbands. This implies that long-term employment of married women—something that became common in white families only after World War II—is potentially a force for change in domestic relationships. But see below, the Conclusion, footnote two, and text, regarding the slow pace of this change. For evidence relevant to the early decades of this century *see* Emily Greene Balch, *Our Slavic Fellow Citizens* (New York: Charities Publication Committee, 1910), p. 359; Manning, *Immigrant Woman and Her Job*, p. 61.

31. Wright, *Children of Wage-Earning Mothers*, p. 43.
32. Anthony, *Mothers Who Must Earn*, p. 147; Wright, *Children of Wage-Earning Mothers*, p. 43; Hughes, *Mothers in Industry*, pp. 180–181; Manning, *Immigrant Woman and Her Job*, p. 70.
33. Van Kleeck, *Artificial Flower Makers*, pp. 84–85; Anthony, *Mothers Who Must Earn*, p. 141; Wright, *Children of Wage-Earning Mothers*, p. 42; Hughes, *Mothers in Industry*, pp. 188–189.
34. Ibid., pp. 176–177.
35. Manning, *Immigrant Woman and Her Job*, pp. 60–61.
36. Wright, *Children of Wage-Earning Mothers*, p. 43.
37. Mary McDowell, "In the Stockyards District," (June 14, 1917), typewritten (Mary McDowell Papers), p. 2; Mary McDowell, "Mothers and Night Work," *The Survey*, XXXIX (December 22, 1917), p. 335. *See also* Illinois, *Hours and Health of Women Workers*, p. 68.
38. National Consumers' League and the Consumers' League of New Jersey, *Night-Working Mothers in Textile Mills*, p. 5. *See also* New York, *Second Report of the Factory Investigating Commission*, Vol. 2, pp. 451–458; U.S., Department of Labor, Women's Bureau, *Women in the Candy Industry in Chicago and St. Louis*, p. 19; U.S., Department of Labor, Women's Bureau, *The Employment of Women at Night*, by Mary D. Hopkins, Bulletin of the Women's Bureau No. 64 (Washington, D.C.: Government Printing Office, 1928), pp. 50–52; Manning, *Immigrant Woman and Her Job*, p. 98.
39. McDowell, "Mothers and Night Work," p. 335. *See also* National Consumers' League and the Consumers' League of New Jersey, *Night-Working Mothers in Textile Mills*, pp. 12–14.
40. Illinois, *Hours and Health of Women Workers*, p. 68.
41. McDowell, "Mothers and Night Work," p. 335; U.S. Department of Labor, Women's Bureau, *The Employment of Women at Night*, pp. 54–55.
42. "Inspection of Night Work by Women at William Carter Company, 33 Morris St., Springfield," n.d., but circa 1918, typewritten. (Consumers' League of Massachusetts Papers, Schlesinger Library, Radcliffe College), p. 4.
43. Wright, *Children of Wage-Earning Mothers*, p. 45.
44. Anthony, *Mothers Who Must Earn*, pp. 163–164.

45. Manning, *Immigrant Woman and Her Job*, p. 56.
46. Wright, *Children of Wage-Earning Mothers*, p. 49.
47. Anthony, *Mothers Who Must Earn*, p. 164.
48. Hilda Smith, "A Study of Fifty Working Mothers," 1915, manuscript (Hilda Smith Papers), p. 7.
49. Anthony, *Mothers Who Must Earn*, p. 165.
50. More, *Wage-Earners' Budgets*, p. 12.
51. Anthony, *Mothers Who Must Earn*, p. 158; Hughes, *Mothers in Industry*, pp. 23–24.
52. Addams, *Democracy and Social Ethics*, pp. 200–201; Herzfeld, *Family Monographs*, pp. 70–71.
53. Monroe, *Chicago Families*, pp. 217–218, 223–224.
54. Hughes, *Mothers in Industry*, p. 194.
55. Manning, *Immigrant Woman and Her Job*, p. 41–42. See also Wright, *Children of Wage-Earning Mothers*, p. 23.
56. Anthony, *Mothers Who Must Earn*, pp. 140, 153.
57. Massachusetts, House, *Report of the Commission on the Support of Dependent Minor Children of Widowed Mothers*, H. Doc. 2075 (Boston, 1913), p. 149.
58. Wright, *Children of Wage-Earning Mothers*, pp. 17, 24; Hughes, *Mothers in Industry*, p. 198; Manning, *Immigrant Woman and Her Job*, p. 42.
59. Manning, *Immigrant Woman and Her Job*, p. 42.
60. Wright, *Children of Wage-Earning Mothers*, p. 24.
61. Sophonisba P. Breckinridge, "Neglected Widowhood in the Juvenile Court," *American Journal of Sociology*, XVI (July 1910), pp. 60–61; U.S., Congress, Senate, *Report on Condition of Woman and Child Wage-Earners*, Vol. 2, pp. 383–384; Wright, *Children of Wage-Earning Mothers*, p. 23; Hughes, *Mothers in Industry*, pp. 23–24.
62. Janet Geister, "The Industrial Day Nursery," n.d., but 1919, typewritten (Records of the Children's Bureau, Record Group 102, National Archives), pp. 8–9.
63. Barbara Bartlett to Grace L. Meigs, May 16, 1918 (Records of the Children's Bureau).
64. "Health," 1908, typewritten (Mary McDowell Papers), p. 3.
65. Herzfeld, *Family Monographs*, pp. 52–58; Wright, *Children of Wage-Earning Mothers*, p. 17.
66. Anthony, *Mothers Who Must Earn*, p. 155.
67. Ibid., p. 12.
68. Margaret O'Brien Steinfels, *Who's Minding the Children? The History*

and Politics of Day Care in America (New York: Simon and Schuster, 1973), p. 34.

69. Geister, "The Industrial Day Nursery," p. 5; "Mushrooming Day Nurseries," n.d., but c. 1918, typewritten (Records of the Children's Bureau), p. 2; Helen Glenn Tyson, Foreword to *Mothers in Industry,* by Gwendolyn S. Hughes, p. xv.

70. Barbara Bartlett to Julia Lathrop, February 15, 1918 (Records of the Children's Bureau). *See also* Wright, *Children of Wage-Earning Mothers,* pp. 18–19.

71. Grace L. Meigs, "Memorandum for Julia Lathrop with Regard to Day Nurseries in Factories, Especially the Munitions Factories," April 4, 1918, typewritten (Records of the Children's Bureau), no pagination; Geister, "The Industrial Day Nursery," p. 11.

72. Geister, "The Industrial Day Nursery," p. 9.

73. "Mushrooming Day Nurseries," p. 1.

74. Barbara Bartlett, "Mary Crane Day Nursery: Interview with Miss Myrna Brockett and Mrs. Gillum," January 4, 1918, typewritten (Records of the Children's Bureau), no pagination.

75. Ibid.; Barbara Bartlett, "Interview with Miss Ellen L. Foley, Superintendent of Visiting Nurses Association, Chicago, Illinois," November 28, 1917, typewritten (Records of the Children's Bureau), p. 2.

76. Ibid., p. 1.

77. Barbara Bartlett, "Interview with Miss Brocket and Mrs. Gillum at the Mary Crane Day Nursery," November 30, 1917, typewritten (Records of the Children's Bureau), p. 2.

78. Helen McKee Brenton, *A Study of Day Nurseries, Made for the Chicago Association of Day Nurseries* (Chicago: n. pub., 1918), pp. 48–49.

79. Helen Glenn Tyson, foreword to *Mothers in Industry,* by Gwendolyn S. Hughes, p. xv.

80. New York, Commission on Relief of Widowed Mothers, *Report of the New York State Commission on Relief of Widowed Mothers* (Albany, 1914), p. 46.

81. Woods, *The City Wilderness,* p. 253.

82. Helen Brenton to Julia Lathrop, Sept. 16, 1917 (Records of the Children's Bureau), p. 3.

83. Woods, *The City Wilderness,* p. 252.

84. Anthony, *Mothers Who Must Earn,* p. 152.

85. Long, *Labor Force,* p. 297.

86. Anthony, *Mothers Who Must Earn,* p. 24.

87. Hughes, *Mothers in Industry,* p. 75, 87–88.

88. Manning, *Immigrant Woman and Her Job*, p. 23.

89. Massachusetts, House, *Report of the Commission on the Support of Dependent Children of Widowed Mothers*, p. 146; Elizabeth L. Hall, *Mothers' Assistance in Philadelphia: Actual and Potential Costs: A Study of 1010 Families* (Hanover, N.H., Minneapolis, and Liverpool: The Sociological Press, 1933), p. 16.

90. More, *Wage-Earners' Budgets*, pp. 42–43, 144–145; Chapin, *The Standard of Living Among Workingmen's Families*, p. 191; Massachusetts, House, *Report of the Commission on the Support of Dependent Minor Children of Widowed Mothers*, p. 147; Mary E. Richmond and Fred S. Hall, *A Study of Nine Hundred and Eighty-Five Widows Known to Certain Charity Organization Societies in 1910* (New York: Russell Sage Foundation, Charity Organization Department, 1913), p. 16; Anthony, *Mothers Who Must Earn*, p. 139; New York, *Report of the New York State Commission on Relief for Widowed Mothers*, pp. 22–24; True, *The Neglected Girl*, pp. 128–129; Odencrantz, *Italian Women*, pp. 200–201; Little and Cotton, "Budgets of Families," p. 138; Hall, *Mothers' Assistance in Philadelphia*, pp. 16, 25.

91. Mary Kenney O'Sullivan, manuscript autobiography, n.d., typewritten (Schlesinger Library, Radcliffe College), p. 194.

92. Anthony, *Mothers Who Must Earn*, pp. 27–28.

93. Lubove, *The Struggle for Social Security*, pp. 53–54, 57–59.

94. Helen Glenn Tyson, foreword to *Mothers in Industry*, by Gwendolyn S. Hughes, p. xiv.

95. Hall, *Mothers' Assistance in Philadelphia*, p. 89.

96. Massachusetts, House, *Report of the Commission on the Support of Dependent Minor Children of Widowed Mothers*, p. 147; Richmond and Hall, *A Study of Nine Hundred and Eighty-Five Widows*, p. 20.

97. Alice L. Higgins and Florence Windon, "Helping Widows to Bring Up Citizens," in *Proceedings of the National Conference of Charities and Correction* (1910), quoted in Richmond and Hall, *A Study of Nine Hundred and Eighty-Five Widows*, p. 20.

98. Massachusetts, House, *Report of the Commission on the Support of Dependent Minor Children of Widowed Mothers*, p. 154.

99. New York, *Report of the New York State Commission on Relief for Widowed Mothers*, pp. 50, 126.

100. Massachusetts, House, *Report of the Commission on the Support of Dependent Minor Children of Widowed Mothers*, p. 148; Richmond and Hall, *A Study of Nine Hundred and Eighty-Five Widows*, p. 22; New York, *Report of the New York State Commission on Relief for Widowed*

Mothers, pp. 136–139; Hall, *Mothers' Assistance in Philadelphia*, p. 32.

101. Anthony, *Mothers Who Must Earn*, pp. 124–125.

102. Smith, "A Study of Fifty Working Mothers," pp. 6–7, 11.

103. New York, *Report of the New York State Commission on Relief for Widowed Mothers*, p. 35.

104. Manning, *Immigrant Woman and Her Job*, p. 57.

105. Hall, *Mothers' Assistance in Philadelphia*, p. 32.

106. Ibid., p. 33.

107. U.S., Congress, Senate, *Report on Condition of Woman and Child Wage-Earners*, Vol. 2, p. 377; ibid., Vol. 5, pp. 56–57.

108. U.S., Congress, Senate, *Report on Condition of Woman and Child Wage-Earners*, Vol. 5, p. 57.

109. New York, *Report of the New York State Commission on Relief for Widowed Mothers*, p. 58.

110. Anthony, *Mothers Who Must Earn*, p. 153; Consumers' League of New York, *Behind the Scenes in a Hotel*, p. 36.

111. New York, *Report of the New York State Commission on Relief for Widowed Mothers*, pp. 56, 64.

112. Ibid., p. 57.

113. Massachusetts, House, *Report of the Commission on the Support of Widowed Mothers*, p. 66.

114. Ibid., p. 51; New York, *Report of the New York State Commission on Relief for Widowed Mothers*, p. 59.

115. Hall, *Mothers' Assistance in Philadelphia*, p. 36.

116. Anthony, *Mothers Who Must Earn*, p. 153.

117. Addams, *Democracy and Social Ethics*, pp. 200–201; Herzfeld, *Family Monographs*, pp. 50–51, 70–71, 114–115; Eastman, "The Temper of the Workers Under Trial," p. 566; Woods and Kennedy, *Young Working Girls*, pp. 49–50; Anthony, *Mothers Who Must Earn*, pp. 20–21, 156–157; New York, *Fourth Report of the Factory Investigating Commission*, Vol. 4, pp. 1579, 1667; Odencrantz, *Italian Women*, p. 204.

118. More, *Wage-Earners' Budgets*, p. 138.

119. Kazin, *Walker in the City*, p. 68.

120. See, for example, Ware, *Greenwich Village*, p. 409.

121. Herzfeld, *Family Monographs*, p. 50; More, *Wage-Earners' Budgets*, p. 136; Byington, *Homestead*, p. 108; Frank Hatch Streightoff, *The Standard of Living Among the Industrial People of America* (Boston and New York: Houghton Mifflin Company, 1911), p. 140; Woods and Kennedy, *Young Working Girls*, p. 55. Odencrantz, *Italian Women*, p. 163; Little and Cotton, "Budgets of Families," pp. 28, 100.

122. Massachusetts, *Report of the Commission on Industrial and Technical Education*, pp. 91–92; Byington, *Homestead*, p. 60.
123. Herzfeld, *Family Monographs*, p. 51; Woods and Kennedy, *Young Working Girls*, pp. 44–45.
124. Thomas Jesse Jones, *The Sociology of a New York City Block*, Columbia University Studies in History, Economic and Public Law (New York: Columbia University Press, 1904), p. 115; Hughes, *Mothers in Industry*, p. 99.

CONCLUSION

1. Mirra Komarovsky, *Blue Collar Marriage* (New York: Vintage Books, 1967), pp. 65–67.
2. For a summary of recent studies, *see* Rubin, *Worlds of Pain*, pp. 228–229, nn. 6–11.
3. Teresa Levitan, Robert F. Quinn, and Graham P. Staines, "Sex Discrimination Against the American Working Woman," Survey Research Center, Center for Research on the Utilization of Scientific Knowledge, University of Michigan, mimeographed (Ann Arbor, 1970), p. 23.

Bibliography

MANUSCRIPT SOURCES

Cambridge, Mass. Schlesinger Library. Radcliffe College. Consumers' League of Massachusetts Papers.

———. Schlesinger Library. Radcliffe College. Ethel M. Johnson Papers.

———. Schlesinger Library. Radcliffe College. Maud Nathan Papers.

———. Schlesinger Library. Radcliffe College. National Women's Trade Union League Collection.

———. Schlesinger Library. Radcliffe College. Leonora O'Reilly Papers.

———. Schlesinger Library. Radcliffe College. Mary Kenney O'Sullivan Manuscript Autobiography.

———. Schlesinger Library. Radcliffe College. Hilda Smith Papers.

Chicago, Ill. Chicago Circle Campus Library. University of Illinois, Chicago Circle Campus. Chicago Women's Trade Union League Collection.

———. Chicago Circle Campus Library. University of Illinois, Chicago Circle Campus. Juvenile Protective League of Chicago Papers.

———. Chicago Historical Society. Mary McDowell Papers.

———. Chicago Historical Society. Agnes Nestor Papers.

Northampton, Mass. Smith College Library. Smith College. Sophia Smith Collection. Mary Van Kleeck Papers.

Washington, D.C. National Archives. Record Group 102. Records of Children's Bureau.

———. National Archives. Record Group 86. Records of Women's Bureau.

PUBLISHED SOURCES

Abbott, Edith, and Breckenridge, Sophonisba P. *Truancy and Non-Attendance in the Chicago Schools.* Chicago: University of Chicago Press, 1917.

―――. "Women in Industry: The Chicago Stockyards." *Journal of Political Economy*, XIX (October 1911), pp. 632–654.

―――. "Chicago's Housing Problem: Families in Furnished Rooms." *American Journal of Sociology*, XVI (November 1910), pp. 289–308.

Academy of Political Science, Columbia University. *Proceedings of the Academy of Political Science in the City of New York: The Economic Position of Women*. New York: Columbia University, 1910.

Addams, Jane. *Democracy and Social Ethics*. New York: Macmillan Company, 1902.

―――. *The Spirit of Youth and the City Streets*. New York: Macmillan Company, 1909.

Allinson, May. *Dressmaking as a Trade for Women in Massachusetts*. Women in Industry Series No. 9. U.S., Department of Labor, Bureau of Labor Statistics. Bulletin of the Bureau of Labor Statistics No. 193 Washington, D.C.: Government Printing Office, 1916.
(Note: In those few cases where textual clarity requires prominent identification of the authors of government documents, I have listed author rather than sponsoring agency first both in footnotes and bibliography.)

Anderson, Mary, with Winslow, Mary N. *Woman at Work: The Autobiography of Mary Anderson*. Minneapolis: University of Minnesota Press, 1951.

Anthony, Katherine. *Mothers Who Must Earn*. New York: Russell Sage Foundation, Survey Research Associates, 1914.

Armstrong Association of Philadelphia. *A Comparative Study of the Occupations and Wages of the Children of Working Age in the Potter and Durham Schools*. Philadelphia: The Armstrong Association, 1913.

Atherton, Sarah. *Survey of Wage-Earning Girls Below Sixteen Years of Age in Wilkes-Barre, Pennsylvania*. National Consumers' League, Women in Industry Series No. 11. New York: National Consumers' League, 1915.

Auten, Nellie Mason. "Some Phases of the Sweating System in the Garment Trades of Chicago." *American Journal of Sociology*, VI (March 1901), pp. 602–645.

Baker, Elizabeth Faulkner, *Technology and Woman's Work*. New York and London: Columbia University Press, 1964.

Balch, Emily. *Our Slavic Fellow Citizens*. New York: Charities Publications Committee, 1910.

Bergmann, Barbara, and Adelson, Irma. "The 1973 Report of the President's Council of Economic Advisors: The Economic Role of Women." *American Economic Review*, LXIII (Sept. 1973), pp. 509–514.

Bosworth, Louise Marion. "The Living Wage of Women Workers: A Study of Incomes and Expenditures of Four Hundred and Fifty Women Workers in the City of Boston." *Supplement to The Annals of the American Academy of Political and Social Science,* XXXVII (Philadelphia: The American Academy of Political and Social Science, May, 1911), pp. 1–90.

Bowen, Louise DeKoven. *The Department Store Girl: Based Upon Interviews with Two Hundred Girls.* Chicago: Juvenile Protective League of Chicago, 1911.

————. *The Girl Employed in Hotels and Restaurants.* Chicago: Juvenile Protective League of Chicago, 1912.

————. *Our Most Popular Recreation Controlled by the Liquor Interests: A Study of Public Dance Halls.* Chicago: Juvenile Protective League of Chicago, 1911.

————. *The Public Dance Halls of Chicago.* Chicago: Juvenile Protective League of Chicago, 1910.

Bowman, Leroy E., and Lambin, Maria Ward. "Evidence of Social Relations as Seen in Types of New York City Dance Halls." *Journal of Social Forces,* III (January 1925), pp. 286–291.

Brandeis, Louis D., and Goldmark, Josephine. *Women in Industry: Decision of the United States Supreme Court in Curt Muller vs. State of Oregon Upholding the Constitutionality of the Oregon Ten-Hour Law for Women, and Brief for the State of Oregon.* New York: National Consumers' League, n.d.

Breckinridge, Sophonisba P. "The Home Responsibilities of Women Workers and the 'Equal Wage.' " *Journal of Political Economy,* XXXI (August 1923), pp. 521–543.

————. "Neglected Widowhood in the Juvenile Court." *American Journal of Sociology,* XVI (July 1910), pp. 53–87.

————. "Political Equality for Women and Women's Wages." *The Annals of the American Academy of Political and Social Science,* LVI (November 1914), pp. 122–123.

Bremner, Robert. *From the Depths: The Discovery of Poverty in the United States.* New York: New York University Press, 1956.

Brenton, Helen McKee. *A Study of Day Nurseries, Made for the Chicago Association of Day Nurseries.* Chicago: n. pub., 1918.

Bryner, Edna. *The Garment Trades.* Cleveland Education Survey. Cleveland: Cleveland Foundation, Survey Committee, 1916.

Bullock, Edna D. *Selected Articles on the Employment of Women.* New York: H. Wilson Company, 1920.

Bureau of Municipal Research of Philadelphia. *Workingmen's Standard of Living in Philadelphia*. New York: Macmillan Company, 1919.

Bureau of Social Hygiene. *Housing Conditions of Employed Women in the Borough of Manhattan*. New York: n. pub., 1922.

Bushnell, Charles J. "Some Social Aspects of the Chicago Stock Yards: The Stock Yard Community at Chicago." *American Journal of Sociology, VII (November 1901), pp. 289–330.*

———. "Some Social Aspects of the Chicago Stock Yards: The Relation of the Chicago Stock Yards to the Local Community." *American Journal of Sociology,* VII (January 1902), pp. 433–474.

Butler, Elizabeth Beardsley. *Saleswomen in Mercantile Stores: Baltimore, 1909*. New York: Russell Sage Foundation, Charities Publication Committee, 1912.

———. "The Stogy Industry in Pittsburgh." *The Survey,* XX (July 4, 1908), pp. 433–449.

———. *Women and the Trades: Pittsburgh, 1907–1908*. The Pittsburgh Survey, edited by Paul Underwood Kellogg, Vol. 1. New York: Russell Sage Foundation, Charities Publication Committee, 1909.

———. "Work of Women in the Mercantile Houses of Pittsburgh." *The Annals of the American Academy of Political and Social Science,* XXXIII (March 1909), pp. 102–113.

Byington, Margaret F. "The Family in a Typical Mill Town." *American Journal of Sociology,* XIV (March 1909), pp. 648–659.

———. *Homestead: The Households of a Mill Town*. The Pittsburgh Survey, edited by Paul Underwood Kellogg, Vol. 4. New York: Russell Sage Foundation, Charities Publication Committee, 1910.

Chapin, Robert Coit. "The Influence of Income on Standards of Life." *American Journal of Sociology,* XIV (March 1909), pp. 638–647.

———. *The Standard of Living Among Workingmen's Families in New York City*. New York: Russell Sage Foundation, Charities Publication Committee, 1909.

Chicago School of Civics and Philanthropy, Department of Social Investigation. *The Child in the City: A Series of Papers Presented at the Conference Held During the Chicago Child Welfare Exhibit*. Chicago: Hollister Press, 1912.

———. *Finding Employment for Children Who Leave the Grade Schools to Go to Work: Report to the Chicago Women's Club, the Chicago Association of Collegiate Alumnae, and the Woman's City Club*. Chicago: n. pub., 1911.

Clark, Sue Ainslie, and Wyatt, Edith. *Making Both Ends Meet: The Income and Outlay of New York Working Girls.* New York: Macmillan Company, 1911.

Cohen, Miriam. "Italian-American Women in New York City, 1900–1950: Work and School." From *Class, Sex, and the Woman Worker,* edited by Milton Cantor and Bruce Laurie. Contributions in Labor History, No. 1, Westport, Conn.: Greenwood Press, 1977, pp. 120–143.

Commission on Household Employment. *Report of the Commission on Household Employment to the Fifth National Convention of the Young Women's Christian Associations of the United States, May 5–11, 1915, Los Angeles:* n. pub., n. d.

Commons, John R. et al, eds. *History of Labor in the United States, 1896–1932,* Vol. 3. New York: The Macmillan Company, 1935.

Commons, John R. "Labor Conditions in Meat Packing and the Recent Strike." *Quarterly Journal of Economics,* XIX (November 1904), pp. 1–32.

"Conditions in Triangle Shop." *The Survey,* XXVI (April 8, 1911), pp. 85–86.

Connecticut, Bureau of Labor Statistics. *Report of the Bureau of Labor on the Conditions of Wage-Earning Women and Girls.* Charlotte Molyneux Holloway, industrial investigator. Hartford, Conn., 1914.

Consumers' League of Eastern Pennsylvania. *Occupations for Girls: Paper Box Making.* Philadelphia: n. pub., 1913.

Consumers' League of New York. *Behind the Scenes in Candy Factories.* Lillian Symes, investigator. New York: Consumers' League of New York, 1928.

―――. *Behind the Scenes in a Hotel.* New York: n. pub., 1922.

―――. *The Forty-Eight Hour Law: Do Working Women Want It?* New York: Consumers' League of New York, 1927.

Consumers' League of New York City. *Behind the Scenes in a Restaurant: A Study of 1017 Women Restaurant Employees.* New York: n. pub., 1916.

Dinwiddie, Emily W. *Housing Conditions in Philadelphia.* Philadelphia: Octavia Hill Association, 1904.

Donovan, Frances R. *The Saleslady.* Chicago: University of Chicago Press, 1929.

―――. *The Woman Who Waits.* Boston: Richard G. Badger, The Gorham Press, 1920.

Douglas, Dorothy W. "The Cost of Living for Working Women: A Criticism of Current Theories." *Quarterly Journal of Economics,* XXXIV (February 1920), pp. 225–259.

Eastman, Crystal. "The Temper of the Workers under Trial." *Charities and the Commons*, XXI (January 2, 1909), pp. 561–569.

Filene, Edward A. "The Betterment of the Conditions of Working Women." *The Annals of the American Academy of Political and Social Science*, XXVII (June 1906), pp. 151–161.

Fretz, Franklin Kline. "The Furnished Room Problem in Philadelphia." Ph.D. dissertation, University of Pennsylvania, 1912.

Gans, Herbert J. *The Urban Villagers: Group and Class in the Life of Italian-Americans*. New York: Free Press, 1962.

Gillette, John M. "The Culture Agencies of a Typical Manufacturing Group: South Chicago." *American Journal of Sociology*, VII (September 1901), pp. 185–215.

Goldmark, Josephine C. "The Necessary Sequel of Child Labor Laws." *American Journal of Sociology*, XI (November 1905), pp. 312–325.

Gross, Edward. "Plus Ça Change . . .? The Sexual Structure of Occupations over Time." *Social Problems*, XVI (Fall 1968), pp. 198–208.

Hall, Elizabeth L. *Mothers' Assistance in Philadelphia: Actual and Potential Costs: A Study of 1010 Families*. Hanover, N.H., Minneapolis, and Liverpool: The Sociological Press, 1933.

Hapgood, Hutchins. *Types from City Streets*. New York and London: Funk and Wagnalls Company, 1910.

Hasanovitz, Elizabeth. *One of Them: Chapters from a Passionate Autobiography*. Boston and New York: Houghton Mifflin Company, 1918.

Hatcher, O. Latham. *Rural Girls in the City for Work: A Study Made for the Southern Woman's Educational Alliance*. Richmond, Va.: Garrett and Massie, 1930.

Hedges, Anna Charlotte. *Wage Worth of School Training: An Analytical Study of Six Hundred Women Workers in Textile Factories*. Teachers College, Columbia University, Contributions to Education No. 71. New York: Teachers College, Columbia University, 1915.

Henry, Alice. *Memoirs of Alice Henry*. Edited by Nettie Palmer. Melbourne: n. pub., 1944.

———. *The Trade Union Woman*. New York and London: D. Appleton and Company, 1915.

———. *Women and the Labor Movement*. New York: George H. Doran Company, 1923.

Herron, Belva Mary. *The Progress of Labor Organizations Among Women, Together with Some Considerations Concerning Their Place in Industry*. The University Studies, Vol. 1. Urbana, Ill.: University of Illinois Press, 1905.

Herzfeld, Elsa G. *Family Monographs: The History of Twenty-Four Families Living in the Middle-West Side of New York City*. New York: James Kempster Printing Company, 1905.

Hewes, Amy. *Women as Munition Workers: A Study of Conditions in Bridgeport, Connecticut*. New York: Russell Sage Foundation, 1917.

Hodgen, Margaret. *Factory Work for Girls*. New York: The Woman's Press, 1920.

Hoerle, Helen Christine, and Saltzberg, Florence B. *The Girl and the Job*. New York: Henry Holt and Company, 1919.

Hooks, Janet M. *Women's Occupations Through Seven Decades*. U.S., Department of Labor, Women's Bureau. Bulletin of the Women's Bureau No. 218. Washington, D.C.: Government Printing Office, 1947.

Houghteling, Leila. *The Income and Standard of Living of Unskilled Laborers in Chicago*. Chicago: University of Chicago Press, 1927.

Hourwich, Andria Taylor, and Palmer, Gladys L., eds. *I am a Woman Worker: A Scrapbook of Autobiographies*. New York: The Affiliated Schools for Workers, 1936.

Howe, Jane Sheldrick. *All Work and No Play: A Plea for Saturday Afternoon: Stories Told by Two Hundred Department Store Girls*. Chicago: Juvenile Protective Association of Chicago, 1910.

Howe, Louise Kapp. *Pink Collar Workers: Inside the World of Women's Work*. New York: G. P. Putnam's Sons, 1977.

Hughes, Gwendolyn Salisbury. *Mothers in Industry: Wage-Earning by Mothers in Philadelphia*. New York: New Republic, 1925.

Hutchinson, Emilie Josephine. "Women's Wages: A Study of the Wages of Industrial Women and Measures Suggested to Increase Them." Ph.D. dissertation, Columbia University, 1919.

Hutchinson, Woods, M.D. "The Hygienic Aspects of the Shirtwaist Strike." *The Survey*, XXIII (Jan. 22, 1910), pp. 541–550.

Illinois, Bureau of Labor Statistics. *Fourteenth Biennial Report of the Bureau of Labor Statistics of the State of Illinois*. Part II: *Working Women in Factories*. Springfield, 1908.

——. *Fifteenth Biennial Report of the Bureau of Labor Statistics of the State of Illinois*. Part III: *Women Employed in Department Stores*. Springfield, 1910.

Illinois, Industrial Survey. *Hours and Health of Women Workers: Report of the Illinois Industrial Survey, Dec., 1918*. Springfield, 1919.

Illinois, Senate. *Report of the Senate Vice Committee, Created Under the Authority of the Senate of the 49th General Assembly*. N. pub., 1916.

Irwin, Elizabeth A. *Truancy: A Study of the Mental, Physical, and Social Fac-*

tors of the Problem of Non-Attendance at School. New York: n. pub., 1915.

Israels, Belle Lindner. "The Way of the Girl." *The Survey,* XXII (July 3, 1909), pp. 486–497.

Jones, Thomas Jesse. *The Sociology of a New York City Block.* Columbia University Studies in History, Economics, and Public Law. New York: Columbia University Press, 1904.

Kazin, Alfred, *A Walker in the City.* New York: Harcourt, Brace and World, 1951.

Kelley, Florence. "Wage-Earning Women in War-Time: The Textile Industry." Reprinted from *The Journal of Industrial Hygiene,* October 1919. National Consumers' League, n.d.

Kellogg, Paul Underwood, ed. *Wage-Earning Pittsburgh.* The Pittsburgh Survey, edited by Paul Underwood Kellogg, Vol. 6. New York: Russell Sage Foundation, Survey Associates, 1911.

Kennedy, J. C. *Wages and Family Budgets in the Chicago Stockyards District, with Wage Statistics from Other Industries Employing Unskilled Labor.* A Study of Chicago's Stockyards Community, Vol. 3. Chicago: University of Chicago Press, 1914.

Kessler-Harris, Alice. "Organizing the Unorganizable: Three Jewish Women and Their Union." *Labor History,* XVII (Winter 1976), pp. 5–23.

Kingsbury, Susan M. "Relation of Women to Industry." *Papers and Proceedings of the American Sociological Society, Fifteenth Annual Meeting, Dec. 27–29, 1920.* Chicago: University of Chicago Press, 1921.

Komarovsky, Mirra. *Blue-Collar Marriage.* New York: Vintage Books, 1967.

Lauck. W. Jett, and Sydenstricker, Edgar. *Conditions of Labor in American Industries: A Summarization of the Results of Recent Investigations.* New York and London: Funk and Wagnalls Company, 1917.

Laughlin, Clara E. *The Work-a-Day Girl: A Study of Some Present-Day Conditions.* New York: Fleming H. Revell, 1913.

Leupp. Constance D. "Shirtwaist Makers' Strike." *The Survey,* XXIII (Dec. 18, 1909), pp. 383–386.

Levitan, Teresa; Quinn, Robert F.; and Staines, Graham P. "Sex Discrimination Against the American Working Woman." Survey Research Center, Center for Research on the Utilization of Scientific Knowledge, University of Michigan. Ann Arbor, 1970. Mimeographed.

Little, Esther Louise, and Cotton, William Joseph Henry. "Budgets of Families and Individuals of Kensington, Philadelphia." Ph.D. dissertation, University of Pennsylvania, 1920.

Lobsenz, Johanna. *The Older Woman in Industry*. New York: Charles Scribner's Sons, 1929.

Long, Clarence D. *The Labor Force under Changing Income and Employment*. Princeton: Princeton University Press, 1958.

Lubove, Roy. *The Struggle for Social Security, 1900–1935*. Cambridge: Harvard University Press, 1968.

Lutz, R. R. *Wage-Earning and Education*. Cleveland Education Survey. Cleveland: Cleveland Foundation, Survey Committee, 1916.

McDowell, Mary E. "Mothers and Night Work." *The Survey*, XXXIX (December 22, 1917), pp. 335–336.

MacLean, Annie Marion. "The Sweat-Shop in Summer." *American Journal of Sociology*, IX (November 1903), pp. 289–309.

———. *Wage-Earning Women*. New York: Macmillan Company, 1910.

———. *Women Workers and Society*. Chicago: A. C. McClurg Company, 1916.

Manning, Caroline. *The Immigrant Woman and Her Job*. U.S., Department of Labor, Women's Bureau. Bulletin of the Women's Bureau No. 74. Washington, D.C.: Government Printing Office, 1930.

Massachusetts, Commission on Industrial and Technical Education. *Report of the Commission on Industrial and Technical Education*. Columbia University, Teachers College, Educational Reprints No. 1. New York: Teachers College, Columbia University, 1906.

Massachusetts, Commission on Minimum Wage Boards. *Report of the Commission on Minimum Wage Boards*. Boston, 1912.

Massachusetts, Department of Labor and Industries, Division of Minimum Wage. *Wages of Women in the Brush Factories in Massachusetts*. Bulletin of the Minimum Wage Division No. 1. Boston, 1914.

———. *Statement and Decree Concerning the Wages of Women in the Brush Industry in Massachusetts*. Bulletin of the Minimum Wage Division No. 3. Boston, 1914.

———. *Wages of Women in the Candy Factories in Massachusetts*. Bulletin of the Minimum Wage Division No. 4. Boston, 1914.

———. *Wages of Women in the Laundries in Massachusetts*. Bulletin of the Minimum Wage Division No. 5. Boston, 1914.

———. *Wages of Women in Retail Stores in Massachusetts*. Bulletin of the Minimum Wage Division No. 6. Boston, 1914.

———. *Wages of Women in the Paper-Box Factories in Massachusetts*. Bulletin of the Minimum Wage Division No. 8. Boston, 1915.

———. *Wages of Women in Women's Clothing Factories in Massachusetts*. Bulletin of the Minimum Wage Division No. 9. Boston, 1915.

———. *Wages of Women in Hosiery and Knit Goods Factories in Massachusetts.* Bulletin of the Minimum Wage Division No. 10. Boston, 1916.

———. *Report of the Minimum Wage Commission, 1915: Commissioners' Report and Appendices of the Third Annual Report.* Bulletin of the Minimum Wage Division No. 11. Boston, 1916.

———. *Wages of Women in Men's Clothing and Raincoat Factories in Massachusetts.* Bulletin of the Minimum Wage Division No. 13. Boston, 1916.

———. *Wages of Women in Muslin Underwear, Petticoat, Apron, Kimono, Women's Neckwear, and Children's Clothing Factories in Massachusetts.* Bulletin of the Minimum Wage Division No. 14. Boston, 1917.

———. *Wages of Women in Shirt, Workingmen's Garment and Furnishing Goods Factories in Massachusetts.* Bulletin of the Minimum Wage Division No. 15. Boston, 1917.

———. *Wages of Women Employed as Office and Other Building Cleaners in Massachusetts.* Bulletin of the Minimum Wage Division No. 16. Boston, 1918.

———. *Wages of Women in Hotels and Restaurants in Massachusetts.* Bulletin of the Minimum Wage Division No. 17. Boston, 1918.

———. *Supplementary Report on the Wages of Women in Candy Factories in Massachusetts.* Bulletin of the Minimum Wage Division No. 18. Boston, 1919.

———. *Report on the Wages of Women in the Millinery Industry in Massachusetts.* Bulletin of the Minimum Wage Division No. 20. Boston, 1919.

———. *Second Report on the Wages of Women Employed in Paper Box Factories in Massachusetts.* Bulletin of the Minimum Wage Division No. 22. Boston, 1920.

———. *Report on the Wages of Women Employed in the Manufacture of Food Preparations and Minor Lines of Confectionery in Massachusetts.* Bulletin of the Minimum Wage Division No. 23. Boston, 1920.

Massachusetts, House. *Report of the Commission on the Support of Dependent Minor Children of Widowed Mothers.* H. Doc. 2075. Boston, 1913.

———. *Report of the Special Committee Appointed by the House of Representatives of 1913 to Investigate the Conditions under which Women and Children Labor in the Various Industries and Occupations.* H. Doc. 2126. Boston, 1914.

Massachusetts, Senate. Committee on Labor and Industry. *Report of Hearing Before the Committee on Labor and Industry of the Massachusetts Legislature, re Senate Bill 149 and Senate Bill 191.* Boston: Associated Industries of Massachusetts, 1928.

Massachusetts, State Board of Labor and Industries. *Licensed Workers in Industrial Home Work in Massachusetts,* by Susan M. Kingsbury and Mabelle Moses. Industrial Bulletin No. 4. Boston, 1915.

Mitchell, John. *The Wage Earner and His Problems.* Washington, D.C.: P. S. Risdale, 1913.

Monroe, Day. *Chicago Families: A Study of Unpublished Census Data.* Chicago: University of Chicago Press, 1932.

Montgomery, Louise. *The American Girl in the Stockyards District.* A Study of Chicago's Stockyards Community, Vol. 2. Chicago: University of Chicago Press, 1913.

More, Louise Bolard. *Wage-Earners' Budgets: A Study of Standards and Cost of Living in New York City.* New York: Henry Holt and Company, 1907.

National Civic Federation, New England Section. *Report on Unemployment Among Boston Women in 1915,* by Eleanor H. Woods: n. pub., n.d.

National Consumers' League and the Consumers' League of New Jersey. *Night-Working Mothers in Textile Mills, Passaic, New Jersey,* by Agnes de Lima: n. pub., 1920.

National Industrial Conference Board. *Cost of Living in New York City.* New York: National Industrial Conference Board, 1926.

——. *The Cost of Living in Twelve Industrial Cities.* New York: National Industrial Conference Board, 1928.

——. *The Cost of Living in the United States, 1914–1930.* National Industrial Conference Board, 1931.

——. *The Economic Status of the Wage Earner in New York and Other States.* New York: National Industrial Conference Board, 1928.

Nestor, Agnes. *Woman's Labor Leader: An Autobiography of Agnes Nestor.* Rockford, Ill.: Bellevue Books Publishing Company, 1954.

New York, Commission on Relief for Widowed Mothers. *Report of the New York State Commission on Relief for Widowed Mothers.* Albany, 1914.

New York, Department of Labor. *A Study of Hygienic Conditions in Steam Laundries and their Effect upon the Health of Workers.* Department of Labor Special Bulletin No. 130. Albany, 1924.

——. *Employment and Earnings of Men and Women in New York Factories.* Department of Labor Special Bulletin No. 145. Albany, 1926.

New York, Department of Labor, Bureau of Women in Industry. *Hours and*

Earnings of Women in Five Industries. Department of Labor Special Bulletin No. 121. Albany, 1923.

———. *The Health of the Working Child.* Department of Labor Special Bulletin No. 134. Albany, 1924.

———. *Wages and Hours of Work of Organized Women in New York State.* Department of Labor Special Bulletin No. 136. Albany, 1925.

———. *Homework in the Men's Clothing Industry in New York and Rochester.* Department of Labor Special Bulletin No. 147. Albany, 1926.

———. *Chronic Benzol Poisoning Among Women Industrial Workers.* Department of Labor Special Bulletin No. 150. Albany, 1927.

———. *Hours and Earnings of Women Employed in Power Laundries in New York State.* Department of Labor Special Bulletin No. 153. Albany, 1927.

———. *The Paper Box Industry in New York City.* Department of Labor Special Bulletin No. 154. Albany, 1928.

———. *Some Social and Economic Aspects of Homework.* Department of Labor Special Bulletin No. 158. Albany, 1929.

New York, Department of Labor, Division of Women in Industry. *The Employment of Women in Five and Ten Cent Stores.* Department of Labor Special Bulletin No. 109. Albany, 1921.

———. *Women at Work.* Department of Labor Special Bulletin No. 110. Albany, 1922.

New York, Factory Investigating Commission. *Preliminary Report of the Factory Investigating Commission.* 3 vols. Albany, 1912.

———. *Second Report of the Factory Investigating Commission.* 2 vols. Albany, 1913.

———. *Third Report of the Factory Investigating Commission.* Albany, 1914.

———. *Fourth Report of the Factory Investigating Commission.* 5 vols. Albany, 1915.

Odencrantz, Louise C. "The Irregularity of Employment of Women Factory Workers." *The Survey*, XXII (May 1, 1909), pp. 196–210.

———. *Italian Women in Industry: A Study of Conditions in New York City.* New York: Russell Sage Foundation, 1919.

Oppenheimer, Valerie Kincade. *The Female Labor Force in the United States: Demographic and Economic Factors Governing its Growth and Changing Composition.* Population Monograph Studies No. 5. Berkeley: Institute of International Studies, University of California, Berkeley, 1970.

Ormsbee, Hazel Grant. *The Young Employed Girl*. New York: The Woman's Press, 1927.

Parker, Cornelia Stratton. *Working with the Working Woman*. New York and London: Harper and Brothers, 1922.

Pennsylvania, Department of Labor and Industry. *Industrial Home Work in Pennsylvania*, by Agnes Mary Hadden Byrnes. Department of Labor and Industry Special Bulletin No. 3. Harrisburg, 1921.

————. *Conference on Women in Industry: Dec. 8–9, 1925*. Department of Labor and Industry Special Bulletin No. 31. Harrisburg, 1930.

Pennsylvania, Department of Public Instruction. *Report of the Survey of the Public Schools of Philadelphia, Book II: Organization and Administration: Pupils*. Philadelphia: The Public Education and Child Labor Association of Pennsylvania, 1922.

Perry, Lorinda. *The Millinery Trade in Boston and Philadelphia: A Study of Women in Industry*. Binghamton, New York: The Vail-Ballou Company, 1916.

Persons, Charles E. "Women's Work and Wages in the United States." *Quarterly Journal of Economics*, XXIX (February 1915), pp. 201–234.

Powdermaker, Hortense. "From the Diary of a Girl Organizer." *The Amalgamated Illustrated Almanac*. Prepared by the Education Department of the Amalgamated Clothing Workers of America. New York, 1924.

Rainwater, Lee; Coleman, Richard P.; and Handel, Gerald. *Workingman's Wife: Her Personality, World, and Life Style*. New York: Oceana Publications, Inc., 1959.

Richardson, Dorothy. *The Long Day: The Story of a New York Working Girl as Told by Herself*. In *Women at Work*, edited by William O'Neill. Chicago: Quadrangle Books, 1972.

Richmond, Mary E., and Hall, Fred S. *A Study of Nine Hundred and Eighty-Five Widows Known to Certain Charity Organization Societies in 1910*. New York: Russell Sage Foundation, Charity Organization Department, 1913.

Rubin, Lillian Breslow. *Worlds of Pain: Life in the Working-Class Family*. New York: Basic Books, 1976.

Schneiderman, Rose. "A Cap Maker's Story." *The Independent*, LVIII (April 27, 1905), pp. 935–938.

Schneiderman, Rose, with Goldthwaite, Lucy. *All for One*. New York: Paul S. Erikson, 1967.

Smith, Hilda, ed. *The Workers Look at the Stars.* New York: Vineyard Shore Workers' School, 1927.

Smuts, Robert W. *Women and Work in America.* New York: Schocken Books, 1971.

Stearns, Peter N. *Lives of Labor: Work in a Maturing Industrial Society.* New York: Holmes and Meier Publishers, 1975.

Steinfels, Margaret O'Brien. *Who's Minding the Children? The History and Politics of Day Care in America.* New York: Simon and Schuster, 1973.

Strayer, George D. *Report of the Survey of the Schools of Chicago, Illinois,* Vol. V: *Summary of Findings and Recommendations.* New York: Bureau of Publications, Teachers College, Columbia University, 1932.

Streightoff, Frank Hatch. *The Standard of Living Among the Industrial People of America.* Boston and New York: Houghton Mifflin Company, 1911.

Talbert, Ernest L. *Opportunities in School and Industry for Children of the Stockyards District. A Study of Chicago's Stockyards Community,* Vol. 1. Chicago: University of Chicago Press, 1912.

Tanner, Amy E. "Glimpses at the Mind of a Waitress." *American Journal of Sociology,* XIII (July 1907), pp. 48–55.

Taussig, F. W. "Minimum Wages for Women." *Quarterly Journal of Economics,* XXX (May 1916), pp. 411–442.

Tobenkin, Elias. "The Immigrant Girl in Chicago." *The Survey,* XXIII (November 6, 1909), pp. 189–195.

True, Ruth S. *The Neglected Girl.* West Side Studies. New York: Russell Sage Foundation, Survey Associates, 1914.

U.S., Congress, House. *Conditions in the Chicago Stockyards,* by James B. Reynolds and Charles P. Neill. H. Doc. 873, 59th Cong., 1st sess. Washington, D.C.: Government Printing Office, 1906.

U.S., Congress, Senate. *Report on Condition of Woman and Child Wage-Earners in the United States,* Vol. 1: *Cotton Textile Industry.* S. Doc., 645. 61st Cong., 2nd sess. Washington, D.C.: Government Printing Office, 1910.

———. *Report on Condition of Woman and Child Wage-Earners in the United States,* Vol. 2: *Men's Ready-Made Clothing.* S. Doc. 645, 61st Cong., 2nd sess. Washington, D.C.: Government Printing Office, 1911.

———. *Report on Condition of Woman and Child Wage-Earners in the United States,* Vol. 5: *Wage-Earning Women in Stores and Factories.* S. Doc. 645, 61st Cong., 2nd sess. Washington, D.C.: Government Printing Office, 1910.

————. *Report on Condition of Woman and Child Wage-Earners in the United States,* Vol. 12: *Employment of Women in Laundries.* S. Doc. 645, 61st Cong., 2nd sess. Washington, D.C.: Government Printing Office, 1911.

————. *Report on Condition of Woman and Child Wage-Earners in the United States,* Vol. 18: *Employment of Women and Children in Selected Industries.* S. Doc. 645, 61st Cong., 2nd sess. Washington, D.C.: Government Printing Office, 1913.

————. *Reports of the Immigration Commission,* Vol. 14: *Children of Immigrants in Schools,* Vol. 2. S. Doc. 749, 61st Cong., 3rd sess. Washington, D.C.: Government Printing Office, 1911.

————. *Reports of the Immigration Commission,* Vol. 16: *Children of Immigrants in Schools,* Vol. 4. S. Doc. 749, 61st Cong., 3rd sess. Washington, D.C.: Government Printing Office, 1911.

————. *Reports of the Immigration Commission,* Vol. 19. *Immigrants in Industries,* Part 23: *Summary Report on Immigrants in Manufacturing and Mining,* Vol. 1. S. Doc. 633, 61st Cong., 2nd sess. Washington, D.C.: Government Printing Office, 1911.

————. *Reports of the Immigration Commission,* Vol. 26: *Immigrants in Cities,* Vol. 1. S. Doc. 338, 61st Cong., 2nd sess. Washington, D.C.: Government Printing Office, 1911.

U.S., Bureau of Labor. *Boarding Homes and Clubs for Working Women,* by Mary S. Fergusson. Bulletin of the U.S. Bureau of Labor No. 15. Washington, D.C.: Government Printing Office, 1898.

U.S., Department of Commerce, Bureau of the Census. *Fourteenth Census of the United States, 1920,* Vol. II: *Population: General Report and Analytical Tables.* Washington, D.C.: Government Printing Office, 1922.

————. *Fifteenth Census of the United States, 1930,* Vol. II: *Population: General Report: Statistics by Subjects.* Washington, D.C.: Government Printing Office, 1933.

————. *Women in Gainful Occupations, 1870–1920,* by Joseph Hill. Washington, D.C.: Government Printing Office, 1929.

U.S., Department of Labor, Bureau of Labor Statistics. *Employment of Women in Power Laundries in Milwaukee: A Study of Working Conditions and of the Physical Demands of the Various Laundry Occupations,* by Marie L. Obenauer. Women in Industry Series No. 3, Bulletin of the Bureau of Labor Statistics No. 122. Washington, D.C.: Government Printing Office, 1913.

————. *Summary of the Report on Conditions of Woman and Child Wage Earners in the United States.* Women in Industry Series No. 5, Bulletin of the Bureau of Labor Statistics No. 175. Washington, D.C.: Government Printing Office, 1915.

———. *Unemployment Among Women in Department and Other Retail Stores of Boston.* Women in Industry Series No. 8, Bulletin of the Bureau of Labor Statistics No. 182. Washington, D.C.: Government Printing Office, 1916.

———. *Industrial Experience of Trade-School Girls in Massachusetts.* Women in Industry Series No. 10, Bulletin of the Bureau of Labor Statistics No. 215. Washington, D.C.: Government Printing Office, 1917.

———. *Wages and Hours of Labor in the Slaughtering and Meatpacking Industry.* Bulletin of the Bureau of Labor Statistics No. 252. Washington, D.C.: Government Printing Office, 1919.

U.S., Department of Labor, Children's Bureau. *The Working Children of Boston: A Study of Child Labor Under a Modern System of Legal Regulation,* by Helen Sumner Woodbury. Children's Bureau Publication No. 89. Washington, D.C.: Government Printing Office, 1922.

———. *The Working Children of Newark and Patterson,* by Nettie P. McGill. Children's Bureau Publication No. 199. Washington, D.C.: Government Printing Office, 1931.

———. *Children of Working Mothers in Philadelphia,* Part 1, by Clara Mortenson Beyer. Children's Bureau Publication No. 204. Washington, D.C.: Government Printing Office, 1931.

U.S., Department of Labor, Woman in Industry Service. *Wages of Candy Makers in Philadelphia in 1919.* Bulletin of the Woman in Industry Service No. 4. Washington, D.C.: Government Printing Office, 1919.

U.S., Department of Labor, Women's Bureau. *The Employment of Women in Hazardous Industries in the United States: Summary of State and Federal Laws Regulating the Employment of Women in Hazardous Occupations: 1919.* Bulletin of the Women's Bureau No. 6. Washington, D.C.: Government Printing Office, 1921.

———. *Night-Work Laws in the United States: Summary of State Legislation Regulating Night Work for Women.* Bulletin of the Women's Bureau No. 7. Washington, D.C.: Government Printing Office, 1920.

———. *Women Street Car Conductors and Ticket Agents.* Bulletin of the Women's Bureau No. 11. Washington, D.C.: Government Printing Office, 1921.

———. *The New Position of Women in American Industry.* Bulletin of the Women's Bureau No. 12. Washington, D.C.: Government Printing Office, 1920.

————. *Industrial Opportunities and Training for Women and Girls.* Bulletin of the Women's Bureau No. 13. Washington, D.C.: Government Printing Office, 1920.

————. *A Physiological Basis for the Shorter Work Day for Women.* Bulletin of the Women's Bureau No. 14. Washington, D.C.: Government Printing Office, 1921.

————. *Some Effects of Legislation Limiting Hours of Work for Women.* Bulletin of the Women's Bureau No. 15. Washington, D.C.: Government Printing Office, 1921.

————. *State Laws Affecting Working Women.* Bulletin of the Women's Bureau No. 16. Washington, D.C.: Government Printing Office, 1921.

————. *Health Problems of Women in Industry.* Bulletin of the Women's Bureau No. 18. Washington, D.C.: Government Printing Office, 1921.

————. *Women in the Candy Industry in Chicago and St. Louis: A Study of Hours, Wages, and Working Conditions in 1920–1921,* by Mary V. Robinson. Bulletin of the Women's Bureau No. 25. Washington, D.C.: Government Printing Office, 1923.

————. *The Share of Wage-Earning Women in Family Support.* Bulletin of the Women's Bureau No. 30. Washington, D.C.: Government Printing Office, 1923.

————. *Domestic Workers and their Employment Relations: A Study Based on the Records of the Domestic Efficiency Association of Baltimore, Md.* Bulletin of the Women's Bureau No. 39. Washington, D.C.: Government Printing Office, 1925.

————. *Women in Ohio Industries: A Study of Hours and Wages.* Bulletin of the Women's Bureau No. 44. Washington, D.C.: Government Printing Office, 1925.

————. *Women Workers and Family Support: A Study Made by Students in the Economics Course at the Bryn Mawr Summer School.* Bulletin of the Women's Bureau No. 49. Washington, D.C.: Government Printing Office, 1925.

————. *Women in Illinois Industries: A Study of Hours and Working Conditions.* Bulletin of the Women's Bureau No. 51. Washington, D.C.: Government Printing Office, 1926.

————. *State Laws Affecting Working Women: Hours, Minimum Wage, Home Work.* Bulletin of the Women's Bureau No. 63. Washington, D.C.: Government Printing Office, 1927.

————. *The Employment of Women at Night,* by Mary D. Hopkins. Bulletin of the Women's Bureau No. 64. Washington, D.C.: Government Printing Office, 1928.

————. *Woman Workers in Flint, Michigan.* Bulletin of the Women's Bureau No. 67. Washington, D.C.: Government Printing Office, 1929.

————. *What the Wage-Earning Woman Contributes to Family Support,* by Agnes L. Peterson. Bulletin of the Women's Bureau No. 75. Washington, D.C.: Government Printing Office, 1929.

————. *Women in Five and Ten-Cent Stores and Limited-Price Chain Department Stores,* by Mary Elizabeth Pidgeon. Bulletin of the Women's Bureau No. 76. Washington, D.C.: Government Printing Office, 1930.

————. *A Survey of Laundries and their Woman Workers in Twenty-Three Cities,* by Ethel L. Best and Ethel Erickson. Bulletin of the Women's Bureau No. 78. Washington, D.C.: Government Printing Office, 1930.

————. *Industrial Home Work,* by Emily C. Brown. Bulletin of the Women's Bureau No. 79. Washington, D.C.: Government Printing Office, 1930.

————. *The Employment of Women in Slaughtering and Meatpacking,* by Mary Elizabeth Pidgeon. Bulletin of the Women's Bureau No. 88. Washington, D.C.: Government Printing Office, 1932.

————. *The Industrial Experience of Women Workers at the Summer Schools, 1928–1930,* by Gladys L. Palmer. Bulletin of the Women's Bureau No. 89. Washington, D.C.: Government Printing Office, 1931.

————. *Household Employment in Philadelphia,* by Amey E. Watson. Bulletin of the Women's Bureau No. 93. Washington, D.C.: Government Printing Office, 1932.

————. *The Effects on Women of Changing Conditions in the Cigar and Cigarette Industry,* by Caroline Manning and Harriet A. Byrne. Bulletin of the Women's Bureau No. 100. Washington, D.C.: Government Printing Office, 1932.

U.S., Industrial Commission. *Report of the Industrial Commission on the Relations and Conditions of Capital and Labor Employed in Manufacturing and General Business,* Vol. 7. Washington, D.C.: Government Printing Office, 1901.

————. *Report of the Industrial Commission on the Relations and Conditions of Capital and Labor Employed in Mahufacturing and General Business,* Vol. 14. Washington, D.C.: Government Printing Office, 1901.

Van Denburg, Joseph King. *Causes of the Elimination of Students in Public Secondary Schools of New York City.* New York: Teachers College, Columbia University, 1911.

Van Kleeck, Mary. *Artificial Flower Makers.* New York: Russell Sage Foundation, Survey Associates, 1913.

————. *A Seasonal Industry: A Study of the Millinery Trade in New York.* New York: Russell Sage Foundation, Survey Associates, 1917.

————. *Women in the Bookbinding Trade.* New York: Russell Sage Foundation, Survey Associates, 1913.

————. *Working Girls in Evening School: A Statistical Study.* New York: Russell Sage Foundation, Survey Associates, 1914.

Van Kleeck, Mary, and Barrows, Alice P. "How Girls Learn the Millinery Trade." *The Survey,* XXIV (April 16, 1910), pp. 105–113.

Van Vorst, Mrs. John and Van Vorst, Marie. *The Woman Who Toils: Being the Experiences of Two Gentlewomen as Factory Girls.* New York: Doubleday, Page and Company, 1903.

Wald, Lillian D. "Organization Amongst Working Women." *The Annals of the American Academy of Political and Social Science,* XXVII (June 1906), pp. 176–183.

————. *The House on Henry Street.* New York: Dover Publications, 1971.

Ware, Caroline R. *Greenwich Village, 1920–1930: A Comment on American Civilization in the Post-War Years.* Boston: Houghton Mifflin Company, 1935.

Weatherly, V. G. "How Does the Access of Women to Industrial Occupations React on the Family?" *American Journal of Sociology,* XIV (May 1909), pp. 740–752.

Willett, Mabel Hurd. *The Employment of Women in the Clothing Trade.* Columbia University Studies in History, Economics and Public Law. New York: Columbia University Press, 1902.

Wolfe, Albert Benedict. *The Lodging House Problem in Boston.* Harvard Economic Studies, Vol. 2. Boston and New York: Houghton Mifflin Company, 1906.

Wolman, Leo. "Extent of Labor Organization in the United States in 1910." *Quarterly Journal of Economics,* XXX (May 1916), pp. 486–518.

————. *The Growth of American Trade Unions, 1880–1923.* Publications of the National Bureau of Economic Research, No. 6. New York: National Bureau of Economic Research, 1924.

Women's Educational and Industrial Union, Department of Research, in cooperation with the Massachusetts Department of Health. *The Food of Working Women in Boston,* Lucille Eaves, director. Boston: Women's Educational and Industrial Union, 1917.

Women's Educational and Industrial Union, Department of Research. *Industrial Home Work in Massachusetts,* Amy Hewes, director. Boston: Women's Educational and Industrial Union, 1915.

————. *Training for Store Service: The Vocational Experiences and Training of Juvenile Employees of Retail Department, Dry Goods, and Clothing Stores in Boston,* Lucille Eaves, director. Boston: Richard G. Badger, The Gorham Press, 1920.

Woods, Robert A., ed. *Americans in Process: A Settlement Study by Residents and Associates of the South End House.* Boston and New York: Houghton Mifflin Company, 1903.

————. *The City Wilderness: A Settlement Study by Residents and Associates of South End House.* Boston and New York: Houghton Mifflin Company, 1898.

Woods, Robert A., and Kennedy, Albert J. *Young Working Girls: A Summary of Evidence from Two Thousand Social Workers.* Boston and New York: Houghton Mifflin Company, 1913.

Wright, Helen Russell. *Children of Wage-Earning Mothers: A Study of a Selected Group in Chicago.* U.S., Department of Labor, Children's Bureau, Children's Bureau Publication No. 102. Washington, D.C.: Government Printing Office, 1922.

Yezierska, Anzia. *Breadgivers.* New York: Venture/George Braziller, 1975.

Zorbaugh, Harvey Warren. *The Gold Coast and the Slum: A Sociological Study of Chicago's Near North Side.* Chicago: University of Chicago Press, 1929.

Index